BLOOD OF GODS: THE FIRST FIVE VINTAGES

ISBN: 978-1627311601

FERAL HOUSE
1240 W SIMS WAY #124
PORT TOWNSEND WA 98358
WWW.FERALHOUSE.COM
INFO@FERALHOUSE.COM

DESIGN: RON KRETSCH

COVER ART: MORGAN SORENSEN

BLOOD OF GODS

METAL. MAYHEM. WINE.

THE
FIRST
FIVE
VINTAGES

BY RIFF AND ROOT

It's been jokingly said that *Blood of Gods* is a pithy idea that went too far—and then, somehow, not far enough.

Annelise Page

But before we get to the joke, it's best to know where it came from.

THE BLOOD OF GODS STORY

Stacy Buchanan grew up in Walla Walla, Washington, raised on loud riffs, KISS cassettes, and garage-band dreams. His gateway drug was hard rock, funneled through adrenaline-junkie uncles who partied hard and played their records louder. That early love quickly morphed into a hunger for faster, weirder, and heavier sounds—punk, hardcore, and the many tentacled beast known as heavy metal. With few outlets in his small hometown, he turned to zines: self-made, cut-and-paste publications where fandom and creativity collided. That DIY energy landed him freelance gigs at *Alternative Press*, *Thrasher*, and a job at Century Media Records—where he eventually found himself, a la Cameron Crowe's *Almost Famous*, on the Ozzfest tour, working from Los Angeles to Germany, and embedded deep in the heavy music world.

But burnout hit hard. Music, once a love, began to feel like a grind. So, he hit reset and returned home—only to find Walla Walla had transformed into a full-blown wine destination. In eight years, the town had gone from 13 wineries to over 113. It was a different kind of scene, but weirdly familiar. The parallels started stacking up: the language of obsession, the fanatics, the politics of press and distribution, the debates over taste and terroir. Somewhere between a bottle of Cabernet Sauvignon and a Cannibal Corpse record, the joke landed: wine and metal might actually be . . . cousins.

At first, *Blood of Gods* was a novelty. A kitschy zine poking holes in elitism while mashing up two subcultures that rarely share space. Yet what began with tongue firmly in cheek gained teeth—and heart. With artwork from incredible illustrators, interviews with black metal winemakers, and pieces blending humor with reverence, *Blood of Gods* took shape. A feature with Satyr of Satyricon. A Q&A with Maynard James Keenan of Tool. A heavy metal wine name generator. Blind tastings backstage with Paradise Lost. Issue by issue, it evolved.

Then came the moment that changed everything:

BY RIFF AND ROOT

Stacy passed along a copy of the zine to a visiting winery family during a casual encounter. A few months later, the Blue Mountain Humane Society—where *BoG* had donated its proceeds—received a $10,000 donation from the family's charitable foundation, made directly in response to the zine's efforts. The joke had officially grown up.

With each issue, readers, winemakers, and musicians discovered that heavy metal and the wine industry aren't such an odd couple. On one side, you have spikes, patches, denim, and leather. On the other side, slick suits and swirling glasses. But scratch the surface and they mirror each other in striking ways. Both have rockstar personas, gatekeepers, and superfans. Both rely on distributors that can make or break them. Both are at the mercy of reviews, trends, and timing. And both, at their best, are about passion, curiosity, and expression.

Metalheads ask: Who produced this? Was it analog or digital? What bands are listed in the thank-you credits? Wine lovers want to know: Who made this? What was the vintage? How much new oak was used? The questions come from the same place—a hunger to know more, and to love deeper.

Blood of Gods was born not just as a zine, but as a rebuttal. Against wine snobbery. Against metal gatekeeping. Against the idea that these worlds couldn't coexist. As Stacy put it in a *Decibel* interview:

THE BLOOD OF GODS STORY

"There's the excitement, the nerdism, the appreciation, the fun, and the respect of the craft. They are completely equal between wine and metal."

From day one, *Blood of Gods* was meant to be more than a one-trick pony. It celebrates and pokes fun in equal measure. It shifts tones, rotates cover artists, collaborates with tattooers, comic book creators, sommeliers, and winemakers. As Stacy says, sometimes the creation notes are detailed, other times it's just: "Heavy metal and wine. GO."

As the zine grew—from rough-cut debut to a sold-out series spanning dozens of contributors and international acclaim—it never lost its pulse. *Blood of Gods* has appeared in *Wine Enthusiast*, *Decibel*, *SIP*, *Imbibe*, and more. It hosted three annual Merrymaking festivals (donating over $25,000 to Planned Parenthood), launched a subscription service, and featured heavy hitters from both the music and wine world. Still DIY. Still wild at heart.

Where does *Blood of Gods* go from here? Maybe its own wine. Maybe bed sheets. Maybe just more chaos, more joy, more riffs, more vintages. Whatever *Blood of Gods* does, it will do it the way it always has turn up the volume on craft, fandom, and feral creativity—and make space in the tasting rooms and backstage lounges for everyone.

Here's to the next tour.

Bunty May Marshall

Celestial Myth and Alchemy

Celebrating Our Connection with the Incorporeal

SOMETHING WICKED(LY DELICIOUS) THIS WAY COMES:

Winemaking Beyond the Cosmic Energy of Biodynamics

by Will Farley

IN THE MONTH OF BOEDROMION, THE HOLY ROAD OF ATHENS OVERFLOWED with the hallucinogenic kykeon and the sacred, filthy jokes of the pious during the mysterious Eleusinian rituals. Worshippers searched for Persephone, some calling to the Hecate, the three-in-one goddess of magic, "sepulchral, in a saffron veil array'd, leas'd with dark ghosts that wander thro' the shade" (Orphic Hymn #1: "To Musæus") to lend her torches to guide the errant goddess back to her mother, Demeter, and the light of spring.

On Cétshamhain, the first day of Gaelic Summer, mayflowers adorned homes, holy wells were visited, and massive wicker men bonfires, which, according to the Romans, contained animal and occasionally human sacrifices, lit up the night sky for the druidic revelries of Beltane.

Unless you're a neo-pagan or a scholar of ancient history, this is likely the first time you've heard of these quasi-religious practices. But, to those of us in the wine industry, the next one should be familiar: after the spring equinox, under an ascending sidereal moon that stands in flower / light constellations, a cow horn should be filled with a poultice of ground quartz and buried for six months to be imbued with the cosmic forces that will provide an opposite "spray of light" to "spiritual manure" when dynamized. Or, ferment yarrow flowers in a stag's bladder before sidling off to a yoga class.

Sounds similar, doesn't it? While it's only one step off from "Eye of newt and toe of frog," these are the instructions for making biodynamic preparations 501 and 502 and not a medieval grimoire. Lest you worry, it's unlikely we'll see Arianna Occhipinti or Thierry Germain burned at the stake today for practicing witchcraft.

«...biodynamic winemakers join the longstanding human tradition of entreating capricious 'gods' of harvest, fertility, and the cosmos to aid in the quest for metaphorical and literal growth with sympathetic magic.»

What is it about this farming philosophy (often called pseudo-science) that convinced people like Aubert de Villaine (Domaine de la Romanée-Conti) or Anne-Claude Leflaive (Domaine Leflaive) to convert some of the most expensive pieces of real estate to the (previously) niche system?

At its simplest, biodynamics treats the entire farm as one living organism, where plants and animals live in harmony under the watchful eye of man, who administers different preparations as needed. These preparations are made in a way that theoretically allows them to harness cosmic energy and distribute it back to the farm that prepared it. It's a cyclical, seasonal system that deals with the birth, death, and rebirth of all existence.

Denton Watts

But even for the skeptical, wanting to disbelieve in the cosmic import of biodynamics, it's nice to remember what the scientist Carl Sagan said: "The cosmos is all that will ever be." Human beings stand on the "shore of the vast cosmic ocean," and from our tiny vantage point, there are still things that provoke a kind of magic—systems that we can explain that stoke the imagination and some things we can only wonder about.

Where we live, light, minerals, and water are transmuted, breathing life into organic structures that are tended, picked, and fermented by microorganisms that once again transform the substance of the thing before it is again changed by time.

Partaking in ancient mystical practices allows us mayflies, beautiful in our brevity, to come together with those of bygone eras to share the contemplation of the unknown mysteries of human experience. In this way, biodynamic winemakers join the longstanding human tradition of entreating capricious "gods" of harvest, fertility, and the cosmos to aid in the quest for metaphorical and literal growth with sympathetic magic.

Some, like Jason Ruppert, previously the owner/winemaker of Ardure Wines, take this a step further, working two vineyard sites alone regeneratively and employing crystals in his winemaking process to achieve purity driven by spiritual practice at a small scale.

"I get off on geology, and crystals in big clay pots were super sexy to me. This practice goes all the way back to the Egyptians putting gemstones in their goblets for energy. It's super witchy shit.

"I knew I was gonna get laughed at, but I'm a firm believer in it. Same with vibration and sound [in winemaking]. None of this has ever been scientifically proven . . . yet. For me, it's spiritual. I don't actually taste crystals; it's more about the subtle vibrational value, connecting with the earth, my own vibe, setting intention, and putting that into what I'm making."

While some traditional winemakers might scoff at this approach, there are others like Tank Garage Winery that take Jason's example to heart, producing one crystal wine following the Ardure approach: find the right crystals, wash them in the ocean, and charge them in the moonlight before incorporating them into the fermentation process. But for them, this was a story that neatly fits into the larger ethos of Tank Garage, where they are as defined by experimentation as the traditionalists are by their dogma. In their stable of wines, you'll find over forty varieties and everything from traditional Napa fare to wild concepts like zero-zero, carbonically macerated white wines and charged crystal wines. But despite enjoying the process, they don't seem to be true believers.

The real priests and priestesses of cosmic wines live slightly more outside the mainstream than "experimental" but precise winemaking. The winemaker Salvador Batlle Barrabeig runs the aptly named Cosmic Vinyaters in the beautiful hills of Alt Empordà, Catalunya, where, alongside pink quartz crystals, he incorporates concepts borrowed from reiki archetypes, harmonic resonance designed to stimulate fermenting wines, and sacred geometry to protect and encourage his tanks and amphora to stay at their best.

Salvador's explorations are about setting an intention after listening and observing what the earth is trying to tell him. He believes that if you have big expectations you become a slave to those expectations, and he prefers to be open in his approach. He says, "This kind of preparation keeps the wine in harmony, and I'm not saying I do this to make the wine better, but I think it works for me and my wines."

Kyle Bond

Producing a harmonious wine is the best a winemaker can hope for. In this context, harmony means balance. And a balanced wine means that the grapes were deftly guided from budbreak to harvest and through fermentation and aging. To keep his ferments on track, a point of woe for many winemakers (especially those working with native yeasts), Abe Schoener of Scholium Project created his own god.

Today, maneki-neko (Japanese "lucky cats") sit as the watchful gods of fermentation over Schoener's barrels. For his team, "the lucky cat is a sign of the seriousness of our intentions, and also a sign that we know we can't bring about the results by our own actions alone. We have to make some supplication to higher forces."

One of these "higher forces" actually exists under the surface: mycorrhizal networks. These networks are a highly developed symbiotic relationship between fungus and plants that has been demonstrated to be a conduit for nutrients as well as for communication between plants connected to the network. These plants are shown to have increased resistance to pathogens, drought, salt, and heavy metal toxicity while gaining the ability to better synthesize potassium, zinc, and nitrogen. Vineyard managers looking to improve the health of their vineyards take note.

"It's amazing the degree of scientific knowledge we have about the transportation of minerals and plants through these mechanisms. Mycorrhizae is a beautiful example of the interaction between scientific knowledge and mystery. It's human wonder. Explaining it doesn't undercut that they are really amazing or take away from the mystery."

Some vineyard managers, like Mya Tapp and Moss Bittner (formerly of Montinore), have turned to aspects of Korean Natural Farming, which takes advantage of indigenous microorganisms (mycorrhizae included) already present in the soils of healthy vineyard sites. But they've gone one step further and attempted to bridge the gap between spiritual and physical by employing a vineyard reiki consultant.

"Reiki is about bigger systems, it's not just about people," says Virginia Samsel. "It takes a lot of energy to have that spiritual connection, and that's where I come in." Along with Tapp and Bittner, Samsel has a growing cadre of vineyard managers and winemakers (Jason Ruppert among them) that are turning to her to address unknown problems on their sites and provide integrative spiritual solutions.

"I go first to get the personality of the site. I open up and let the site know that I'm here to listen. A lot of my work is translation. I might have some basics from the vineyard manager or owner, but I work as things show up. It can be all of the sudden that this area feels a little blocked. Depending on their personality, they often just start giving me stuff.

"By incorporating spirituality, you are helping that vineyard to have a better sense of self. We are part of the system, helping them transmute. It's not like light energy and earth energy come together to make a blend. Under the cosmic gaze of man, it becomes more. It's about connecting to the ambient energy that's everywhere. Scientifically, it's entanglement theory."

While quantum metaphysics is outside most winemakers' purview, many of the winemakers going beyond biodynamics cite the quantum realm to bolster their ideological practices. This quantum mind state seems to exist somewhere between mysticism and physics. At the moment, the efficacy of any of these practices is unprovable by any measure other than blind tasting. Facilitating this is difficult (but not impossible), as Anne-Claude Leflaive proved in a blind tasting of her 1996 Puligny-Montrachet Premier Cru Clavoillon, where she poured journalists and importers two wines, one conventional, one biodynamic. The biodynamic was the favorite of everyone present.

Only time and rigorous experimentation will tell if these newer methods are a hint into the future of winemaking by way of the deep past.

Abe Schoener leaves with a good word: "The things that seem mysterious are often that way because I just don't know what they are; the mystery needs to be explored. I don't try to use my Cartesian enterprise to control nature through understanding."

So, is it justified to discount a winemaker because they are using methods that can't be validated by traditional scientific means? Absolutely not. These winemakers are trailblazers striving to make the best wines possible, and their dedication to their vineyards is absolute. Whether the meticulous attention to their sites, winemaking, or spiritual intentions provide the balance in their wines is incidental. Really, when the wines are this good, who cares?

ZODIAC

Emily Dunaway-Henrichs

Emily Dunaway-Henrichs, C.S., is the sommelier at Appalachian Vintner in Asheville, North Carolina. She is also smart as a whip with astrology and the written word, so bringing the stars and wine into further alignment is a role she was destined for. The artist Collin Estrada created the chalices for each Zodiac sign, Emily provided the "How" and "Why," and you get to learn which wine makes the most sense for you.

ARIES has always exuded a fiery passion, drive, and ambition unapologetically their own with a conviction that solidifies their self-awareness and position in life. A wine equally representative of those ideals leads straight to Spain, and specifically to Telmo Rodriguez and the Remelluri wines. Recently a huge fan of the Lindes de Remelluri Rioja Vinedos de San Vicente, this wine is confident of the intentional and groundbreaking quality with the perfect baseline of rustic character we all want from Rioja.

Imagine the friend of yours who is your guiding and steadfast principal, the pit bull in your corner, your comfort album. That is a **TAURUS** through and through. Unyielding, logical, tried and true, the epitome of "If it ain't broke don't fix it." Nowhere else in the world did those ideals speak to me more than in Bordeaux, specifically the Left Bank with its more dark and brooding style. Any Left Bank Bordeaux will work for a Taurus, fromyour entry level to any classified growth. This wine (and this friend) will have your back through thick and thin, right now and fifty years from now.

Oh, **GEMINI**. You wonderful social chameleon. You need a wine equally versatile, with many different hats to showcase, which leads us to the wonderful world of orange wine. Glekhuri has been a standout producer for me recently, with everything from their entry level Amber, to the Saperavi. Their 100% Kisi bottling is refined, elegant, unexpected, and yet everything you could ever want from a quality skin-contact wine. With a versatility that could span delicate, light dishes to a heartier pork dish, or even just flying solo in your glass, this needs to be on everyone's "must have" list.

Feeling, absorbing, and eliciting the full spectrum of human emotions is the cornerstone of all **CANCER** sun placements, and no wine has that same effect on me as Tokaji does. Truly, it can be any Tokaji on the market, from Royal Tokaji to Château Pajzos—the raw happiness that envelops Tokaji lovers when it's in the glass is unmatched and a high we all chase after in the world of wine.

Let's be honest—no other zodiac sign is as flashy and bold as our much-loved **LEO**; therefore I can think of no perfect pairing beyond Leo and Napa Valley Cabernet Sauvignon. Loud and ambitious with a need to be seen and heard (and drunk), Leos and Napa Cabernets are unequivocally cut from the same cloth, though my tastes would lean towards any wine orchestrated by the hands of Heidi Barret (Dalla Valle in particular). This sign and wine know who they are, they set the mold, and I don't see them changing their paths anytime soon, because, wherever they are in the world, there are droves of folks clamoring for their unique personalities.

VIRGOs and their exacting nature are truly the engine that runs the world as we know it, just like every single wine coming from the Sinskey vineyards. Abraxas is a wine with exacting precision, the perfect accompaniment to any meal to elevate the entire experience to a trip through the universe's intention for flavor. An Alsatian blend of Riesling, Pinot Blanc, Pinot Gris, and Gewürztraminer, all grown in an unlikely place—Carneros—makes this wine such a standout from the pack and in a league of its own, just like our hot librarian Virgos.

The Aesthetic of Being Extra: A **LIBRA** Memoir. Everything a Libra does is in consideration of what others might think. They love to be the life of the party, the best dressed, and the most liked. And what else embodies this mindset more than an ultra-Instagrammable bottle of Jérôme Prévost La Closerie bubbles (extra points to the Meunier base)? Cheers to life, my Libra friends, because every moment is a celebration, and no expense should be spared.

Looking so innocent and inviting on the outside, yet packing a punch once you dive deeper, you will find a likeness between a bottle of an immensely powerful Barolo and your misunderstood friendly neighborhood **SCORPIO**. Both take some time, a lot of time, to open up and show you how amazing they can truly be. Not for the faint of heart but definitely, for the more refined tastes and those willing to put in the work and patience, a hefty reward awaits you.

For our endearing adventurers, those constantly breaking the rules and living a fiercely independent life, unconcerned with opinions of others, **SAGITTARIUS** deserves nothing less that the perfection of Jean Foillard's Côte du Py bottling of Gamay. Beaujolais and its historical winemaking practices are the epitome of marching to the beat of their own drum, especially given the context of French wine law, and with Foillard's winemaking practices one must wonder if the stars of Sagittarius's archer have a major role to play.

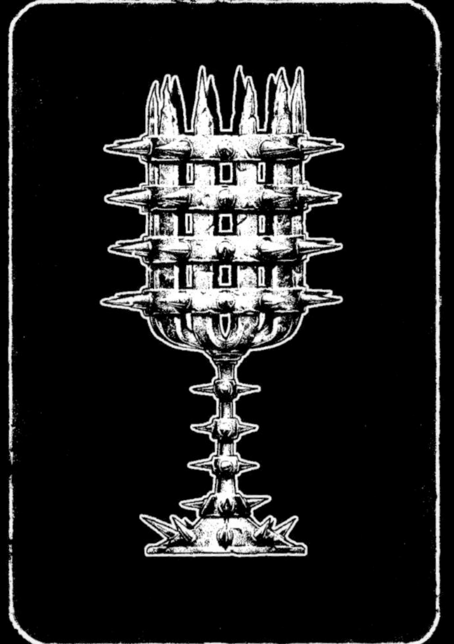

Since my very first days in the wine industry, Syrah has always been characterized by a Dirty Harry–era Clint Eastwood in the sense that it is no-nonsense, rough around the edges, a true hearty, salt-of-the-earth-style wine (affectionately known as the "beef stew" of wine in my heart of hearts). While Clint Eastwood isn't a **CAPRICORN** himself, that character radiates most qualities I know through and through to be a Capricorn, and I won't frill up this description any more than necessary, as I'm sure it would cause our Capricorn friends to roll their eyes and stop reading. So, if you're a Capricorn, drink Syrah. That's it.

AQUARIUS in the zodiac lineup is like ska in the music world: it's quirky, it's weird, but overall enjoyable (humbly asking to not be burned at the stake for this opinion, folks). As my husband is one of those lovable Aquarius oddballs, I would be remiss if I didn't feature one of his favorite wines: Claus Preisinger's Kalkundkiesel blend (Grüner, Pinot Blanc, Muscat Ottonel—unfined/unfiltered/biodynamic). It's unusual, it's odd, but, damnit is it enjoyable. Drink this wine and remember you're not an outcast, you're not weird, you're just doing your own thing and that's one of the best things you can do.

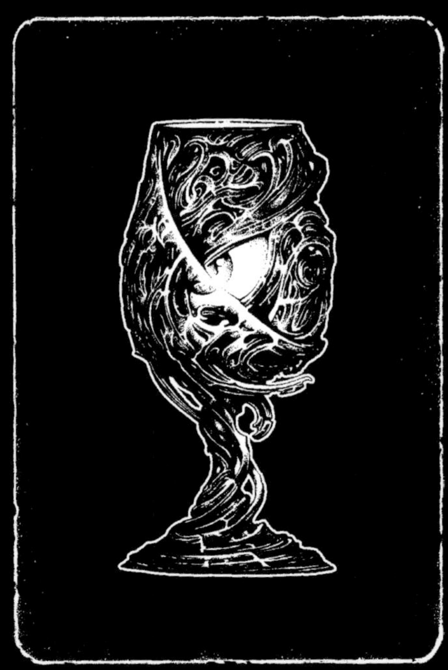

PISCES fall into the emotional realm, dreamers with their heads seeming like they're always in the clouds, and because of this, they are supremely misunderstood. Quick adapters to their surroundings, Pisces embody any Riesling from the most linear and dry examples to a Beerenauslese, but my absolute favorite Riesling is the brilliantly classic J. J. Prum Graacher Himmelreich Spatlese. But for those of us who know Riesling is special because of its ethereal quality and superstar power, we know just how much like a Pisces this misunderstood grape can be.

HARDY WALLACE IS A MADMAN

Interview and photos by James Joiner

In today's social-media-centric society, we all spend too much time doomscrolling through endless smiling charlatans "living their best lives" whilst trying to sell us something. You know the type: eyes enthusiastically wide, cheeks cracking between the conflicting pounds per square inch of a huckster's grin and reality's weight. "Hey guys, it's me! Sooooo . . ." Barf.

The wine world feels particularly rife with wannabe influencers. How are so many "winemakers" constantly foot-stomping Aligoté with Abercrombie-worthy co-eds in vintage SUVs and Blundstones? Here in Sonoma, we see these folks show up at harvests just long enough to "get one for the 'Gram" before scooting off in vanity-plated high-end electric cars for champagne and eggs and it's infuriating, if only because there are so many amazing humans who've actually dedicated their lives to their vision of what wine can be.

One of those humans is Hardy Wallace.

It'd be easy to call Hardy a "breath of fresh air" or some other generic platitude, but it undersells both the man and his mission. You likely know Hardy from his iconic Dirty and Rowdy brand, which championed Mourvèdre before it was a buzzword and put so-called Natural Wine on the map. Or perhaps you remember his blog, *Dirty South Wine,* which gained so much notoriety he found himself winning Murphy Goode's social media contest back in 2009. That's what ultimately transplanted the burgeoning wine writer from Atlanta to Healdsburg, where the fates intervened and he soon found himself learning to make—and, in the process, to break all the so-called rules involved in making—his own wines.

Dirty and Rowdy, for all its success, is now gone. But in its wake Hardy has a new, more fitting partner: his amazing wife Kate. The pair teamed up to launch a new brand, one that speaks closely to and from their hearts: "Extradimensional Wine Co. Yeah!"

Anyone who's seen Hardy's social media knows he's a character. Sporting signature multi-colored eyeglasses, wildly patterned clothing, and trippy camera effects, his often-over-the-top posts (have you ever seen someone use animal impressions to describe Orange Wine? if not, you need to) are subdued only when compared to his own explosive enthusiasm for both wine and life. Yet unlike those carefully calculated personas mentioned above, it's abundantly clear upon meeting Hardy IRL this is no act—Hardy is Extradimensional. A ball of magic energy fueled by a self-charging battery of pure stoke, he and Kate are on a mission to share their beautiful energy, wines, and good vibes with anyone open to receiving them.

Blood of Gods: Okay so what's the deal with Extradimensional Wine Co. Yeah!?

Hardy: Extradimensional means originating outside of the physical reality of the known universe.

As a winemaker, my relationship with wine has always been centered around discovery and pushing boundaries. Kate and I started Extradimensional Wine Co. Yeah! as the answer to the question, "What if, knowing what you know now, you could begin again?"

Our reflections led us to think deeply about many factors, with climate change and our personal relationship with wine resurfacing in each conversation. With years of massive drought, record heat years after record heat years, it is clear that if we want to continue making compelling wines with no adjustments then we have to make a fundamental shift in how we see and make wine.

Part of this process was erasing the often made-up, vinous boundaries, rules, and perceptions that guide much of the industry and instead focus on making the best wines that even in the most challenging of years can touch the soul and endure. We want to capture what California is all about—the energy that we feel from living here and working with iconic vineyards, and the depth and weightlessness that comes through these soils, vines, and wines. The term "California Energy Wine" is written on our tasting room wall and pretty much sums it up.

BoG: How did you go from tech sales to iconic natural winemaker?

H: I spent twelve years in an unhappy spot and very much trapped in a tech sales / marketing career. I fell into it after college and was afraid to leave it. The only part of the job I enjoyed was entertaining clients where we had many beautiful meals and drank great wines. I started writing up the bottles and various wine experiences on my blog *Dirty South Wine*. The blog got tons of traction and was well received in the height of those blogging days.

Fast forward to late '08, early '09, when the economy started melting down, and my boss called me up to let me know I was to be laid off. I remember that moment vividly, and, though terrifying, it was one of the best moments of my life. I was set free, and my soul knew I would move full time into wine.

In early 2009, Murphy Goode winery announced a contest, "A Really Goode Job." The original iteration felt like the *American Idol* of wine social media, and as soon as I heard about it I knew it was my ticket into the wine business and that I was going to win it. I did.

The gig brought me to Healdsburg, and after I finished out my six-month contract I switched directions to work for Kevin Kelley of the now-defunct Salinia and the Natural Process Alliance (the NPA). Kevin was so far ahead of his time in many distinct ways and his wines were my absolute favorite. At the NPA, we made different blends each week that we hand-bottled in Klean Kanteen bottles and only distributed within a 100-mile radius of the winery. These wines were delivered to accounts weekly like the old-school milkman and all the empties brought back to the winery for sanitizing and refilling.

The NPA wines were in both Michelin-starred restaurants and groundbreaking natural wine bars. I ended up in charge of making the blends and deliveries and through these weekly drop-offs established meaningful relationships (which I still value to this day) with many of the best sommeliers and buyers in the San Francisco Bay area. While working at the NPA, Kevin encouraged me to make my own wines, and I dove in and started Dirty and Rowdy. Our first wine was a variety-defying semi-carbonic Mourvèdre from a 3,000-foot-high desert vineyard in Santa Barbara County. People not only loved it but were ready for it and wanted more—it propelled Dirty and Rowdy, and we grew and explored many alternative expressions of California Mourvèdre and well beyond.

After about two years with Kevin, I wanted to expand my skill set and went to work for icons like Ehren Jordan of Failla, Cathy Corison of Corison, and Ann Kramer at Shake Ridge Ranch. All natural labels aside, I am currently making incredible, tiny-production (sub 2,000 cases) wines without any additions except minimal SO_2 that both natural- and non-natural-wine lovers are fired up about and are sharing with others all over the world.

BoG: How did you learn to make wine? How come you're so darn good at it?

H: I was fortunate to work with great winemakers and learn on the job. On the beyond-the-box side, I know what lights me up both in wine and in the world. I seek that often beautiful (sometimes frightening) place where subject objects fail to exist and where we experience moments of infinite wonder. To me, I find thinking creatively, outside of typicity, and having a point of view that isn't bound to or by made-up constraints as the only way for me to exist.

BoG: Do you still have a blog?

H: Does anyone? Just kidding. In some ways, I wish I did. I like the format. It feels like a podcast of the written word. If I did have a blog, it probably wouldn't be straight-up for wine and likely would be for poetry, psychedelics, parenting, and ukulele . . .

BoG: Tell me about the full-sense and smell wine tastings. How did that happen? What makes it special?

H: I have been studying aromatics and rare fragrances over the last few years and began to explore how they interact with wine and with the human psyche. This exploration led to the design of the Extradimensional Wine and Aroma Energy Experience. This is a first-of-its-kind wine tasting, which is really an aromatic crossing that incorporates wine, music, and a variety of sensational oils in a multi-sensory wine tasting. In doing this, the participant smells, tastes, and most importantly feels (both physically and emotionally) a deep sense of awe and bliss. It's a full deep-end dive driven by the olfactory system, and it offers participants the opportunity to tune in and be present while getting more from wine than they ever imagined.

There's serious and beautiful stuff to explore here.

BoG: What role does music play in your life and winemaking?

H: To me, wine is music in slow motion. After studying Hindustani and North Indian Classical music for fifteen years, winemaking feels similar. North Indian Classical music is filled with awe-inspiring subtlety. There are complex time signatures, beautiful structures, and intricate rhythmic crescendos that bend the perception of time. Dancing within all that structure is mind-boggling improvisation and spontaneous composition. Wine is the same thing just in a longer rhythmic cycle.

BoG: Explain how wine is more than just booze.

H: At its best, wine is a connection from the center of the earth to the center of the cosmos. From the geological forces that create our physical terroir to the atmospheric events that drive growing and ripening. Wine and winemaking can act as a connection between these happenings. Even further, wine can be a way to help us understand ourselves. The aromatics alone can act as time machines bringing us back to moments that we can relive again.

BoG: In an era of mega-conglomerates, what keeps you making unique and magical wines instead of just cashing in on some dumb red blend with a gothic label and selling it to Gallo?

H: As an industry (and as in pretty much all industries) we face this either/or because these are the larger system drivers that keep it all binary—the stay small or the go big, feed the masses and sell. But really in our case it's a vision thing. As in a way of seeing. It's also a scale and design thing. I have the privilege of making "unique and magical wine" because I didn't begin making wine from any pressure point or planned arrival point. What we do is not formulaic, which is what is often the requirement to swim in certain seas. I'm essentially playing live music in real time at a set time in the calendar year defined by natural elements (most of which are beyond my control) with a band of growers that I feel honored to have relationships with. This isn't a linear process, it comes with a specific skill set, and it involves taking risks. All of this keeps me doing what I'm doing and it's fun as hell!

In all seriousness though, I do believe there are buyers out there that understand what we are doing, know the data (especially with regards to shifting markets, demographics, and climate change), and envision Yeah! as a potential answer. Imagine Yeah! Wine written on the side of a fleet of electric-powered trucks delivering psychedelic-inspired fine wine across the USA. You can't get much better than that.

BoG: What's up with you and Mourvèdre?

H: Mourvèdre is my kindred spirit. To me, it is the grape that has the most diverse spectrum of flavors, frequencies, and expressions. It is the base of the most beautiful rosé wines in the world and also produces some of the most intense, powerful, and brooding reds. All that space in between is the Mourvèdre-verse and there is so much to explore.
Along with its wide range of expressions, its thicker skins and later budding make it more resilient than many varieties in California.

At this point, I've bottled somewhere around 70-75 Mourvèdre-based wines from different parts of California on radically different terroirs. I love the way it expresses site.

BoG: What doesn't the world know about you that you want it to?

H: That my work is all really a love poem and a song that I hope makes it into the hearts and the glasses of as many people as possible. 🍷

METAL MOMENTS

IN WINE MYTH, HISTORY, AND PRACTICE

BY WILL FARLEY

ILLUSTRATION BY SHAUN FRIEND

Every metalhead has had a lightbulb moment when they realize that music can be more than the bubblegum-soaked pop drivel spoon-fed by top-forty radio disk jockeys. For me, it was somewhere between catching Gwar on Jerry Springer eloquently defending creative expression in heavy metal and my first taste of divine madness after being moved by a riff so heavy that it felt like headbanging a monolith. Whatever prompts the realization that you can reject the corporate butt-rock for something sludgy and feral should be celebrated and memorialized. Your moment could be the stepping stone for others.

Wine has similar moments of ecstasy, and, as with heavy metal, there are wild myths, strange practices, and feuding personalities that give it character. So it's not really strange that metalheads turn into wine fans, just a twist of fate. Like great albums, wine is crafted. There are foundational myths that add color to the experience, and it can get you brutally inebriated.

The pages of mythology and history are splattered with the blood of gods and mortals that shaped the world, inventing wine as they bled into the primordial dirt. Blood of Gods revels in the divine inspiration that comes from wine and heavy metal, so I've assembled a collection of metal moments in wine myth, history, and winemaking practice to give those on the fence (and the already-converted) even more reasons to enjoy imbibing.

The right combination of music, story, and wine can make the most skeptical pop-listening, craft-beer-guzzling normie appreciate the blood of the gods. Drink in the sordid details with some of my favorite wine and music pairings that match every moment.

The Birth of Dionysus - God of Wine and Ritual Madness

Before inventing wine, the god of wine had to be born. And while many of the pagan gods sprang from the feet of broken bodies and scattered titanic gore, the birth of Dionysus (the god of the grape harvest, wine, and ritual madness) was an especially metal moment in mythology.

His mother was the mortal Semele, a Phoenician princess of renowned beauty and daughter of one of the first human heroes, while his father was Zeus, the sky-father, the god of lightning and ruler of all the Greek gods on Mount Olympus. When Zeus's wife, Hera, discovered the affair, she was enraged. Disguised, she caused Semele to doubt Zeus's divinity and demand that he prove his godhood by revealing his true splendor. Zeus reluctantly agreed, sealing Semele's fate.

In his true form, Zeus radiated power, and Semele began to bleed from the ears and eyes. When Zeus produced his thunderbolts, she was torn in two down the middle, exposing the still-developing Dionysus. To save his unborn son, Zeus cut open a hole in his thigh, gently placing the fetus there and sewing him in until he was mature enough to survive birth.

Pairing:

Wine: Domaine Hauvette Alpilles Blanc "Jaspe" is a 100% Roussanne wine from southern France that tastes like a thunderstorm on a seaside farm. It's a celebration that unto us the god of wine has come, and it will evoke a lament once the bottle is empty.

The Invention of Wine

The satyr Ampelos probably shouldn't have bragged that he was better at riding animals than the goddess Selene (famous for driving the chariot of the moon across the sky). When she heard, she was enraged. In her anger, she bewitched the bull Ampelos was riding, which threw him into the air and skewered him through the heart. Being gored is a brutal way to go. Being gored by a raging bull that was bewitched is an especially brutal way to go.

But Ampelos and Dionysus were close, and, as his broken body lay splayed in the dirt, it was transformed into grapevines. The blood leaking out of his gaping chest wound changed hue ever so slightly and became the first vintage of wine. Dionysus mourned and then drank deeply of his friend before sharing this discovery with god and mortal alike. Maybe this will give you something new to think about when you drink something a sommelier has described as "blood red."

Pairing:

Wine: Paolo Bea's Sagrantino di Montefalco Pagliaro is absolutely savage. The unrelenting tannins, the spice, the tobacco, the searing acid, and the plush fruit harmonize into a brutal melody fit for the gods—a worthwhile tribute to the first vintage and the fallen Ampelos.

Music:

"Hesperus" by Windhand - The sludgy guitar and slow tempo drive home the emotional heft of the lyrics that are mourning just as Dionysus mourned.

Bacchanalia

Not all metal is doom and gloom, and not all wine moments are about murder and death; sometimes, there's drunken debauchery and licentiousness too. In ancient Rome, Dionysus went by another name: Bacchus, and Bacchus became the center of massive cults dedicated to divine madness.

This state of madness changed from cult to cult but wasn't just about getting fucked up. Bacchanalias are probably most famous for the orgiastic aspects, but they were way wilder than just tame group sex. At some bacchanalia, animals were torn in half and eaten raw. This reenactment of Bacchus's birth was a means to becoming more enthusiastic. The real meaning of enthusiasm is to have one's body taken over by divine madness. Bacchus demanded that his followers cede control to his will. I know that metal fans can relate to the feeling. Sometimes, when the music is playing and the riffs are heavy, the spirit speaks and you can't help but headbang enthusiastically with the music that now controls you.

Pairings:

Wine: Agrapart & Fils "Venus" Blanc de Blanc Brut Nature Millesime is a vintage champagne from a single vineyard in Avize. Venus is the name of the horse that plows the field. It's textured, with an unbelievable depth. A champagne that moved me to enthusiasm.

Music:

Infest the Rat's Nest by King Gizzard and the Lizard Wizard - The whole record is heavy, thrashy, and full of blast beats, guitarmonies, and gang-vocal-filled choruses that portend our incoming destruction at the hands of wealthy interlopers. The lyrics from the song "Superbug" could just as easily be about COVID-19 as about Bacchus and his divine madness.

Black Masses and Theophagy (the Eating of a God)

There's nothing more metal than a Black Mass. Since Ozzy's early invocation of "Generals gathered in their masses / just like witches at Black Masses," the Black Mass and the occult have been inextricably linked with heavy metal culture. A Black Mass takes the elements that Christians believe to be holy and inverts them using profane simulacra. There's no correct way to hold a Black Mass. I'd recommend having lots of wine as sometimes it's about getting drunk off the wine (the blood of a god). But some would say it's necessary to sacrifice an animal and have sex on the altar. A Black Mass is really a heavy metal Choose-Your-Own-Adventure of sorts.

Germanic and Roman pagans criticized the Christians by calling them cannibals because of their obsessed fixation with torture devices and the belief that they were literally eating the body and drinking the blood of their god. So the components of a regular mass are shockingly metal as well. Wicked.

Pairings:

Wine: David Duband Nuits-St-Georges 1er Cru "Les Proces" is a blood-red wine with a meaty ferocity and savory character. With all the talk about drinking blood, this is a wine that will surprise and delight. Just enough mineral iron to make you think of the last time you bit your lip a little too hard.

Music:

"War Pigs" by Black Sabbath - This is the song that launched heavy metal music into the firmament and forever linked it with the occult. Drink up and turn it up.

"I wanted to marry the history and the myth of the bacchanal with its origins as a women's cult and later scandals of ritual murder, and the lusty satyrs/Pans that appear in later art. I took inspiration from the cluttered compositions of Norman Lindsay and used my signature graveyard rave palette to help create vivid points of interests and guide you from party in the front to sacrifice in the back."

—Bo Bradshaw

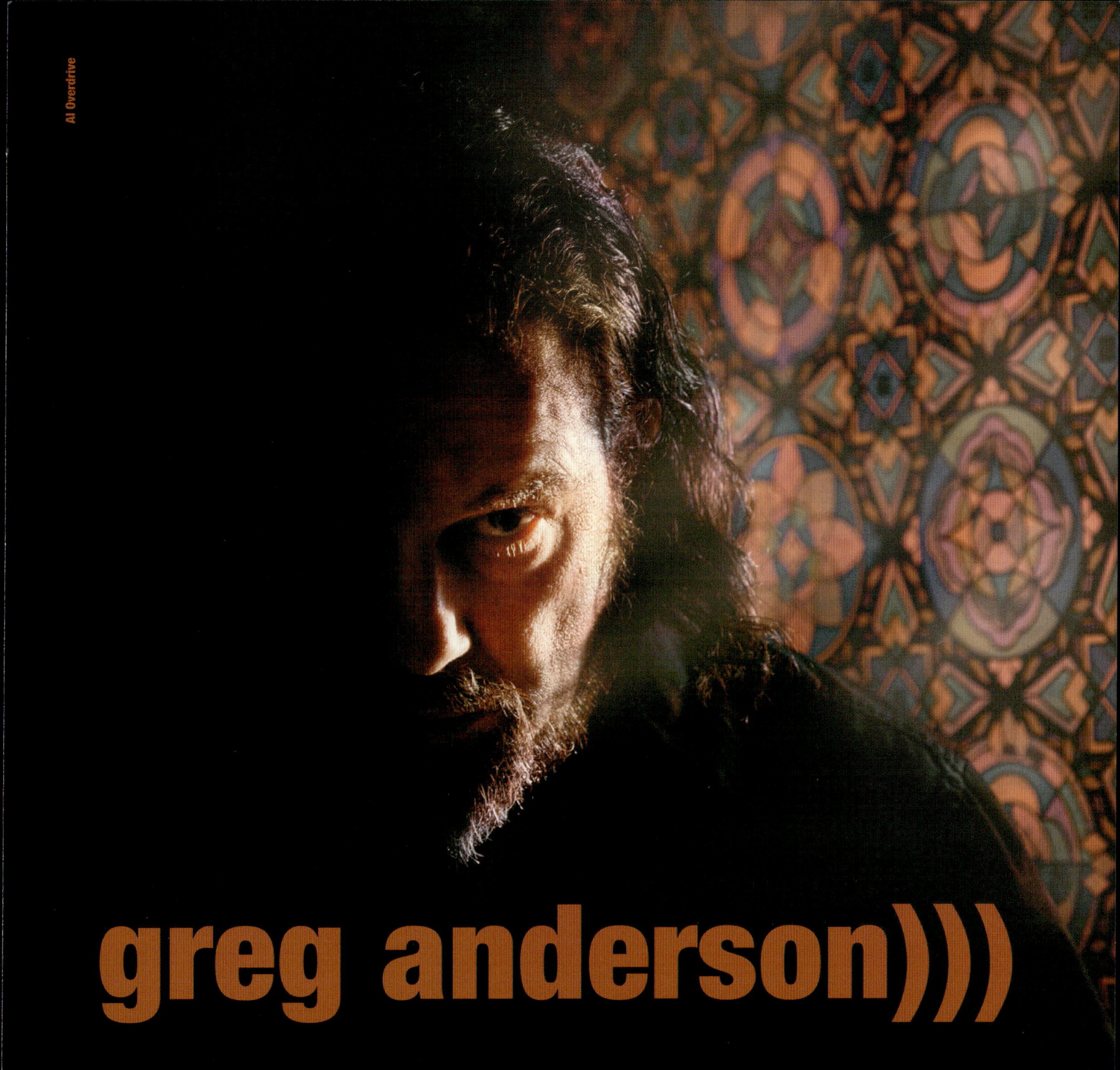

Al Overdrive

greg anderson)))

Conceptualized and formed in March of 1998,

sunn O)))

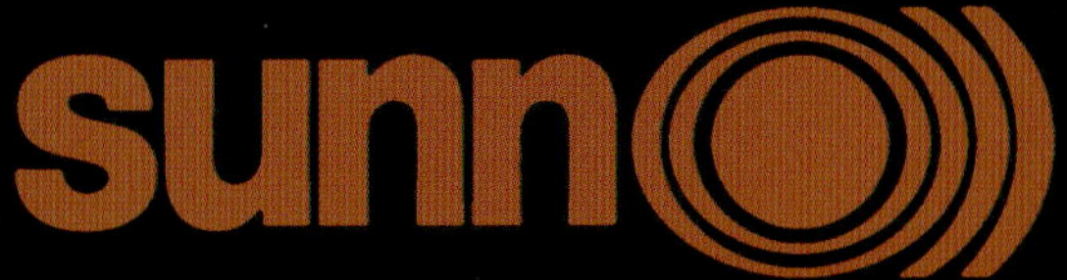

has been challenging the ways we think about music ever since.

>>>>>

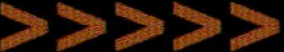

DESCRIBED BY THE BAND AS, "A SYNTHESIS OF DRONE, METAL, MINIMALISM AND maximalism verging on pure sonic ecstasy. They induce meditative trance states in the listener through the power, beauty and color of sound pressure emanating from their legendary backline of valve amplification and their Earth shaking tectonic compositions of existence, dedicated to the mysteries of life and the cosmos." Led by Greg Anderson, owner of Southern Lord Records, the appreciation of textures, nuance, subtly, and volume are qualifiers that bridge the gap between the sonic spectrum that Sunn O))) peddles in and wine appreciation. But the crossover doesn't end there . . .

Blood of Gods: What's your experience with wine?

Greg: For a time period, from probably about 2004 till 2018 I would say, it sort of became the drink of choice for Sunn O))). We would actually have bottles of wine on our rider. Usually we would have a curated list or a choice of what we'd like to have, typically local or French. We would specify a nice bottle of wine, no cheap stuff, and not only have it on our rider for us to have in the green room or backstage, but we would also usually have two bottles of wine on stage as well that were open, and we would drink them throughout our set. It was something that for us was part of the atmosphere—it's what we chose and preferred to enhance our mood or our vibe for the live shows. And then outside of Sunn O))) it was, for a long time, something that I preferred. I never was a huge beer drinker, and neither was Stephen [Ed.: O'Malley, other core Sunn O))) member]—it's not something I ever really connected with or got into. Wine has played an interesting role with Sun O))) over the years. Having the wine together before, during, and after the show is something that's sort of been a part of the process.

BoG: That makes total sense to me. Especially with your music, there's a meditative quality, it's something to zen-out to and ruminate on. I was thinking about concepts like "Ritual" and "Ceremony" and those aspects you've described with your live performances—and even with the robes you wear—it's doing something with intention.

Greg: Wine and the effect it has on me, and I think for Stephen as well—and it also lends itself to the music, it's sort of this deeper feeling. It's kind of slow to me, it has a lot of depth to it, so that is something that's been inspirational for us.

BoG: Like with your music in Sunn O))), there is that depth and complexity, and it's certainly an investment of time, but I think it's rewarding if you're willing to put in that investment.

Greg: It's so true. It is about time, it's not something that often comes to you right away. It's not immediate. And the band is in itself that way, as far as time goes, as well. This has been an ongoing collaboration between Stephen and I for over twenty-five years, so it's something that we've developed over time as well. To get kind of nerdy and over-analyze: there's decay in what we've done as well, just as in fermentation in wine.

BoG: Or noble rot.

Greg: Noble rot—absolutely! That's definitely happening. Stephen and I really try to respect and recognize the beginnings of what we did and incorporate that always. Obviously, it has decayed or rotted over time, but that's something, especially with our last studio full-length, the *Life Metal* record, that was really our acknowledging and celebrating our roots and where we came from and attempting to incorporate that into the overall sound. And that obviously has ties correlating with wine and the winemaking process as well.

BoG: I imagine a good number of folks reading this who are into wine might not be familiar with Sunn O))) and like with some wines your music can be an acquired taste, so for someone who's hearing about Sunn O))) for the first time, where would you recommend people start with your music?

Greg: I would suggest someone come experience the group live, to be honest with you. I sometimes look at Sunn O))) as this two-headed beast, where there's the performance side and then there's the recorded side. And they obviously have a lot of similarities but there are a lot of differences as well, and I think, maybe more than a lot of bands, the live show and performance is an experience that, once you dig in and you experience it, you realize that it is different from the albums that we have available.

But then, as far as an album goes, I would say that *Monoliths and Dimensions* has a lot of diversity and has a lot of strong characteristics of what the group is about. There are also vocals on that record from Attila Csihar, known for his work with Mayhem. I think at that time—that record came out in 2009—it was a bit of a crowning achievement for us. We spent so much time . . . we actually spent a few years making that record and working on it. With the time we spent, just in the trenches with that record, we wanted to create something that was the ultimate documentation or representation of the group and I'm really proud of that record. There's a lot of really bold moves and choices that we made on that record that were different from anything we had done before, and a lot of the stuff was beyond or transcended what we had done live as well. And those ideas that we recorded and captured sort of paved the way for us for the next nine years or so, and a lot of the live performances that we did were based off of themes and concepts from that record; a lot of those shows were with Attila as well. So that would be an entry-point, I'd say.

Al Overdrive

And the last record we did, *Life Metal*, that we recorded with Steve Albini, was really, to me, a step into re-establishing the group. We reevaluated what the group was to us shortly after our twentieth anniversary as a band, and, as I was mentioning before, it was acknowledging and celebrating our past, as well as looking, as we always strive to do, to a different direction than the recordings before it.

Either of those two records, or the live show—which I think is really important to feel Sunn 0))) because to me that's really a huge part of what we do: the physical aspect of it and the volume and feeling the vibrations of the sound. There's a lot of people that maybe don't connect with the studio records—it's not something that works for them—but seeing it live is such a different beast. I would say it's nearly impossible not to be affected by it somehow—whether it's positive or negative—but it's definitely not something where you just go, "Meh . . . I don't know . . ." It demands your attention, and it grabs you, and sometimes that is pleasurable for people, and I am really grateful for the people affected by it, but then there's also people that it's not for them, it's not an experience they want to have.

BoG: I just saw Nine Inch Nails live, and there was this realization during the concert that, "This is the loudest I will probably ever hear this song." My home stereo, my car stereo, nothing is going to touch these decibels . . . but the huge sound system and PA, and feeling the vibrations was cleansing, cathartic, and energizing.

Greg: That's the other thing to mention: the records, they have limitations as far as the sound systems that they're played on, and of course that varies from person to person, listener to listener. But the live experience, you can look at it as: it's curated by the group. We have our sound person that we work with who's really important to the performance as well, and of course working with the PA that you have in the venue—but that PA has also been discussed and signed off on by the band and the sound person weeks before the show happens. So everything there is more like the ultimate experience of the sound, because it really is curated and authorized by the band.

Unfortunately, nine times out of ten, the way that people listen to music usually falls short. Especially these days with earbuds and headphones and stuff like that—and I have no problem with that, I'm not saying that's the wrong way to listen to it, I listen to music that way all the time—but unfortunately it doesn't always represent and transfer the music the way we would like. So that's why the live performance for us is so important to the group.

POGGIO ANIMA

POGGIO ANIMA is a joint venture between one of Tuscany's rising stars, Riccardo Campinoti of Le Ragnaie in Montalcino and his U.S. importer Ronnie Sanders of Vine Street Imports. The idea is straightforward: to source great vineyards from existing relationships and produce a real wine that conveys a place and a grape. These wines are not bulk wines or leftover juice from a winery; instead, they are the result of long-standing relationships with reputable and respected growers throughout Italy. Why the ancient pagan labels? There is an everyday dichotomy between good and bad in the world. Looking for balance in all things (including wine) is a vital quest for many. The Eastern ideology of *yin/yang* is the core of this "balance" in the Poggio Anima concept. Fusing this Eastern belief with Western philosophy is apparent when you look at the contradiction of red and white (wines), good versus evil (demons versus angels) and modern ideas with old world winemaking practices (catchy, fun packaging with classic old-world wine). The white wines are named after archangels, while the reds are named after fallen angels. Each wine was specifically named for the persona of the grape, region, or style of the wine. Each wine hails from one variety, a single vineyard, and represents its indigenous place of origin. This is real wine, from a real place, made by real people. >

Courtesy of Ronnie Sanders

Blood of Gods: Heavy metal and ancient history, specifically religion and mythology, have often proved to be a complementary pairing. How do you view the connection between these two and wine?

Ronnie Sanders: I think the great thing about making wines in Italy is that you have not only the great historical aspect of winemaking but you also have an extra emphasis on religion, which many in the metal world may see as a type of mythology. When we first came up with the idea of Poggio Anima's branding, it was more about the dichotomy of red versus white, good versus evil, etc. Italy being the hub of Catholicism, we loved the irony of using the Old Testament names for fallen angels and archangels as a little poke at religion. Tuscany, where my partner and his winery is based, during the Renaissance period, was the one Italian region that was always at odds a bit with the Church. That was also a part of the thinking. When we started Poggio Anima back in 2008, this was pretty controversial at the time. I remember some of the first reactions we had to the packaging in Italy was literal shock, and maybe a bit of confusion. Our bottlers thought that we were nuts. It was different days back then, and before the natural wine boom, which of course changed the way people look at packaging, and everything is so much looser now than back in 2008, but we certainly shook people up, which, of course, was the point.

BoG: I'd imagine that some typical wine drinkers who aren't familiar with the story behind the winery might be a little spooked or confused by the labels—what's some of the funnier reactions you've gotten?

RS: For sure we had some people who had some pretty extreme reactions. I can remember some accounts that, once they knew what some of the names were, they wouldn't stock the wines. That was pretty rare, though. We really look at the fine wine retailers, wine bars, and restaurants as our main customer base, and for every buyer that wouldn't buy the wines we had five that would buy them just because of the names or the labels. I remember showing the wines to a restaurant called Patois in New Orleans and the sommelier, Lorenzo, who I've met once or twice, as soon as he saw the labels, he lifted his shirt and showed me his enormous "Satan on the Throne" tattoo that was about thirty inches on the side of his midriff. I think he ran with the wines by the glass for a while. Also, the girl that Lorenzo was dating at the time actually got the Lilith Primitivo label image tattooed on her shoulder.

POGGIO ANIMA
GABRIEL
PECORINO TERRE DI CHIETI
INDICAZIONE GEOGRAFICA TIPICA

BoG: What was your first "music moment" when you discovered a taste for underground/ extreme music?

RS: I definitely not only have some defining moments but also defining people in my life that helped me discover extreme music. My first memory, though, is when I was nine or ten, and already taking guitar lessons and listening to classic rock, getting and listening to Black Sabbath's "Black Sabbath" song and record. I listened to it on my bed while looking at the cover and being totally freaked out and almost afraid. That song still kind of freaks me out. The second big moment was when I was in tenth grade in 1981. There was a girl that I was friends with that I sat next to in homeroom. She left ninth grade for summer break as a "normal girl" and came to school the first day of our sophomore year as a punk—hair dyed platinum blonde with black in the front, the whole look with the clothes etc.—and I was blown away. She was totally into music and told me about how she got into punk rock. The next day she brought in a cassette for me; the first side was Crass's *Penis Envy* and the second side was the Dead Kennedys' *Fresh Fruit for Rotting Vegetables*. At the time I was super into bands like Led Zeppelin, the Who, Rainbow, Black Sabbath, etc., and this tape literally blew my mind. To this day that Crass record still leaves me in awe.

The third big moment was my freshman year of college at the University of Hartford. There was a guy who was in the art school in my dorm that was totally into metal. I was at the time a full-on punk kid and this guy, whose name was Rob Abrams but quickly got the nickname of "Satan," was listening to bands like Celtic Frost, Mercyful Fate, and Venom. He used to wear a Venom black leather jacket with the spikes and all the works. He and I became pretty good friends. He turned me on to all the metal and I turned him onto bands like Black Flag, Bad Brains, and the Misfits. In fact, he painted a Black Flag *My War* jacket that I still have today. Ironically, Black Flag and Venom played together at my local concert spot from growing up called the City Gardens in Trenton, New Jersey. The Black Flag sound guy recorded all of the banter from Cronos that he uttered to crowd during the show and put it together for the amusement of the Black Flag guys and it's actually on YouTube and absolutely hilarious.

The last big thing was hearing Norwegian black metal for the first time. I was already listening to death metal bands like Death, Cannibal Corpse, and Deicide, as well as bands like Pantera and Sepultura, but hearing Mayhem and Emperor for the first time was a revelation. I always had a love for bands like Bauhaus and Joy Division, as well as old-school prog rock, and here was a music that had the brutality of American death metal with the goth vibe of Bauhaus and Christian Death with some progressive chops as well. I loved bands like Yes, King Crimson, and Genesis (Peter Gabriel era) and with bands like Enslaved, Behemoth, and Opeth, as well as so many others, moving from black or extreme metal into prog metal—that, for me, is the best of both worlds. I think those bands today are the ELPs and King Crimsons or Frank Zappa or Mahavishnu Orchestra of the 1970s. You want heavy? Go listen to Mahavishnu's *Between Nothingness and Eternity*. That record is heavy.

BoG: Similarly, what was your first "Ah-ha!" wine moment when you realized that wine was something special for you?

RS: I was very fortunate that my father was super into wine. When I was in high school, we had wine on the table for dinner almost every night and I was always allowed to have a glass. This was during the '80s and the wine world was totally different back then, but wines like Lynch Bages and Leoville Barton were always on the table. I started collecting wine with my dad after I graduated from college. He unfortunately died young, when I was around twenty-four. He left me with about 3,000 bottles of mostly Bordeaux, with a little bit of Rhône and Burgundy, but all great stuff. He bought very well. I still have probably most of it and lots have become almost too valuable to drink. I need to send my daughter to college in a few years and the rest may get sold then; it's hard-to-find, perfectly-stored-since-released Bordeaux.

BoG: What principles from underground music have helped you in the wine world?

RS: Really what music taught me most is that packaging sells records and wine. As a kid, before the internet, I used to love going to the record store and buying albums without having any idea of what they sounded like. Sometimes it resulted in finding records that stay with you for life, like Iron Maiden's *Killers* (yes, I still think Paul Di'Anno is the better singer), and other times I ended up buying Meatloaf's *Bat out of Hell*, which totally freaked me out. The album art is fantastic, but the music sounded like show tunes. That one I gave to my sister, who loved it.

Wolves

in the Throne Room

IN HIS 1962 BOOK *PROFILES OF THE FUTURE*, ARTHUR C. CLARKE FAMOUSLY STATED THAT "Any sufficiently advanced technology is indistinguishable from magic." That quote speaks to the nature of technology and where its advancement can lead us. But in many creative pursuits, whether it is creating raging, epic black metal or delicious wine, more and more folks are suspecting that perhaps nature has already been at this magical event horizon, or beyond it even. It's been posited that the harmony of living systems, holistic practices, and the seasonal rhythms of nature already provide a solution that advancements in technology are unable to answer. **WOLVES IN THE THRONE ROOM**, based in Olympia, Washington, demonstrates that these principles and biodynamics can extend beyond their predominant realm of wine and into music while taking inspiration from, and seeking connection with, the magic of nature.

Blood of Gods: With Wolves in the Throne Room, it should be mentioned that ritual, connection with nature, transformation, and alchemy, just like in wine, play strong roles. To people new to your band and music, how do you describe the themes that are important to you and your craft?

Aaron Weaver: We've been a band for nearly twenty years, so the inspiration and the method shifts with the phase of life. Each record springs directly from the experience of life in the moment. So it's quite sad, beautiful, and magical to go back through our discography and feel myself at those points in time. That being said, there has been a constant thread that we will not waver from: the music springs directly from our connection to the landscape of Cascadia. We simply listen to the voices of the spirits here and convert the vibrations into music through the lens of our human experience and individuality.

BoG: You've had a couple beer collaborations—and a mead one as well—but we think it's time for a Wolves in the Throne Room wine. If you were to collaborate with a winery, what type of wine do you envision?

AW: Nathan, Kody, and myself have pretty similar tastes in wine and we like to drink wine on stage, so it would have to be something really refreshing and invigorating. A red wine, quite dry. It would ideally be from a vineyard in the Pacific Northwest. I've got a long-standing interest in regenerative agriculture, so I'd advocate for a wine grown according to biodynamic principles. I've got my quibbles with Rudolf Steiner (I'm allergic to dogma and religious ossification of the mystery), but he was certainly an influence on my thinking as a young man.

BoG: Recording an album—or even an intense metal show—and making wine have been likened to each other, both having an element of "controlled chaos." There are some etiquette and "rules," but there's also that unpredictable component where magic or mayhem could erupt at any moment. Do you see similar parallels in your experience?

AW: Definitely. As I understand it, winemaking is a collaboration between the soil, the plants, the vintner, the elements and the microbes that transform the crushed fruit into wine. I certainly approach music from the same vantage point. My collaborators are certain trees and plants. Animal spirits and esoteric forces perceived in vision and dream. Inspiration is mysterious and exists most powerfully in the space within the yin and yang of controlled technique and chaotic abandon. All the arts, winemaking and music included, must be tapped into this current.

BoG: Sometimes fans and creators, whether of wine or metal, can experience burnout, creative blocks, or fatigue—does this ever happen for you? Do you ever require a palate cleanser, a recalibrating "North Star," or some kind of respite to reignite the passion?

AW: Usually, I build something out of wood. I worked as a carpenter for years before Wolves in the Throne Room was a full time job and I'm pretty good at it. Building a house is not too different from making a record. The same attention to detail, skillful crafting, and stamina is required to be successful. I'm a bit of a serial house builder. I like funky, unpermitted dwellings made of natural materials. After we've completed a record or another big project, I like to build something new or make changes to existing structures.

BoG: I'd imagine a good number of folks reading this who are into wine might not be familiar with Wolves in the Throne Room, and, like with some wines, your music can be an acquired taste, so for someone who's hearing about your music for the first time, where would you recommend people start with Wolves in the Throne Room?

AW: I'd suggest listening to our most recent full-length record, called *Primordial Arcana*. This is the record I'm most proud of because it marked the beginning of a new era for Wolves in the Throne Room. It's the first record that we produced entirely at our own recording studio in Olympia, without any outside producer or engineer. We also got very into video production for this record. We made two music videos ourselves which are quite good. So many bands slide into an easy creative rut after ten-plus years, but I'm proud to say that we will always challenge ourselves to go deeper into the music to find that fresh spring of creativity.

Founded by Jesse Schmidt and Hal Iverson, Gjallerhorn Winesmiths is quickly becoming one of the most exciting names in Washington state wine. Backed by a solid reputation and experience honed at other renowned wineries, this new venture is one to watch. And let's be honest–the name itself is worth remembering (go ahead, say it out loud: "Y'all-er-horn"–pretty fun, right?). With their unique approach and impressive beginnings, great things are already unfolding from this duo.

Blood Of Gods: There's such a strong thematic backbone to Gjallerhorn—the runic imagery, the ethos and spirit. What is the significance of this to you?

Gjallerhorn: We knew we didn't want to name our winery after ourselves. We are both Scandinavian in heritage and that felt like a genuine theme to us that we could really explore. In origin, our initial attraction was to the phonetic sound of Gjallerhorn (pronounced like y'all-er-horn) despite the inevitable difficulty people will have reading or pronouncing its spelling. It's an epic theme with lots of iconography to play with. We really enjoy tying each bottle to a rune symbol. Each rune means something different and specific, and we have a story for why each wine has a specific symbol. For example, our Chardonnay is named for the rune "Berkana," which symbolizes birth and new beginnings. Chardonnay was the first wine that we started making on our own—it will always be special to us.

Jon Kaplan

BoG: Your past experience for many years at Quilceda Creek, one of Washington state's most "cult" wineries, is almost entirely not mentioned. Surely this was intentional—can you chat a bit about that decision?

G: We are super grateful to have had some incredible learning opportunities involving Cabernet Sauvignon at Quilceda Creek. To have had such great experiences at such a storied winery is a gift, but we aren't ones to ride coattails. We want this brand to succeed on its own merits rather than an association to our previous employer. Shedding the moniker "the guys from Quilceda" has been a part of our journey. We're proud that the first wines we made under this brand were Chardonnay, Syrah, Grenache, Viognier, and Merlot—all wines that a Cabernet-dominant house like Quilceda Creek doesn't make. Of course, our winemaking history has served to pique some initial interest, but the expression, integrity of the wine, and how the wines perform is entirely a product of our efforts. We have our own unique vision for what these wines should be, we have incredibly high internal standards for them, and these are wines "of place" through our lens only.

BoG: Does it feel like you're starting over in a way? If so, what's most exciting and inspiring about that? Conversely, what's been the most challenging or daunting?

G: We wouldn't be anywhere without the gifted growers and the dynamic sites they have all cultivated. We sought out old-vine Wente clone Chardonnay planted in 1977 at Roza Hills, knock-out Merlot planted in 1992 by Washington wine legend Mike Saur at Red Willow, silky and lush Rocks Syrah from Rockbar vineyard in Milton-Freewater, and some incredibly precise and dynamic Rhône varietals from Olsen Vineyard. How can one have a pulse and not be excited about that? Conversely, we recognize the wine industry is in a weird moment right now. It was daunting to have the courage to just start the damn brand and follow our passion. We are entering our fifth vintage with this label. We started small and have grown slowly each year. We still make less than 100 cases of each varietal. There are a lot of struggling vineyards and wineries out there just barely hanging on. We aren't chasing any bullshit short-term trends. We aren't getting our wines scored. We aren't investing in influencers on Instagram. We are planting our flag in great sites, focusing on consistency, and creating intense flavors. That's what we feel is possible in our wine region. But we do recognize that it's not a guarantee, and this may not resonate in these strange times. But at least there's integrity in this approach, ya know?

"We aren't chasing any bullshit short-term trends. We aren't getting our wines scored. We aren't investing in influencers on Instagram. We are planting our flag in great sites, focusing on consistency, and creating intense flavors."

BoG: Scandinavian culture is almost synonymous with Vikings, which is to say: beer and mead. What would you say to make that case for wine to be more a part of this equation?

G: Wine grapes are now grown in Norway! We also know that Vikings expanded well into winegrowing areas of Europe for centuries. Can't you imagine them taking nips from the monk's casks? In modern-day Nordic cuisine—the amazing seafood, hearty meat and potato dishes—those meals beg for wine. No shade thrown on beer though: most of our end-of-the-day decompressions and conversations will involve a beer or five. But beer can't quite replace the passion, complexity, and intrigue that wine offers.

BoG: You reference the Poetic Edda on your website—which is essentially ground zero for all Norse mythology and legends—the name Gjallerhorn is the horn that signals Ragnarok . . . In short, there's some heavy and powerful concepts, but how heavy are your music-listening habits? What's spinning in the cellar during harvest?

G: We aren't sure if it's the hardest musical collection, but we listen a combination of pretty classic rock and really vibey, stoner rock stuff. Black Angels, King Gizz, Thee Oh Sees, Delta Spirit, My Morning Jacket, Tool, Soundgarden, Pearl Jam, Kyuss, the Doors, Zeppelin, Hendrix, Pink Floyd, Cream, Sabbath, Neil Young. Jesse is actually in a band called King Mammoth, which is a psychedelic rock band that has played all around Seattle. Music and vibe are incredibly important to us to set the tone of harvest and to inform our joy in it.

BoG: You poured at the *Blood of Gods* Third Annual Merrymaking in the summer of 2024. Having never attended before, what were your thoughts, key take-aways, and highlights? (Don't worry, we'll keep our ego in check)

G: We can't wait to do it again! It was such a great time, and we were blown away by the response from industry folk, but also metalheads that were in a world of their own enjoying great libations and great live bands. All of the vendors had incredible offerings and were nice as hell. The live music blew the doors off of the place at the end of the night and feeling the energy of the crowd was such a cool experience. When BoG can facilitate such a great lineup of bands, vendors, and winemakers, it's a recipe for a barn-burner. What a cool event to build community!

ANDREW KRAHNKE

CRADLE OF FILTH'S CAPTIVATING FRONTMAN, DANI FILTH,

IS AN EQUAL-OPPORTUNITY LIBATION LOVER WITH A PENCHANT FOR PROSECCO. HOWEVER, UNLIKE MOST MUSICIANS TO GRACE OUR PAGES, HE NOT ONLY IMBIBES THE NECTAR OF THE VINE, HE SUBTLY INCORPORATES IT IN HIS LYRICS WITH POETIC SKILL.

>>>

IKOSIDIO

Blood of Gods: So how big of a wine fan are you? Where are you on the libation spectrum, from beer, spirits, wine, etc.

Dani: Umm . . . alcohol? [Laughs] I've gone through phases of liking white wine for some strange reason, I really like chilled white wine. But then I went totally off it. I don't mind red from time to time, but I just find it too heavy. But I love Prosecco. I can drink Prosecco like water—I don't know why—I think it's the "fizz." But I can easily finish two bottles without even batting an eyelid, really [laughs].

BoG: We did a tasting with Nick and Aaron from Paradise Lost and they shared their unique perspective that, being from the U.K., like you are, there's definitely a cultural precedent where it's often generalized as being more of a beer-drinking culture, where there's not the history, like in France or Italy, and they felt like over time it's been warming up to wine-drinking.

D: Well, wine-drinking is big in the U.K., it's just that we're not a prolific grower of the vine. We do have vineyards around where I live, and in the south of England as well, such as Devon and Cornwall. The rest of England just doesn't really bode well for growing it. I mean, of course, yeah—south of France, Spain, Italy, it's all Mediterranean country, so you get great weather so, of course, yeah, plenty of wine to be had there.

BoG: Going into the lyrical side of things, this is kind of an exciting first, because most of the time the musician we're speaking with is a fan of wine, but the music and lyrics are completely a different deal, but with Cradle of Filth you have incorporated wine into your lyrics, most notably in *Dusk . . . and Her Embrace* but also in various points throughout your discography. It fits in so well with your themes of myth, history, romance, and sagas. How do you see it fitting into your repertoire?

D: Well, it's a euphemism for blood, isn't it? Yeah, so it comes up in all kinds of religious aspects during our lyricism. The wine of harlotry, utilizing it as a sacrifice. Early on, it was always—since you mentioned *Dusk . . . and Her Embrace*—it was always the vampiric element that wine was brought up into the lyrics. I mean, I wouldn't lean on it, I wouldn't say it was an important subject matter in our lyrics, it's just one of those things that gets alluded to from time to time.

BoG: So, I'm going to title this "I Drink the Blood-Red Wine ..." from one of your lyrics, and it seems very fitting. But what's the first lyric of yours that jumps to mind that includes mention of wine?

D: On the new album, "Drunk on the wine of the mass of fornication" I believe is one of the lines from "Black Smoke Curling from the Lips of War."

IKOSIDIO

BoG: Was there ever a moment that jumps out to you about being interested in wine, or was it more a blur . . . ?

Dani: Not really, no, sorry to be boring about it. But yeah, like I said, I enjoy a glass of wine but I'm not religious about it. I mean, I've been wine-tasting in France and in Spain . . . But actually, I do find some people to be a bit irritating about it. I just find it a little bit pompous, to be honest. I know some people who have wine cellars, and I don't think they can tell the difference between one bottle and the next, unless it's very obvious, ya know, "This one's got black currant and plum . . . This one's got red currants and jam." I think if you enjoy wine, you enjoy wine and the taste and it's each to their own. Sometimes you can get a five- or six-pound bottle of wine, and it could be equally as good as one that you'll find for fifteen or twenty pounds.

BoG: Absolutely. And that's the point that came up when talking with Daniel from Watain—where most times it's not about how expensive it is or how limited the wine is or the points or score it received. Sometimes it's pure circumstance: who you were with or where you were at. It could have been an old friend's house across the world, and you had some good stories and memories to share, and some nondescript wine greased the wheels of conversation.

D: Yeah, absolutely. It's definitely a very social drink. I mean, it's not really a pub thing for me. If I go into the pub, I'll have a Guinness or a nice lager or beer. But if it's at home with friends it's a different matter—it would be wine.

BoG: You had a good point, though, that it can be a bit of a pompous, irritating thing, and that's certainly one of those examples where I see some snobs in metal and there are some snobs in wine, as well as gatekeepers in both: "You're not evil enough, you're not smart enough, you don't know enough." Do you see any of that as it pertains to Cradle of Filth? I guess "elitists" would be the best word . . .

D: Elitists, yeah, definitely. Yeah, of course, you get the people who think they have a monopoly on your music or the genre in which they think your music is based. People who were like, "Oh no! I can't stand that band. They were only good before they got signed," or, "They were only good on their demo tapes." It's totally an elitist reaction, it's childish. I mean, it's all in the eye, er, palate, of the beholder, isn't it? And you should do what you want and enjoy what you want.

SPELLS, SPIRITS, AND SIPS: A MAGICAL GUIDE TO WIZARDS, WITCHES, AND WINE

Five master somms select which wines pair with these six famous wizards and witches from the literary canon.

Andrew Myers, M.S. ▬ Jackson Rohrbaugh, M.S. ▬ Nick Davis, M.S.
Justin Moore, M.S. ▬ Doug Frost, M.S., M.W.

Illustrations by Devin Forst

GANDALF

***The Lord of the Rings* by J. R. R. Tolkien**

The wise and powerful wizard who plays a crucial role in the fight against Sauron.

AM: Gandalf is a straight-up stoner, so I trust he's looking to get torn up and crash like a well-fed Hobbit, but he's also a classy bitch. I'd take him to Henri Bonneau "Celestines" Châteauneuf-du-Pape. It's got class and plenty of bang for the many bucks it takes to get one. It is also 80% likely to stain his beard in a most metal way \m/\m/

JR: Mithrandir, a.k.a. the Wielder of the Flame of Anor, is a destiny-shaper. He uses brilliant light to defeat enemies and inspire men and elves. He sparkles with wit and wisdom. Gandalf would drink Champagne, that most regal, helpful, and versatile of wines. Also, Glamdring would be the perfect sword to saber a bottle of Bal Roger.

ND: Bollinger Vieilles Vignes Françaises Champagne 1989. A Champagne as rare and extraordinary as the Grey Wizard himself, Bollinger Vieilles Vignes Françaises is the ultimate tribute to Gandalf's timeless wisdom and unwavering strength. This vintage Blanc de Noirs, crafted from ungrafted vines that survived the phylloxera epidemic, exudes an unparalleled elegance and depth. The fine mousse of the wine carries aromas of brioche, toasted hazelnuts, and dried fruit, weaving a narrative as intricate as Gandalf's own journey. Much like the wizard's ability to inspire hope in the darkest times, this Champagne leaves an indelible impression of light and endurance.

JM: Storm Crow loves his pipeweed, but when he's in it to cross-fade, only Gamay will do. He quells his parched palate with Bonnet Cotton "100% Cotton" Côte de Brouilly, straight from the bottle.

DF: "He that breaks a thing to find out what it is has left the path of wisdom." We live in an era that celebrates the notion of "if it ain't broke, break it," and there is no question that certain folks have benefited from this tendency. Gandalf was a red wine lover, and it seems to me that he would enjoy wines of a place. Some might connect him with "natural" wines, but most "natural" wines are so filled with extraneous, winemaking flavors that they express little or no sense of place. Sorry; that's just how it is. I associate someone like Gandalf with wines that profoundly express their origin, and most of us think of Burgundy in that regard. I vote for Vosne-Romanée and, since you asked, Meo-Camuzet's Vosne-Romanée.

MALEFICENT

Sleeping Beauty and *Maleficent*

a dark fairy often considered a witch, especially in her live-action reinterpretation.

AM: I'm going with Rombauer Chard. Yep. She seems most evil and just cougar-y enough to drink this foul witches' brew of sadness and impending divorce.

JR: Maleficent would drink Red Burgundy. Svelte, beautiful, and deadly—a walking enigma. Maleficent was oft-misunderstood and, while capable of great generosity and intrigue, could also turn on you in an instant. I don't know if there's a wine more capricious and capable of harm than Red Burgundy. I mean, I could spend $1,000 on a bottle right now, open it, and be disappointed that it's nowhere close to being ready to drink. And then I'm pretty sure the bottle would grow horns and wings and begin cackling maniacally.

ND: Cappellano Stravecchio Barolo Chinato 1967. For a dark enchantress like Maleficent, only a wine steeped in mystery and magic will suffice. Cappellano Stravecchio Barolo Chinato, a rare elixir of Barolo infused with quinine, herbs, and spices, perfectly mirrors her beguiling yet sinister nature. This potion-like wine dances between bitterness and sweetness, its layers of dried flowers, exotic spices, and medicinal depth casting a spell on all who taste it. The wine's complex and otherworldly character reflects Maleficent's ability to enchant, seduce, and strike fear, capturing her duality in a single, unforgettable sip.

JM: She obviously imbibes with super sexy, deep, dark and brooding wine. Must be Stella del Campalto Brunello di Montalcino.

DF: Here we are back to the age-old notion of misogyny, in a character obsessed with her beauty and youthfulness. She feels disrespected and so condemns an infant to death. But there's more: Disney's Maleficent was modeled on Vampira, who was modeled on the Charles Addams character of Morticia. In the Disney version, she has a husky, deep (hmm, almost male) voice, leading one to question her gender, or perhaps are we talking trans again? See what happens when you ask me these questions? What wine? Fucking First Growth Bordeaux, of course. You remember how Nixon would drink Château Margaux and serve everybody else Cru Bourgeois. Very Maleficent of him.

MERLIN

Perhaps the most famous wizard of all time, Merlin is a central figure in the tales of King Arthur, known for his wisdom and magical abilities.

AM: A gentleman by most accounts. I believe he would enjoy a polite glass of Raveneau, Montée de Tonnerre while supping on eye-of-newt soup.

JR: In Merlin's tower, the various and sundry handblown flasks must have contained the spoils of English trade and conquest—there's no doubt Merlin had an early iteration of Claret, probably pulled from one of King Arthur's own barrels, potentially captured in a raid on the French coast. This would be the oldest-school style of Bordeaux: closer to a dark rosé in color, with lovely tannin, and most likely a field blend made from the main Bordeaux grapes like Cabernet Sauvignon and Merlot, but all the obscure and extinct ones too. Anyone up for a blend of Petit Verdot, Hourcat and Moustozères?

ND: Egon Müller Le Gallais Riesling Auslese Goldkapsel Wiltinger Braune Kupp 1975. Merlin's timeless wisdom and mystical charm are captured perfectly in the golden brilliance of Egon Müller's Auslese Riesling. Hailing from the legendary Wiltinger Braune Kupp vineyard, this wine is nothing short of magical, with its dazzling interplay of sweetness, vibrant acidity, and profound minerality. Aromas of ripe peach, honey, and crushed slate rise like an incantation from the glass, invoking the essence of Merlin's alchemy. As it evolves on the palate, its complexity deepens, much like the wizard's own intricate lore, making it a wine to savor and contemplate.

JM: This wizard is the OG and slams OG juice. His lips are often stained red with Domaine J. L. Chave Hermitage. King Arthur and the whole round table would approve.

DF: Well, the easy answer would be a bottle of Napa's Blackbird, since "merle" is a French term for a blackbird. But Merlin is a complicated jumble: was he fathered by an incubus? Does his name suggest that he is in fact a madman (look it up)? There is something dark at work and so I want to go to one of the darkest wines I know: Julio B. Bastos Alicante Bouschet, from Portugal's Alentejo.

BABA YAGA

From Slavic folklore and various adaptations

A witch who lives in a house on chicken legs, blending the line between helper and hindrance in stories.

AM: Kirkland bag-in-box Pinot Grigio. She lives in a house with chicken legs, so it's not like she has a strong design aesthetic or sense of taste. I'm pretty sure she's just looking for a cheap buzz.

JR: All I know is that Keanu Reeves, who plays my favorite "version" of Baba Yaga in the John Wick series, really digs great Australian reds. So, if Baba Yaga (you gotta pronounce it "Bebeh Yeygah," like the Russian mobsters do in the movies) was sitting down to a nice dinner of New York Strip, I'd be reaching for a great Shiraz like Hill of Grace or Rockford Basket Press. Yum! I'm sure the actual Baba Yaga wouldn't mind a dark red potion like that either!

ND: Grgić Vina Plavac Mali Pelješac 2008. Rooted in the rugged terrain of Croatia, Grgić Vina's Plavac Mali embodies the earthy, untamed spirit of Baba Yaga. This bold and rustic red wine, with its robust tannins and notes of dark berries, dried herbs, and a hint of coastal saltiness, evokes the wild forests and unpredictable nature of the witch's domain. Fermented with minimal intervention, the wine carries an ancient energy, reflecting Baba Yaga's connection to primal forces and Slavic traditions. Each sip is like stepping into her chicken-legged hut—mysterious, captivating, and just a little unsettling.

JM: This creep is a total hipster, soooo ... orange wine, duh. Not just any orange wine, "amber wine" in the style of Georgia, the oldest wine-producing country on this planet. Chona's Marani Kisi-Mtsvane Amber, Kakheti, Georgia

DF: The ubiquitous wicked old witch in fairy tales is deeply relevant in our misogynistic culture; the Salem witch trials seem long ago today, but the idea of strange women with spooky powers who must be guarded against is, IMHO, just another version of gender terrorism. And, since you asked, idiots like Nancy Mace denying people their basic rights (to pee, no less) are continuing that shameful trauma; let people speak and be free, whatever their gender. So, this one is easy: I recommend Chrysalis Norton from Jenni McCloud in Virginia. I hope she'll forgive me for connecting her with Baba Yaga; I think she'll understand why I did so. I recommend her wine too.

DUMBLEDORE

The Harry Potter seires by J.K. Rowling

The wise and enigmatic headmaster of Hogwarts.

AM: Definitely a well-aged Madeira. I can't imagine he'd get into his cups. Strikes me more as a distinguished gentleman that would rather sip one glass of something amazing.

JR: Dumbledore would most definitely drink enigmatic wines of contemplation. Dumbledore would drink aged, old-school Barolo of the highest quality—think Rinaldi, Giacomo Conterno, and Giuseppe Mascarello. Barolo is the Bertie Bott's Every Flavor Bean of the wine world: you don't always know if it's going to be savory, fruity, lush, or sour, and that's why we keep coming back for more. For someone who loves speaking in riddles as much as Dumbledore, I can't think of a grape he'd rather drink than Nebbiolo.

ND: Justin Vineyards Isosceles Reserve Paso Robles 1996. Dumbledore, the wise and compassionate headmaster of Hogwarts, deserves a wine that balances intellect and heart. Justin Vineyards' Isosceles Reserve is a masterful blend of Cabernet Sauvignon, Merlot, and Cabernet Franc, with layers as intricate as the wizard himself. Notes of black currant, cassis, and cedar unfold alongside whispers of graphite and a touch of earthiness, creating a wine that is both powerful and approachable. As it opens in the glass, the wine reveals even more depth, mirroring Dumbledore's ability to guide with strength and kindness, offering a moment of quiet reflection amid life's chaos.

JM: When not pounding the potion of despair, he needs something serious to keep his crystal goblet wet. He drinks magnums of Il Carnevale Caberlot from Tuscany.

DF: What would Dumbledore drink (WWDD)? Truthfully, Echolands Winery Albus (Sauvignon Blanc-Semillon blend, partially barrel fermented) is named Albus not merely because it's Latin for "white" and that was more fun to say than "white." Instead, I have two daughters who instantly took a shine to our Albus, because they knew that was Dumbledore's first name. And that's really why I did it.

SARUMAN

The Lord of the Rings by J. R. R. Tolkien

The once-great wizard who turns to darkness, serving as a major antagonist.

AM: Aglianico. It's known as "the Dark Monarch" of wines. That's metal as fuck. Saruman could be his own solo black metal band à la Xasthur.

JR: The hour is later than you think. Saruman seeks power, influence, and to place his name among the greats. Saruman definitely drinks Napa Cabernet. I mean, just look at some of Napa's biggest and most impressive wineries. There's definitely an Orthanc-like sheen to many of them, all black glass and custom-poured seamless concrete. If Saruman represents striving for power, he definitely enjoys the aspirational-wealth vibes of America's most prominent and powerful wine region. Now to just keep those trees on the fringe from burning . . .

ND: Pegasus Bay Gewürztraminer North Canterbury 2010. Saruman's descent into darkness is reflected in the layered and intense character of Pegasus Bay Gewürztraminer. This wine's unctuous texture and aromatic complexity offer an initial allure of beauty and sophistication, much like Saruman's once-noble persona. Exotic notes of lychee, ginger, Turkish delight, and rose petal create an air of opulence, but beneath lies a powerful and almost overwhelming core. As the wine unfolds, its richness can feel excessive, much like Saruman's greed and ultimate corruption. It is a pairing that captures his journey—a story of brilliance marred by ambition and betrayal.

JM: Being a white wizard, this mf primarily crushes white wine so his beard stays fresh. He's a geezer, so he likes that old-man juice but nothing basic. Few know this, but he's actually gluten-sensitive so he gets his bread from a former baker turned winemaker, Genot-Boulanger. Puligny-Montrachet Les Foilitiere 1er Cru is in his chalice.

DF: One of Tolkein's greatest and most terrifying characters embodied a rationalizing, self-interested fascism that was well-known to Tolkien (and might remind people today of a few folks). The ability to believe in something corrupt simply because it can be justified by pretzel logic, lazy disrespect, and contrarian and petulant anger reminds me of so many poorly made wines with excessive oak, lofty alcohols, and funky "natty" aromas. People rave about such wines, though I don't see them having more than a glass or two before they move onto something that actually tastes good. But people can fool themselves into just about anything, it seems.

SCOTT FLANDERS

D-I-Wine

Nonconformity and Do-It-Yourself Mentality

BLOOD OF GODS
WHAT'S SO
PUNK
ABOUT
WINE
?
NICOLE GOUX

THE PUNK ETHOS MAY NOT SEEM IMMEDIATELY CONNECTED TO THE WORLD OF WINE, BUT ITS CORE IDEALS ARE FUELING SOME OF THE MOST EXCITING INNOVATIONS IN THE INDUSTRY. A DO-IT-YOURSELF SPIRIT, A DRIVE TO CHALLENGE THE STATUS QUO, AND A COMMITMENT TO CREATIVE EXPRESSION AND INDEPENDENCE ARE INSPIRING WINEMAKERS AND BRANDS TO BREAK FREE FROM OUTDATED TRADITIONS. WE'VE SELECTED A FEW EXAMPLES TO EXPLORE THE QUESTION "WHAT'S SO PUNK ABOUT WINE?"

ERIC WAREHEIM & JOEL BURT, OWNER AND WINEMAKER, LAS JARAS

COURTESY OF LAS JARAS

TO US, PUNK ROCK IS MORE THAN A GENRE OF MUSIC, it is a full-on aesthetic worldview. The early days of punk rock in New York City were a backlash to the glossy, overproduced, and predictable music that arena-rock bands like the Eagles were playing. Every band had a fucking Wurlitzer on stage and someone playing a flute. Punk showed you can do it with a trio and only knowing three chords on the guitar. Punk rock was a way to explore new sounds and harness raw energy. Not surprisingly, the recent world of wine has had a similar arc.

When I went to school to study winemaking in the early 2000s, my professors were obsessed with making wines that were free of flaws and faults.

>>>>

Wine publications and their critics also had a stranglehold on the industry and only awarded high marks to wines that were rich and oaky. This led to a worldwide homogenization of wine where each was analogous to your most despised Eagles song. I was blessed with early wine mentorship from an old-school curmudgeon who hated high-alcohol wines and loved European wine, and by the time I graduated from university I was primed to join the nascent "real wine" movement. This movement, along with the "pursuit of balance" movement, was a way to express that wines from California can have moderate alcohol, apparent acidity, and modest use of new oak; in other words: DRINKABLE WINE. Winemakers in this scene were generally interested in minimal-intervention winemaking as well, such as native yeast fermentations. Much of this movement merged with the natural-wine movement and that is where things started to get a little crazy and very punk rock.

I think of the natural-wine movement as having first and second waves. The first wave was mostly producers that were trying to make terroir-driven wines that resembled the benchmarks of their region (Bourgogne, Rhône, Loire, Sicily, etc.) but fermenting naturally and only using organic or biodynamic grapes and avoiding the use of chemicals in the cellar, except for sometimes sulfur. In the second wave came the iconoclastic wines that define the current era. These are the wines that can be quite wild like our "Superbloom," which is unlike any traditional wine where it is a carbonic co-ferment pink wine that tastes like a watermelon Jolly Rancher sprinkled with celery salt, or the kombucha-esque pet-nats that quench everyone's thirst in Palm Springs. When Eric and I started Las Jaras, we were interested in exploring and producing wines that conform to minimal-intervention winemaking but also deliver pleasure and are easy to drink. That puts our wines in both waves of the natural-wine scene, but we are focused on continually elevating the quality, exploring new styles, and making new statements. We are kinda post-punk/math rock. Just like punk rock, I think we'll see lots of variety in this space (some natural winemakers even like Phish!), and hopefully no corporate bullshit!

CHRISTIAN TSCHIDA, OWNER AND WINEMAKER, TSCHIDA

I ALWAYS ASKED MYSELF, "WHICH MOTHERFUCKER said that white wine had to taste like water with flavor and red wine needs 14.5% alcohol to be a good one?" At the age of twenty-five, after analyzing my first red, the authorities called me (they never call) and politely "recommended" to not bottle a wine like this—with 12.2% it would be too light, too fresh, and very special in taste. Of course I bottled it, and the unique wine was sold out after a couple of weeks. Some years later, exactly this fresh style of red was the next big shit, and my life started to become even more crazy when our family vineyards started to look like a green jungle after treating it my way for years. People started to call me an enfant terrible. They said I was killing the family vineyards and wasting the best grapes. Then, after six vintages of experimental vinification, I released my first macerated white. In Austria it was like driving at 130 mph against a wall. This was the next big question mark until the now world-famous restaurant Noma in Copenhagen discovered my "Himmel auf Erden Maischevergoren" for their menu. Now in my forties, I feel more punk than ever before—still searching for the Holy Grail, still a very nasty boy.

COURTESY OF CHRISTIAN TSCHIDA

COURTESY OF CAMILLE LINDSLEY

CAMILLE LINDSLEY, HAGS, NEW YORK CITY

THERE ARE FEW THINGS THAT INTEREST ME MORE ABOUT subcultures than their favorite acquired tastes. These preferences often appear, at first glance, to be strange, counterintuitive, or even ironically chosen. However, my appreciation for music that others might label as "completely unlistenable" is entirely genuine. When I first got into wine, there were more than a few acquired tastes that other sommeliers prided themselves on that struck me as counter to what a "real somm" would dare drink, let alone encourage others to try. Like the beloved-by-some Einstürzende Neubauten, Harvey Milk, Bauhaus, or other bands that I initially found unpleasantly challenging, some of my favorite wines were ones I came around to after initially writing off. I found myself enamored with lush yet much maligned Merlot, sweet Auslese Rieslings from Germany with the ABV of an IPA, and sherries of all kinds. Maybe because of my love of acquired tastes in music, I have a soft spot for wines that are "underdogs" of the wine world. Perhaps one day my one-woman crusade to get more people to drink more sweet wines will convert a couple people to the sweet side of acquired tastes.

DR. JAMIE GOODE, *SUNDAY EXPRESS*

COURTESY OF JAIME GOODE

ON THE SURFACE, WINE DOESN'T SEEM very punk. It has a conservative air to it, and it's often associated with wealth, status, and the respect of centuries of tradition. And I once got invited to an event in Napa where the dress code was "wine country casual." Definitely not punk. But wine has its counterculture. It gets under the skin of all sorts of people, and some of the best wines are made by younger, self-supporting winemakers with a very punk attitude. Rent some space in a cellar, borrow equipment, buy a few tons of grapes, and let your imagination run riot. Try new winemaking techniques (or, indeed, just doing less). You don't need a fortune to start your own project, as long as you aren't working in the most famous wine regions, with celebrity grape varieties. Some of my favorite wines began life as home-brew projects from young winemakers with a day job at a larger winery. The punk side? Well, questioning the status quo, for a start. Doing things without fancy equipment but improvising and riffing simply with what's available. On the surface, things might look chaotic and unruly, but usually these people know exactly what they are doing, and it takes a great deal of skill to make wines with little intervention and without the safety net of the usual bag of tricks. These young winemakers are making lesser-known varieties famous, and they are bringing attention to regions that previously were frequently overlooked. Forget fancy Napa Cabs, or wine country casual: we want something grittier, more authentic, and more fun.

VICTOR MELENDEZ

THE HEAVIEST MOMENTS OF SUB POP RECORDS

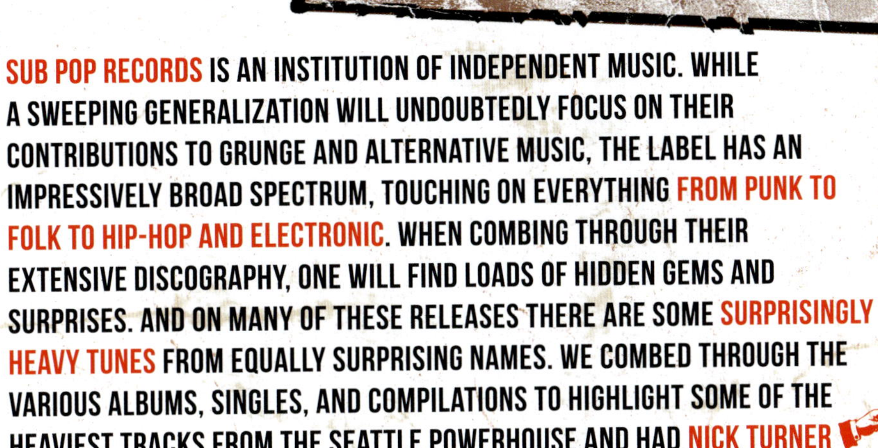

SUB POP RECORDS IS AN INSTITUTION OF INDEPENDENT MUSIC. WHILE A SWEEPING GENERALIZATION WILL UNDOUBTEDLY FOCUS ON THEIR CONTRIBUTIONS TO GRUNGE AND ALTERNATIVE MUSIC, THE LABEL HAS AN IMPRESSIVELY BROAD SPECTRUM, TOUCHING ON EVERYTHING FROM PUNK TO FOLK TO HIP-HOP AND ELECTRONIC. WHEN COMBING THROUGH THEIR EXTENSIVE DISCOGRAPHY, ONE WILL FIND LOADS OF HIDDEN GEMS AND SURPRISES. AND ON MANY OF THESE RELEASES THERE ARE SOME SURPRISINGLY HEAVY TUNES FROM EQUALLY SURPRISING NAMES. WE COMBED THROUGH THE VARIOUS ALBUMS, SINGLES, AND COMPILATIONS TO HIGHLIGHT SOME OF THE HEAVIEST TRACKS FROM THE SEATTLE POWERHOUSE AND HAD NICK TURNER FROM SUB POP'S A&R AND SALES DEPARTMENTS WEIGH IN WITH HIS QUICK TAKES ON THE TEN SONGS THAT TOPPED OUR LIST.

COURTESY OF NICK TURNER

1. SLAYER, "ABOLISH GOVERNMENT"

FROM THE SLAYER/T.S.O.L. SPLIT 7" *SINGLE*, 1996

Thrash metal gods Slayer paid tribute to their hardcore punk influences on their 1996 album *Undisputed Attitude*, which featured covers of D.R.I., Verbal Abuse, Minor Threat, etc., plus a few punky originals. "Abolish Government/Superficial Love" is Slayer's take on two tracks by Huntington Beach reprobates T.S.O.L., with the latter's original 1981 versions on the B side. It's a fitting homage to the '80s underground explosion that inspired both Slayer and Sub Pop. And . . . IT'S FUCKIN' SLAYER!!!

2. SOUNDGARDEN, "ROOM A THOUSAND YEARS WIDE"

7" SINGLE, 1990

Soundgarden had a stunning amalgam of '70s heavy rock and post-punk experimentation from the get-go, and their talents are on full display in this raw version of "Room a Thousand Years Wide." It's a wild and grimy trip, with guitars that slug and chug, propulsive yet unpredictable rhythms, Chris Cornell's inimitable wail, and a frantic sax solo. A more polished version wound up on the band's breakthrough album, *Badmotorfinger*, a year or so later.

3. HANDSOME, "CAN'T CONNECT"

FROM THE "SWIMMING" *7" SINGLE*, 1995

This groove-oriented rock tune by Handsome is a perfect snapshot of a particular moment in the '90s when players from the prior decade's hyper-aggro hardcore scene were exploring more varied—but no less loud—modes of expression. With one member each from post-hardcore legends Quicksand, emo standard-bearers Jets to Brazil, art-metallers Helmet, and fearsome New York hardcore icons Cro-Mags, Handsome's pedigree says it all. The era's sound has proven durable, with bands like Turnstile putting their own spin on it today.

4. GODFLESH, "WOUND '91"

7" SINGLE, 1990

Godflesh came out of the late-'80s U.K. grindcore scene alongside Napalm Death (Godflesh founder Justin Broadrick's former band), Extreme Noise Terror, and Carcass. But while those bands went for land speed records, Godflesh waded in molasses, using their drum machine and atonal guitars to create an agonizing crawl. "Wound '91" harkens back to their crushing early material, while A side "Slateman" hints at the shoegazey melodies of Godflesh's influential later releases.

5. TAD, "STUMBLIN' MAN"

FROM *8 WAY SANTA*, 1991

TAD is responsible for some of the heaviest riffs of the Seattle scene, and some entertaining album-art stories as well! "Stumblin' Man" has it all: a low-frequency dirge, snarling vocals, and a tale of a down-and-out fellow with nowhere to go but further down and further out. Singer, guitarist, and founder Tad Doyle is a true gem of Northwest music, and he's still out there making tunes, producing, and supporting new bands.

6. UNSANE, "VANDAL X"

7" SINGLE, 1990

Long-running New York trio Unsane let loose two of their trademark noise-rock assaults on this 7" for the Sub Pop Singles Club. "Vandal X" pounds the ears for just under two minutes and splits the moment it has made its point, as all good punk songs should. The cover features a naked person cowering in the corner of a blood-splattered room; the image, rendered in black and white, is tame in comparison to the gleefully gory full-color images that adorn Unsane's albums.

7. ROLLINS BAND, “EARACHE MY EYE”

7" SINGLE, 1990

The Singles Club gave—and still gives!—the label many opportunities to work with friends and fellow travelers in the world of underground music, and this release is a fun highlight. Ex-Black Flag frontman Henry Rollins brings his warlike intensity to Cheech Marin’s parody song from the ’70s stoner film *Up in Smoke*, resulting in a thunderous hard-rock romp. A wonderful rejoinder to all who accuse Rollins of being too serious. And, for those who prefer it DEAD serious, there’s his spoken-word dive into alienation and solitude on the B side!

8. ZEKE, “JACK TORRANCE”

7" SINGLE, 2000

The first of three blasts of joyfully aggressive punk from Zeke’s Singles Club release, this *Shining*-inspired tune makes the Ramones sound like prog rock. The B side pays tribute to another horror classic, *Evil Dead*, and the whole record clocks in at almost exactly three minutes. The cover features Tad Doyle doing his best Jack Nicholson impression, an image that was lovingly co-opted for a Father John Misty shirt in recent years. Genre films have been a fruitful influence for many Sub Pop artists: check out Mudhoney’s biker-movie sample on *Superfuzz Bigmuff*, Clipping’s two horror-rap concept albums, and Weyes Blood’s slasher-film video for “Everyday.”

9. PALLBEARER, “ATLANTIS””

7" SINGLE, 2019

Arkansas doom-metal troupe Pallbearer graciously contributed this melancholy banger to Sub Pop’s thirtieth-anniversary reboot of the Singles Club. As much as we adore the go-for-the-throat approach of Zeke and Unsane, we still have plenty of room for more expansive approaches to the heavy stuff. In “Atlantis,” Pallbearer’s mix of punishing doomy riffs and plaintive prog-rock passages make for a lovely combination.

10. NIRVANA, “NEGATIVE CREEP”

FROM *BLEACH*, 1989

A little band from Aberdeen, Washington, that really could have gone somewhere if anyone had paid attention. Much has been made of Nirvana’s knack for pop hooks—and rightly so—but they could be super heavy when they wanted to be. With agonizingly bendy guitar lines, stop-start rhythms, and a chorus anchored by a pummeling double-kick beat, “Negative Creep” sounds like a musical approximation of seasickness. But, like, in a good way.

VICTOR MELENDEZ

IS JASON WILSON PUNK?

is Wine Writing? are you? Am I?

COURTESY OF JASON WILSON

THAT'S A HARD MAYBE. SO WE GAVE THE FOOD/TRAVEL/WINE WRITER THE LIGHTNING ROUND TO ASCERTAIN STREET CRED. >>>>>
(VISIT HIS WEBSITE: EVERYDAYDRINKING.COM)

BLOOD OF GODS: Your newsletter and articles deftly push back on bullshit regularly. I think this can be a great spearhead to dethrone figureheads in ivory towers, but, in your view, how can typical audiences push back when encountering someone who is trying to peddle/espouse something that is clearly bullshit?

JASON WILSON: People always comment on my having a "no bullshit" approach or, as you say, that I "push back on the bullshit," but I guess I don't really see it that way. Obviously, yes, there's a ton of bullshit in the wine business. But mostly I just ignore the bullshit. Ultimately, I feel like the only way to successfully fend off bullshit is to ignore it. Which is why my approach is more about celebrating and advocating for things I believe represent quality and value. Certainly, I've done my share of rants. But I really do try to limit how often I'm the ranting curmudgeon. It's much easier to write a snarky takedown than to write a piece expressing sincerely why something is really good, and I like to focus on the latter as much as possible.

> "OH, YOU MEMORIZED THE THIRTEEN GRAPES USED IN CHÂTEAUNEUF-DU-PAPE? COOL, BRO. YEAH, I FORGOT FOUR OF THE GRAPES, BUT I HAVE GOOGLE ON MY PHONE SO I'M GOOD."

BOG: Hypothetical scenario: 1) Wine Scores/Points. 2) Terroir Deniers. 3) Wine Certification/Credentials Programs (i.e. WSET, Court of Master Somms, etc.)—you get to pick which of these three topics gets banished from wine discourse forever—which one hits the road and why?

JW: Wow, I mean, you could make a case for all three. Terroir Deniers are idiots and so will eventually banish themselves from the discourse. Wine scores are lame, but as long as they're done with integrity they're harmless. They help some (mostly older) people in their wine-buying, I guess. It's not the scores themselves but particular critics that are the issue. I guess if I had to pick, I would say certifications and credentials because, at this point, I don't really know what they're actually for. A lot of the exams just seems like spending a lot of time and money to prepare for a wine version of Trivial Pursuit. Oh, you memorized the thirteen grapes used in Châteauneuf-du-Pape? Cool, bro. Yeah, I forgot four of the grapes, but I have Google on my phone so I'm good. One problem with the credentialing is that it reinforces the idea that wine needs gatekeepers. The second problem is that it continues to normalize the idea that wine is something you need to be educated on, that it's this topic you need to study if you want to enjoy it.

BOG: Asking questions, challenging the status quo, do-it-yourself attitude, and speaking your mind—with volume and heart—is at the core of punk, metal, hardcore … just like your writing. So just how crazy are your music-listening habits compared to your feisty articles about wine, food, and travel?

JW: Hahaha, I think I may have rather boring music tastes. I wish I could tell the Blood of Gods audience I listen to Norwegian black metal or Finnish death metal. But my metal era was very short, in the late 1980s South Jersey, culminating with maybe Dio or Cinderella. I still occasionally listen to the skate punk and grunge of my youth, stuff like the Descendents, Minor Threat, the Faction, Agent Orange, Hole, L7, the Gits, and more contemporary ones like Fidlar, Bleached, the Orwells, etc. but not as often. Though I have interrogated this in an essay for Everyday Drinking, I am decidedly not punk.

When I write now, I mostly listen to some sort of EDM: house, techno, ambient, trance, big room, whatever. I never totally know the definitions of the various rave-y sub-genres, but I like it all. When I write I need that wall of sound and repetition and absence of lyrics. When not writing, I listen to a mish-mash of pop punk, eurotrash, '60s French pop, '90s hip-hop, reggaeton, alt-country, emo, and what some friends call "whiny" alt-rock. Which I don't think is fair, but there we are. When I was recently on a long drive in Spain, I put on a playlist called something like "Sad Girl Starter Kit" and after an hour of listening to Mitski, Phoebe Bridgers, Beach Bunny, Angel Olsen, Haley Heynderickx, Mazzy Star, etc. my travel companion finally was like, "I'm going to throw myself out of the car if we keep listening to this," and she put on disco. That's fine, agree to disagree, but I do love that kind of sad music.

"IF WE WANT WINE TO MOVE FORWARD AND GROW THE ENGAGEMENT AND ACCEPTANCE OF A WIDER AUDIENCE, WINE COMMUNICATION CERTAINLY HAS TO BECOME LESS EMBARRASSING."

BOG: What is going to be the next big trend in wine, or the next biggest hot-button issue?

JW: I've been saying it for a while, but the whole idea of mainstream wine is changing. That $11.99 wine the industry is trying to sell us just isn't engaging younger wine-drinkers. Look at the numbers worldwide—there's an overproduction of middling wines. The emerging generation of wine drinkers wants something that's either a) even cheaper (wine in cans, wine in boxes) or b) well-made, good-value wine that's more expensive. For the latter, we keep seeing study after study saying that the younger generation drinks less but spends more. And for the former, the wine industry doesn't seem to understand that it's competing at the lower end with seltzers, High Noon, and other shit in a can.

BOG: Based on feedback, what has been your spiciest hot take of an article you've written, and why do you think it elicited such responses?

JW: I think my recent piece entitled "Does Wine Writing Have to Be So Embarrassing?", in which I call out the way that legacy, general-interest publications (in this case the New York Times) covers wine—I used the Times Magazine's recent profile of Oregon winemaker Maggie Harrison as the main example. Basically, I asked why wine can never be covered like any other normal part of culture, but instead always has some false conflict or narrative foisted on it. I definitely got more comments, emails, and likes on that than other pieces. I don't know why, though. I've definitely called out other things more aggressively in the past. Maybe it's a question that's been on a lot of other people's minds. If we want wine to move forward and grow the engagement and acceptance of a wider audience, wine communication certainly has to become less embarrassing.

Maison Jérôme Lefèvre

"Controlled chaos" is a phrase that has often danced around the phenomenon of heavy music, be it punk, metal, or hardcore, particularly in the live setting. There's a loose organization to the goings-on of live shows, but the unexpected always pits order against disorder and what ensues is the exhilarating stew where the magic happens. It's also an apt metaphor for the process behind making wine. Champagne producer Jérôme Lefèvre has one foot firmly in each scene and years of experience in both to draw parallels and valuable crossover lessons between the two.

Blood of Gods: What was your first "music moment" when you discovered a taste for underground/extreme music?

Jérôme Lefèvre: I was introduced to heavy metal very early, at the age of seven. I was given some records (AC/DC, Deep Purple) by one of my uncles because I was fascinated by the album covers and the band pictures. I grew up in a village, so I had never seen such looks. I don't know where it comes from, but I've always been interested in pictures. I got into this music that was totally new for me, and I soon discovered Iron Maiden, Judas Priest, Motörhead. *The Live after Death*, *British Steel*, and *Bomber* albums had a very strong impact on me, and those records still count among my favorites today. But due to my generation and entering my teenage years, I immediately came to thrash metal and punk, especially American hardcore punk, and then the grindcore and death metal scenes that emerged from punk and thrash. I was deep into a range from Black Flag, the Misfits, Discharge, Bad Brains, Poison Idea, Slayer, D.R.I., Suicidal Tendencies to the whole extreme metal scene: Napalm Death, Repulsion, Carcass, Death, Master, Autopsy, Morbid Angel, Obituary, Bolt Thrower, and others. I formed a grindcore/noise band named Dismal Death where I used to sing and play the guitar. I could say punk and metal had a strong effect on me and the way I think. Hardcore punk and grindcore also opened my perceptions. There was a noise aspect that really attracted me. There were also extremely short songs, a bit the way bands like S.O.D. or Negative Approach did, and I love it. It's strange when you get into that at fourteen! But later this made me able to understand contemporary and experimental composers like Olivier Messiaen, John Cage, Stockhausen, or La Monte Young—as well for jazz and electronic music.

BoG: Similarly, what was your first aha wine moment when you realized that wine was something special for you?

JL: My family has been grape-growing in Champagne for generations, but my interest in wine came quite late. I discovered contemporary art through Raymond Pettibon—he did the art for Black Flag and was kind of a hero for me. So when I saw in an art magazine and this guy was showing his œuvre in art galleries and museums of contemporary art, I told myself that scene is necessarily very cool. I did research to understand what the fuck was "Contemporary Art," and I studied art. I did a career as an art critic and curated some exhibitions and it's only in this context that I tasted very interesting Champagne and Burgundy wines. I never tried truly good wines before. From that moment I told myself wines could also be objects of contemplation as well as painting, poetry, or some music could be. I decided to do wine myself from a very tiny family domain instead of just selling the grapes. So I converted the domain to organic, I created the brand, I did the first cuvées, and you know the rest.

For a moment, I did both activities together. The year I did my first wines, in 2013, I also curated an exhibition about the links between contemporary art and extreme metal. It was named "Altars of Madness" and took place first in Luxembourg and then in France, showing works of artists like Damien Deroubaix, Matthew Barney, Banks Violette, Harmony Korine, Steven Shearer, Mark Titchner, Torbjørn Rødland, and some others. We also added historical figures in the show: Gee Vaucher from Crass and the root of the grindcore aesthetics; Larry Carroll, who did the major art works for Slayer; and works from the nineteenth-century Norwegian artist Theodor Kittelsen as the root of the black metal aesthetics. I asked for documents (flyers, demos, art covers) from musicians such as Mick Harris, Fenriz, and Jeff Walker for the catalog. It was really cool to do this. Now I do only wine.

BoG: One of the things I love about Delalot is that the branding, appearance, and aesthetic are very refined and polished, so it might be a surprise to some in the wine world that you're into punk, metal, and hardcore. Do you ever feel like a fish out of water?

JL: That's true. I wanted something very "in the usual codes" because my approach at the vineyard was already very singular. It's a very small domain, and I wanted to work it not only organic but also without any machines. It was already kind of a challenge to do so, and really unusual in Champagne, which is quite conservative.

But here resides the link between my approach and extreme music: the way I work the vines and I do the wines are strongly inspired by the readings of people like Masanubo Fukuoka, Henry David Thoreau, or Aldo Leopold. It might seem strange but I know my interest in these statements also comes from bands like Crass, Discharge, Napalm Death, and D.I.Y. politics. This is really the link between my wines and extreme metal. There is both an intellectual and political approach. It goes further than sustainability or working organic. I always have some Thoreau and Fukuoka books in the winery.

BoG: What principles from underground music have helped you in the wine world?

JL: First I would say thrash metal and punk introduced me to my future reading and understanding of Thoreau, Fukuoka, and some others. That was huge for me. Today I work the vineyard without any machines, all by hand. I don't really care about doing something "punk," but for me it's a very D.I.Y. approach. The less machines I use, the more independent I am. For sure it also gave me a kind of independent way of thinking. This is a quality of the underground scene: once you've gotten into it, you're not afraid of being far from the mainstream. You just don't care about the mainstream. But I'm a composite of all the things I've experienced. That's also what is cool with wine: a good wine is an experience and that's why it's precious. Because we are all made by our experiences—that's what really counts in life. And again, I'm convinced wines can be objects of contemplation.

BoG: "Controlled chaos" is a phrase I've often heard to describe the melting pot of energy and influences at punk and metal concerts. It also seems to be a great descriptor for winemaking in that you're working with nature's biological and chemical agents. Can you talk about the parallels between the two?

JL: Exactly. It even starts in the parcel. Grape-growing is already kind of controlling chaos because it

can have a lot of directions and you have to choose yours depending on the wines you want to do at the end. Now I work the different parcels differently from each other.

Then, winemaking is of course controlling chaos because if you don't you will make vinegar. When you do natural or strictly organic wine, you work a very raw material, a living material. And to get the best from it there's an alchemy. If you're good you can do stunning wine. Michelangelo said the sculptures are already in the marble blocks and only a good artist is able to pull them out. I think it's the same for wine. Grapes ferment easily, wine is already there, but the quality of the winemaker really makes the difference. The terroir and the grapes deserve your intelligence and your concepts to make great wines. Especially now. Music is very different. You can do music without any chaos, you can simply sing a song or whistle. But music is also controlled noise. When you start an instrument it's always chaotic, but you learn to control it. I really like the way John Cage included noise and wrote about this. Distortion is also interesting because you choose to include noise. Here also you decide noise is beautiful. It had been a big challenge for thrash bands and their engineers to play fast with distortion and to sound clear at the same time. It's like when you decide to include faults to your wine because you really want it. Some faults could be the best things you can do to your wine.

All photos courtesy of Jérôme Lefèvre

Have Wine, Will Cocktail

By Max Reese

Over 500 years ago, some say the first wine cocktails were summoned from nothingness. >>>

Adahlia Cole

Early iterations showcased wealth and luxury—fine wine, eggs, cream—ingredients few could afford, beautifully displayed in crystalline glassware. One of these early cocktails took a name, the Syllabub. The Syllabub was born from yule celebration, a reminder of the many gifts the year had bestowed. Before the American cocktail had taken stage, the Syllabub lurked in the minds of those wishing to showcase decadence, a layering of white wine, cream, sugar, and lemon—an inspiration for alcohol-laden holiday treats that exist to this very day. As time passed, grander displays of decadence displaced the Syllabub. Opulent showcasing of self-fortitude became the star of alcoholic yuletide cheer. Eggs and cream now took center stage, wine fell to the wayside, and spirit took its stead. Eggnog was born. The Syllabub faded into cookbooks and was nearly forgotten—but, like many things thought forgotten, the Syllabub learned to live in the darkness, until it was time to rise again.

The Syllabub
by Unknown

1 oz. lemon
2 oz. granulated sugar
4 oz. white wine
2 oz. heavy whipping cream
Zest of half a lemon

Whisk ingredients together until integrated. Pour into serving vessel. Allow cream to separate and rise to the top of the beverage in a cool place until serving.

Matt Stikker

Kaia Sauter

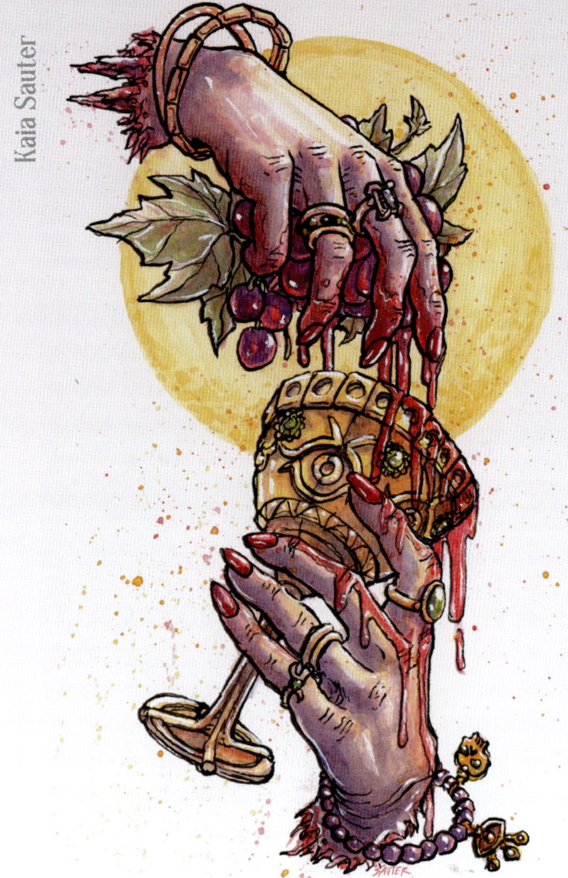

The Bishop
by Jerry Thomas

The year is 1755. A cocktail, the Bishop, lies within the pages of a tome, *The English Language Dictionary*: "A cant word for a mixture of red wine, oranges and sugar." Time abandons the Bishop, but in 1862 the Bishop surfaces again. A concoction of red wine, lime, sugar, and rum from a far-away land. Now we ask, "Who has the bishop become?"

The Bishop holds a glass of red communion wine clutched tight in his sweaty hand. With each sip, under the guise of holy worship, he explores a secret curiosity of exoticism and the modern world.

1.5 *oz. Jamaican rum*
1 *oz. red wine*
.25 *oz. lime juice*
.25 *oz. cane syrup* 1:1

Combine ingredients in a cocktail shaker topped with ice. Shake until cold. Strain into a chilled wine glass.

Wine is decadence in purest form, and in cocktails it has donned many faces. I now present an abomination born of these two characters of the past—a shrine to wine in the form of pure lust for inebriation. The Syllabub and the Bishop will now take hands, become one, and live forever in these texts.

The Beelzebub
by Max Reis

3 oz. dry red wine (dry white can also be used as a substitution or variation)
1 oz. overproof Jamaican rum (e.g., Golden Devil)
.5 oz. lemon
.75 oz of a 50/50 mix of quality sherry (e.g., Pedro Ximénez) and cane sugar simple syrup
1 bar spoon whole milk powder

(Before making individual cocktails, premix a 50/50 blend of sherry and simple syrup, based on the number of drinks you're preparing for the session.)

Add ingredients to a shaker tin with a small amount of pebble ice. Shake until the ice is no more. Add the cocktail to an unholy vessel and top with pebble ice. Forget the past and worship the future.

Adahlia Cole

Ogre Rosé
ED LUCE

D.I. WINE

WE ASKED CURTIS DUFFY, BEST KNOWN FOR WINNING MULTIPLE MICHELIN STARS AND JAMES BEARD AWARDS, AND APPEARING ON *IRON CHEF* (IN ADDITION TO BEING A METALHEAD),

COURTESY OF CURTIS DUFFY

AND JUNE RODIL, MASTER SOMMELIER AND THE ONLY PERSON TO HAVE RECEIVED THE RESTAURANT OF THE YEAR AND SOMMELIER OF THE YEAR ACCOLADES IN *FOOD & WINE* MAGAZINE HISTORY.

COURTESY OF JUNE RODIL

SOME ADVICE AND THEIR THOUGHTS ON FOOD AND WINE PAIRINGS FOR ANYONE TO TRY:

BOG: DURING THE PANDEMIC LOCKDOWN, AND IN ITS CURRENT STATE OF FLUX, MORE AND MORE PEOPLE HAVE BEEN EXPANDING THEIR SKILLS AND ROUTINES AT HOME IN THEIR KITCHEN. WAS THIS THE SAME FOR YOU?

JUNE RODIL: WHILE I WOULD ABSOLUTELY LOVE TO SAY, "YES, THAT'S ME!" INDEED IT IS NOT. I LEAVE A LOT OF THE KITCHEN SKILLS TO MY HUSBAND. I GOT REALLY GOOD AT MANEUVERING DEFTLY THROUGH ONLINE ORDERING APPS AND BUYING TO-GO FROM LOCAL RESTAURANTS. HOWEVER, I WILL SAY, BECAUSE I'M EVER THE OVER-ORDERER, WE GOT SUPER CREATIVE AT RE-IMAGINING LEFTOVERS INTO NEW DISHES. BASICALLY OUR OWN VERSION OF CHOPPED BUT WITHOUT THE TIME CONSTRAINTS 'CAUSE . . . COVID.

CURTIS DUFFY: I DON'T HAVE A LOT OF TIME OFF OR FREE TIME, SO SUNDAYS ARE MY DAY OFF. IF I'M COOKING AT HOME, THAT'S GOING TO BE MY DAY WHERE I'LL PREPARE SOME THINGS FOR THE FAMILY FOR A FEW DAYS. AND THOSE ARE THE DAYS WHERE WE'LL JUST PUT ON VINYL RECORDS, AND MY WIFE AND I SOMETIMES LIKE TO PLAY A GAME LIKE, "ALL RIGHT, CLOSE YOUR EYES AND PULL SOMETHING OUT OF THE COLLECTION." AND WE'LL PLAY IT, BOTH SIDES, THE FULL RECORD, AND WE'LL DO THAT A COUPLE TIMES THROUGHOUT THE DAY. THERE'S JUST SOMETHING ABOUT THAT OLD LP THAT JUST CRACKLES AND POPS AND IS JUST VERY NOSTALGIC FOR ME

›››››

because that's what my father did, with records, and a lot of my record collection is from him. So we'll pull out old stuff, sometimes there's new stuff, or there will be stuff like NWA in there so it's a random pick sometimes, which is fun because sometimes you might go, "Ahh, I didn't really want to listen to this . . ." But then, as it goes, and we kind of have a rule that once you pick it, you gotta play the whole album. Sometimes you don't want to hear the whole album, but we do.

BOG: Because a lot of folks have been taking the first steps to expand their food and beverage knowledge as a result of the pandemic, are there any wine and food pairings you'd recommend for those who are first-timers, or are wanting to try something fun and new, that are easy to do with ingredients/items they'd find around the home?

JR: Start small—like single-item foods—and go from there and definitely sip and taste as you go to expand your palate and tastes. Remember—this is for you. While there may be tried and true suggestions or universal takes on pairings, it really is more about what your personal palate prefers. Second reminder: what your palate prefers also depends on how you are at the moment, what happened during your day, and what you're craving. Food and wine are fluid (no pun intended) and change with us and our preferences. Be honest with yourself of what you like and dislike and have fun with it! The above being said—here's some hot takes:

POPCORN + CHARDO (A.K.A. BUTTER CHARDONNAY)

Love it. Live it. Inhale it . . . And then change it up and add to it. Compound that popcorn with other flavors and see how it changes the pairing. The combos are endless.

- The go-to: cacio e pepe popcorn: black pepper + Parm
- Piemonte style: truffle oil (or salt) + pecorino
- Spice it up with sriracha + furikake (one of my all-time favorite seasonings in life)
- More umami: soy sauce + furikake
- Salty sweet: salt + honey

FROZEN FRENCH FRIES + BASICALLY ANYTHING SPARKLING

Literally do the same as above! Start with just the vessel (a crispy and delicious fry and begone you weirdo greasy-floppy-wilty-fry lovers) and go from there—your pantry is your oyster. Anything from ketchup, mayo, special sauce to poutine—but remember to taste as you go and find how the flavor pairings change. Document your faves! And one last thing: as you add to your data (yes, get scientific about it if you like!), I would suggest opening that second bottle (or third—they do last more than a day in the fridge, y'all) and comparing a few different wines and the dishes and items you have to just constantly layer that info together because there is never one good choice when it comes to pairing food and wine. And it's always better with good company.

CD: I think most people who drink wine can safely say they like a specific varietal of grape, right? So a lot of people might say, "I love Pinot Noir because it's really soft and it's easy to drink, it's very fruit-forward." Some people will be like, "No! I really like the old California Cabernets that are huge and robust, and got a lot of body to it, a lot of tannin to it." I'm a huge advocate of just saying, "You know what—find what you like to drink, and I don't really care what you pair with it. As long as you're enjoying it!" That's the beauty of it, behind the whole "white wine needs to go with fish" or "red wine needs to go with meat and pasta." I don't necessarily agree with that. There's a lot of heavy white wines that would go incredibly well with something that's gamey and bloody, like duck and squab and things like that. It's something that we practice in the restaurant quite a bit. The majority of my menu is on the lighter side, and if you're going to have ten different glasses of wine—if you do the pairing—probably seven of them are going to be on the white side, and very light red wines at the very end. You should drink what you want to drink, when you want to drink it, and if you want to drink a huge Bordeaux with pepperoni pizza, why not? What are the rules? Who says that those two don't go together? It might be a beautiful pairing where this pizza place—wherever you are in the world—has the most amazing buttery crust that cuts the tannins right out of a Bordeaux, and makes it an amazing pairing. Who's to say that would never work?

BOG: For the more bold and daring: what are some unconventional, weird, or just plain fun wine pairings that you'd recommend?

JR: Here are some go-to high-low pairings that I absolutely love. Again, I am a horrible cook, so, as you can see, this is sort of stuff out of a 7-Eleven and what I can get out of my favorite grocery store (a.k.a. the walk-in at my restaurants). So the high tends to be the wine and the low tends to be what I stop and get at my local corner store on the way home because I am utter trash.

BUGLES ORIGINAL + CAVIAR + SOUR CREAM + WHITE BURGUNDY (AND IF YOU WANT A LOW-END WHITE—AN OAKY CHARDO)

A riff on a caviar plate classic of a starchy blini (the base), the crème fraîche (the creamy glue/binder), and of course the caviar (the sine qua non, if you will—the essential thing, the good-good as we like to call it that's pearly, salty, lofty intensity cannot be manipulated and the other components are mere vessels for its majesty). These flavors are bold and the sour cream and that strong corn/cornchip flavor of the Bugle only steps it up a notch, so grabbing an oaked Chard (be it the four-digit Montrachet of your dreams or the $20 oaky Chardo at your local grocer's) are bound to make great pairings. Both will have power and intensity to the max but in different ways but are sure to stand up and carry the weight and burst of flavors in these tasty treats). Fun tip: rather than Bugle fingers, build your Bugle caviar treats like ice cream cones to mimic the famous salmon cornettos of celebrity chef Thomas Keller's iconic amuse-bouche at the French Laudry and Per Se.

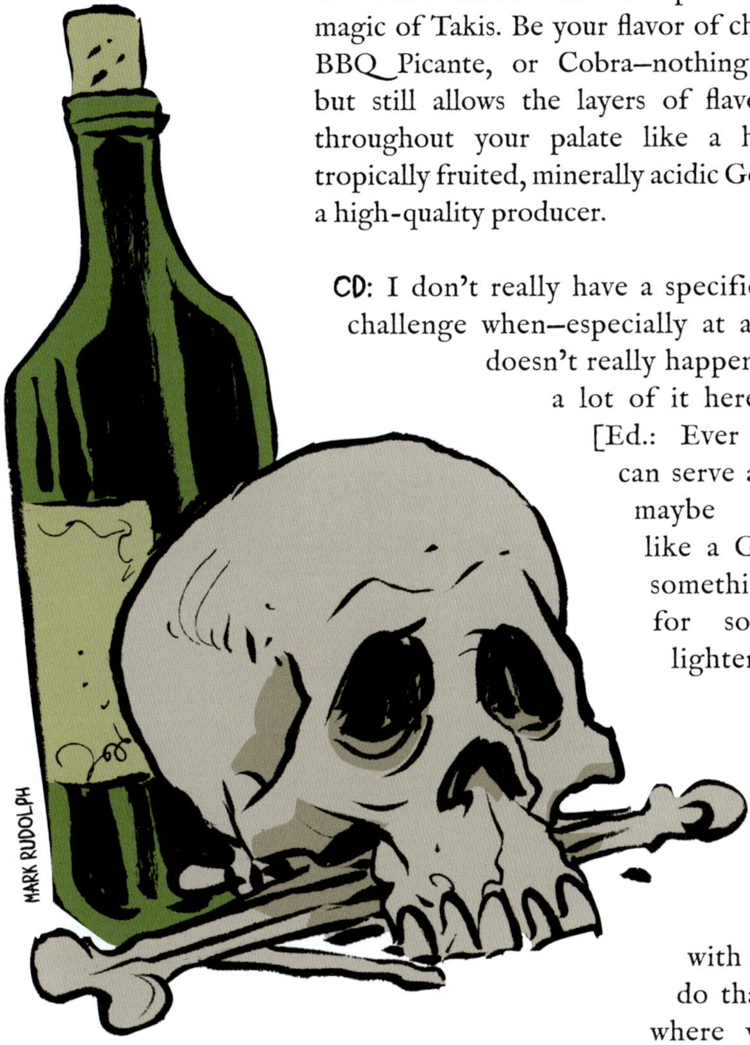

KRAFT STRING CHEESE + MONTRACHET (I SAID WHAT I SAID)

Grand cru for a grand time. Listen: if you spend your money on Montrachet, you're not gonna have enough money to have a high-end tasting menu. In fact, the perfect setting could be Netflixing, chilling, and drinking that bottle by yourself—ever slowly as the story that you've seen many times unfolds (I am seriously thinking of the movies *Pretty in Pink* and *Pride and Prejudice* right now)—while savoring those magic movie moments combining with the new epic romance of the best Chardonnay in the world taking your favorite red-sauce Italian snack by storm. It's just like the movies above—rich frat boy is actually more than he seems and he teaches wrong-side-of-the tracks Molly Ringwald that it's great to be yourself and be loved for it. Mr. Darcy seems too erudite and closed off but fun, witty, and independent Elizabeth Bennett can really unlock a new, open side of him. A sum of all their parts, they are better matched together. All hail the love story of fried cheese and magnificent chardonnay!

MARK RUDOLPH

TAKIS + AUSLESE GERMAN RIESLING!

(And, 'cause it never gets old, please listen to this song by these kiddos: "Hot Cheetos and Takis")

Ever want to slam the sweet, liquid gold and bubbly-scratchy-burny sensation of a Coca-Cola Classic after a bag of hot Cheetos or Takis as a kid? Look no further, adult self, than sweet liquid gold of Auslese Riesling to wash down the hot-powdery-mystical-spiced-magic of Takis. Be your flavor of choice Angry Burger, BBQ_Picante, or Cobra—nothing tempers the heat but still allows the layers of flavor to be expressed throughout your palate like a high-end, complex, tropically fruited, minerally acidic German Riesling from a high-quality producer.

CD: I don't really have a specific one, but I love a challenge when—especially at a restaurant, and it doesn't really happen often but we push a lot of it here at the restaurant [Ed.: Ever in Chicago]—you can serve a crazy white wine, maybe from Germany—like a Gewürztraminer or something—that is meant for something on the lighter side, maybe fruit-forward, that you can just serve with a piece of red meat or something classically meant to go with something red. We do that quite a bit here, where you'll go through the pairing, you'll get almost to the end of savory, and they'll hit you with a couple of red wines, but then your final savory course is paired with a crazy white wine that is just off the charts. And I love that, and that challenges us as humans, us as chefs, the sommelier team, it challenges everybody to look for those because those are interesting and it's exciting from the guests' standpoint because they never would have thought of it that way, or maybe they have but they wouldn't expect it to work and it's just a beautiful thing when it's "Man! I would have never have thought of that!" When you can surprise a guest like that, especially the ones that think they're just, like, this wine god or whatever, it's awesome when you can smack 'em in the face a little bit.

I FEEL IT BUILDING

J. Bayer 2021

WOW, THIS OLD CASETTE HAD SOME OF MY FAVORITE BANDS ON IT - ALL THE BEST DISCHORD STUFF

IT HAS IGNITION SLANT SIX... GRAY MATTER... AND THE FAITH VOID SPLIT EP.

UHHH... 'DISCHORD?'

DISCHORD?

OH, YOU MEAN THE LABLE MINOR THREAT IS ON? YEAH, I LOVE DISCHORD

ME TOO! WHAT OTHER BANDS DO YOU LIKE? BEST?

HMM, THAT A TOUGH ONE. I'D HAVE TO SAYY..

THE ONE THAT HAS TO BE SONG MINOR THREAT - BY THE BAND MINOR THREAT

LOOK OVER THERE!

LIKE AN ANGRY GOD - IAN McCAYE BURSTS FORTH FROM THE PIT WHERE HE'S LAIN IMPRISONED FOR EONS

INHALE

TISSSS

TISSSSSS

PÄR STRÖMBERG

More often than not, when celebrities dip their toes into other business ventures outside of their known trade, it's hard for them to shake their primary identity. George Clooney's Casamigos tequila is great, but it's not what puts him on magazine covers. Similarly, loads of bands and musicians sell their image and branding on cheap bottled libations, make some money, but it's never anything to outshine their main careers. That's why it's awesome to know Pär Strömberg. His primary career is as a writer and artist—that's what he's known for. But one of his passions is metal. It ultimately feels like he's the proverbial "inside man" for extreme metal—an ally adding legitimacy to underground sounds amongst the rank and file of the wine world. >>>>

BLOOD OF GODS: Why metal and wine?

PÄR STRÖMBERG: Well, you have Sigurd "Satyr" Wongraven from Satyricon, you have Maynard from Tool/Puscifer/A Perfect Circle, Les Claypool from Primus . . . you have Charles Smith in Washington State, you have Eliane Delalot and Vincent Maries of No Control in France and Noble Rot in England. You have so many many more rock musicians and other people in art and the arts industry that are deeply involved in wine. Most of the winemakers I've met have a deep interest in music. Many are punk or metal fans and it's no surprise. I think the DIY mentality in art, music, and, in this example, winemaking, are crucial. We're not talking mega-brands, we're talking true bands and artists. If you, as a fan, still think that black metal is about burning churches, blood, and death worship, get into this century. I was a (small) part of its beginning in Sweden, and I see fans today, just like punks, are becoming a style rather than getting the idea, and it's sad to see. It has always been about a feeling, an art form, a way of life that includes rather than excludes. Includes other art, music, influences and especially includes the idea of being open to other people and other impressions.

Most of the winemakers I meet have a deep interest in music; many are punk or metal fans, and it's no surprise.

BOG: So where did your interest in wine originate?

PS: My wine story starts in Amsterdam back in early 2000 with my best friend, and nowadays wine guru, Roger Dorresteijn, who happens to be the CEO of record label Epitaph at their European office. We used to hang out, go to gigs and art shows, and we had a lot in common. One day he took me to a wine-tasting of premier white Burgundy wines and I was instantly hooked. After this encounter, Roger saw my joy and invited me to several dinners with his bands on tour in Europe, wining and dining exclusively, and for me, that punk has so much taste and knowledge, was an epiphany for me. Ever since, Roger and I go see bands together all over, but never without a couple of proper bottles before.

BOG: How are you currently involved in wine? Where can readers follow your writing and work?

PS: Today I work as both an artist/painter and as a wine writer. The combination is to die for. Wherever I go, I can strike up a conversation in no time. Besides being a musician, which I'm not, I think being a chef, lawyer, doctor, artist, or something within wine is unbeatable when it comes to other people's opinions and interest in your position. I paint, therefore I am. I write about wine, therefore I remain insane . . . or sane?! I mainly write in Swedish nowadays, for web platform Winetable.se, but I used to write about wine in English for *Totally Stockholm*, a sort of expat magazine where I had my wine column, "In Vino Präntas," for about seven years. I'm also a contributor for Swedish wine magazine *Törst*.

BOG: Rather than a musician who's very much in the public eye, known for their craft, and folks might not know of their love for wine so much, you're somewhat the reverse: a wine writer who has a love for extreme metal. Are your wine industry peers surprised when they discover some of the more extreme music you're drawn to?

PS: This is an interesting question, and, because punk music brought me into this world, I can only say that I think punk and metal, and beyond, are more like wine and winemaking than hip-hop and R&B could ever be. Most of the winemakers I meet have a deep interest in music; many are punk or metal fans, and it's no surprise. I think the DIY mentality in art, music, and, in this example, winemaking are crucial. What I can do, both as an artist and a writer, is to influence or open eyes for people. There are so many non-mainstream things to discover, and if you are like me, an independent thinker, be a goat, not a sheep.

BOG: There are always exceptions to the rule, but generally, wine-lovers have a very discerning palate but haven't caught the bug for extreme or underground music. At the same time, metalheads are diehard about their highly specialized niche of music yet haven't applied that passion to a taste for wine. What's missing from either side to give them a push to explore?

PS: Again, I think creative people, in whatever genre, try to explore the very most of their potential. On the other hand, there are people with the same need of impulse, impression, and expression, but however—and unfortunately—can't create themselves. What music and art can do for people like this is immense. I believe that this can be found in many more aspects of life. In winemaking, I mean true and honest winemaking, there's a very beautiful circle of life. Spring with growth and budding, summer with blooming and ripening, autumn with harvest, and winter with catharsis and the closure and an awaiting rebirth in the coming spring. I love this, and especially when it gives the most delicious and intriguing produce there is: the fermented grape. To get back to the very question, I think of this "life circle with catharsis" as the spring of life that is ever-existent in music and art lovers, whichever (art) they happen to prefer.

BOG: Trends and innovation always seem to be met with suspicion in both wine and metal, where their respective audiences generally respect the more time-proven institutions and practices. However, can you mention any new developments in wine and in metal that get you excited and keep your curiosity engaged?

PS: I believe that in very specific art or music genres, followers and artists, actors or whomever are serious about their specific interests. I see this in philosophy, psychology, religion, and in culture studies as well. If you are certain about ideas, idealism and dogmas easily take over. Suspicion to news is at place, however—people that are goats always tend to influence sheep. If the audience doesn't want to identify as sheep, they have to start their own shit. But, in the end, there are many great goats who make great stuff in the world, and there are even more sheep that don't necessarily have to bow their heads, but they will maintain the need for leaders. As with metal fans, they will always be ready for what is good or great, selectiveness has made them come this far. Good art, good music, good brews, and good wine will always remain!

Ikosidio

BOG: There are many elements about wine that are still being studied and researched. While several aspects, such as biodynamic practices, may have anecdotal support, the scientific mechanisms (if any) behind their effects on wine quality are not fully understood. Would you rather have these still-unknown aspects of wine fully understood or do you prefer to leave certain things a mystery?

PS: I have a strong belief in science, but art doesn't require science to exist. Wine, as I perceive it, is a product of human craftsmanship, built on history, passion, and respect for nature, terroir, climate, and the unique sense of place the winemaker inhabits. Some aspects need to remain somewhat mystical to preserve their allure. I am not interested in mass-produced wines; I want to know where the vines and grapes were grown, and I want to feel the vision and craftsmanship of the winemaker in my glass, whether it stems from traditional methods, anthroposophical agriculture, or adherence to the lunar calendar. An ecological and holistic approach to creating anything from nature can only be beneficial.

BOG: What is your favorite "truth is stranger than fiction" anecdote or fact about wine that blurs the line between science and science fiction?

PS: It probably began when I made my first batch of homemade wine from the grapes on my in-laws' patio. The vines, originating from Romania, were planted over thirty years ago, and we have no idea what variety they are. There are two different types, both producing green (white) grapes. My kids helped stomp them with their little feet right after harvest, and we put the juice and skins into a jar. I didn't expect much from this small experiment, but it started to ferment, and in time it transformed into wine—though not particularly tasty, it became an amber-colored alcoholic beverage. I felt like Jesus, turning water into wine during a wedding in Cana of Galilee, which isn't far from the truth, considering I was born on Christmas Day too. 🍷

Seekers of the Truth

Vanguards, Iconoclasts, and Trailblazers

CHARLES

Few figures embody the renegade spirit of *Blood of Gods* quite like Charles Smith. With a past rooted in punk rock, a present grounded in wine, and a philosophy that fuses both with fearless clarity, Smith has long operated outside the safe lanes of convention. He's made a career—and a name—not by asking permission, but by trusting instinct, taking risks, and staying relentlessly true to his voice. In this conversation, he riffs on everything from the poverty-forged roots of punk to the soul of winemaking, the pitfalls of elitism, and how integrity—not approval—is the measure of success.

Illustrations by Alex Murd

SMITH

AGAINST CONVENTION, WITH CONVICTION

BLOOD OF GODS: I've been wanting to get you in *Blood of Gods* since the first issue, but I'm glad it happened now because that one's long sold out, and now there are a lot more people reading.

CHARLES SMITH: You don't know people are paying attention, and then all of a sudden they get you. And it's like, I didn't know people were paying attention to what I was doing, I was just doing my thing, hoping they would pay attention, but I didn't really take an account of who was paying attention, I just kept doing it. I think it's maybe like that in music: you're just focused on what you're doing—next thing you know there's an audience out there in front of you and you're like, "Where the fuck did all these people come from?!"

BoG: We regularly ask people, "What's So Punk about Wine?" What are your thoughts about how punk ideals informed your approach to wine?

CS: "What's so punk about wine?" Well, the one thing is that so few people exhibit what *is* really punk about wine in the wine world. Same thing about music—there's a lot of beige out there. But when you decide to factor in your own individual voice, it's kind of like, "I don't know how to play guitar—I got a guitar and I started playing it. I got some other people to make noise with. Eventually we made a sound together." And I think it's the same thing. You have nothing to lose, you can only go forward, and that's what's really punk about it—you decide to have your own voice, and you're not really paying attention to what other people do, but you learn from the history of what people are doing—you have that to draw from—and create something that's purely your own. And I would say that's very rock 'n' roll or that's really punk. But also, a lot of times it comes out of poverty and out of shitty situations. Like me, I came from poverty and shitty situations, so I had nothing to lose, but to go forward. You're not afraid of your own voice 'cause that's actually all you have. What have you got to lose? There's nothing to lose.

BoG: And also, as far as punk ethos, challenging the status quo, pushing back against convention, and asking questions—do you see that paralleled in your experience?

CS: Yeah, absolutely. You have a pretty good lay of the land, and you can decide what your truth is going to be, and typically it's not going to be the collective truth of everyone else. Punk is more well-informed than the vast majority of people because they actually pay attention, because they're into it, you know? They're on it, man! And to really be on it means you have to be in the moment, and to be in the moment does not allow for convention, it creates risk. And with risk there is reward. And that's where the excitement happens.

BoG: That kind of ties into the old adage of "He who dares wins."

CS: Yeah, the act of actually doing it is the exciting part. Succeeding is like, "Next." There's no excitement, there's no satisfaction. And then it becomes dull or numb and, "What am I going to do? Hit repeat, and do this over and over again?" I think the cooler things in wine are through innovation, which is something that doesn't really happen in wine. I mean, you can't call a one-liter box or a can innovation. That's just another thing to put wine in. Finding new ways to express something that's been done for hundreds of years can be a really difficult thing without trying to be different or being an individual, because it is. And it has to be. Me, I did this Pinot Noir project [Ed.: Golden West], and you know ... don't tell me you can't do it. But apparently everybody else in Washington state for the most part believed that you can't do it. So they said, "Yeah, okay . . . blah, blah, blah . . ." Then they packed their little suitcase and went back home and watched the evening news. I went out in the middle of nowhere, unpacked my suitcase, and said, "What the fuck can we do out here?" and, "Let's make it happen." So now I have 500 acres of Pinot Noir in the ground. And you know, I didn't invent it, I just decided to do it where the other people decided not to. That's pretty punk rock. Is that definitely a risk? Fuck yeah. It's trusting that there are people out there that feel the same way that you do, and they're going to find you by putting your voice out there.

BoG: What do you do when doubt or fear creeps in? When you take these risks, are you ever scared?

CS: Oh yeah! Man, there's no guarantee. There are no guarantees with anything. I think, when you're calculated, I think you can do it, but it's kind of like paint by numbers. When I want to do something that turns out to be innovative, I kind of have this idea, like, "Okay, I check this box, I check this box . . ." I take care of every part of it, and it's bulletproof for me in integrity, then I can move forward with certainty knowing that, without promise, but certainly, it's good. Because I'm thinking about the people and what they want and I'm responding to not just an inner voice but also the connectivity. This isn't about me, it's about the collective "we." And that's why I say, when you know those people are out there, you know that eventually they're gonna hear you. And that's who you want to get in contact with. So, yeah, there's absolutely a "Holy fuck! I can't believe I'm doing this!" and it's like, "Okay, everything I thought connects, and they get it." And that is really cool when you're heard.

BoG: Absolutely. I think it's like a Venn diagram where one circle is the part that satisfies you personally, on a deeper, creative, maybe even spiritual, level, and the other circle is what your fans and followers like and want, and where they overlap is the sweet spot.

CS: Well, the cool thing is that if "your people" is everybody, you're able to put something out there that taps into something in every type of person, it's not just a focus for a certain group. I make my wines for everybody, and if you want them—we may have very different interests—but if you like what I'm doing, and you get it, we have a relationship. And that is really cool. I think about everybody, "What do the people want?" and then give them it with integrity, intent, and purity, and no compromise. And then if it turns out to be commercial—let's say you're a band and you've been slugging away forever, playing in shitty places, and you're really tight, and you've got a lot of people that love you, and all of a sudden you get huge—and then they're all like, "You've betrayed us!" I mean, how did they betray you? Because more people like what you like?! They're not betraying anybody. As long as you're not betraying yourself, and you can look in the mirror and go, "Yeah, this is my truth." There's no betrayal.

BoG: By the way, I saw you're wearing a Melvins shirt, and I remember when I first heard the Melvins, I was probably a young teenager in middle school or high school, and it was scary.

CS: It's heavy!

BoG: I think it was maybe *Stoner Witch* or something, and it was so sludgy and brutal ... but it brings to mind my short fuse for elitists where I'll be at a wine event or a tasting and I'll see these pedantic wine snobs or elitists trying to flex their wine knowledge or palate, but then they'll turn around and turn on something like the Dave Matthews Band . . .

CS: (laughs) Oh my god.

BoG: . . . and—disclaimer: I know it's all subjective, but when I see Charles Smith is wearing a Melvins shirt or a Dead Moon shirt, I think, "Alright, cool, he's good. He checks out. The good taste isn't limited to his wine-tasting palate."

CS: Well, I mean, I've been around for a long time. I turned eighteen in '79, so I had hard rock and heavy metal, and then I had new wave and punk rock, and then metal metal, then dirtier and slower music in the '90s, and all the way through . . . so my wardrobe is basically reflective of the years, it's not because I found my new favorite thing. You eventually figure out what you wear and what suits you. I don't even know how old this Melvins t-shirt is. I think it's probably fifteen to twenty years old, I don't know. I was exercising in it earlier, I needed a shirt, and I don't buy Lululemon, so what the fuck? Maybe the Melvins should start their workout line.

BoG: It's been mentioned before that winemaking can be like a punk concert where there's a sense of "controlled chaos"—where things can get wild and crazy and there's an element of danger and uncertainty, but it can also come together to create something beautiful.

CS: Well, it takes on a life of its own. So you've seen these really big shows where disastrous things happen. Nobody is wishing this, but it takes on a life of its own and it can go to an inevitable crash, but on the other hand most nearly every single night it goes in a completely different way, where everyone fosters togetherness and somehow they find themselves in that moment—individually and in a group—together, which is pretty badass.

BoG: That's a perfect example. It usually harmonizes. People usually police themselves or find their own rhythm. But I think of the Rolling Stones concert at the Altamont Speedway, where shit gets crazy, the ferment goes bad, or in their case someone gets stabbed. And that's where it can jump the track, like a stuck fermentation, or a bad yeast is introduced, and it can get nasty . . .

CS: I think you trust the process. If you know that you're prepared, you get ready for it, and then you just do it with reckless abandon. Understanding the process, and that you cannot control it all, and when you do try to control it all, you take away some of the passion and emotion of it, and for me making wine without heart is not even worth doing. I think it's the same thing being around musicians and bands—if you don't go out there every night and put out everything that you want to put out and leave everything on the stage, then what the fuck are you doing there? Make room for somebody else. If there's something that's honest and personal, we'll react most likely.

BoG: Whenever you encounter elitism, how do you deal with it?

CS: I just usually walk the other way. I do my own thing. I know what's going on, but I'm not really watching everybody else run their game, I'm too busy doing my own, and that's how I contribute to the whole world of wine, by being completely engaged in doing my thing, and I'm just a piece of it. It's not for a lack of thinking other people aren't talented and there's not good wine or nice people, but I'm just doing my own thing. And if I get to cohabitate and work with other like-minded people and collaborate and so forth, then that's really cool. And I can appreciate people that are doing it in a different way than what I'm doing, but these private clubs and these private organizations and, "I hang out with this person. You hang out with this person . . ." It's like, "Man, I'm

just making wine." And if I'm in Walla Walla, then I'm a part of the wine community there 'cause I grow grapes and I started making wine in '99. We find our tribe wherever we go, and they can be very different from yourself, but there's something that they carry around that's inherently the same as you. It's very easy for me to name people that I really like what they're doing, mostly when it comes to wine, and really relatable in other things I'm interested in, and I just think they're badasses in what they're doing because of the integrity in which they do it.

BoG: Great quote!

CS: Yeah—the integrity in which they do it. And that's the deal with hard rock, metal, doom metal, black metal . . . you know that this is most likely never going to be big, but this is purity for you. It's ground zero, it's the heart of darkness in everything, and you are compelled to do this because this is inherently who you are. And that's why if I'm at a show, or Copenhell or whatever, I'm always looking for the smaller stages near people, because their intent is right there in front of you and it's so great. You get this so well in music, particularly in hard rock and metal music, because there's a blueprint for it and finding their own way within this, where it's already a crowded field, and feeling that you have your own voice and you are being true to yourself—that makes you a part of the collective of the whole thing. And that is your participation in it, and that is my participation with everybody else in the wine world that I know, don't know, hang out with, don't hang out with, appreciate their work, don't appreciate their work . . . my contribution is contributing myself to it. That's it.

BoG: What tunes are you digging lately?

CS: Recently, nothing new musically. I just decided that I was going to pretty much start every day with Black Sabbath's first record, it seems to be resonating with me for the last month. And so at least one day I've been putting on Black Sabbath's *Black Sabbath* and it's been really, really working for me right now. I think listening to those guys bang it out, it seems kind of simpatico with where my head's at right now. And right now, getting revved up and getting ready for harvest, this is the way to go into it—with a little bit of swagger and anticipation and the excitement of when it's gonna happen. And I guess right now my soundtrack for it is Black Sabbath.

Courtesy of Brian Slagel

Brian Slagel

METALBLADE RECORDS

"Founded by Brian Slagel in 1982, Metal Blade Records has brought wave after wave of powerful, innovative, and often genre-defining music to the ever-hungry metal masses. It is this ethos that has seen Metal Blade build up a stunning and diverse catalogue, weather the various storms facing any independent label, and in an age of declining record sales boast the most successful years of its existence as it cruises into its fourth decade," writes Dan Slessor on the Metal Blade site. Fortunately for us, Brian's taste and talent for finding crucial heavy tunes also crosses over into appreciation for primo vino. >>>>

Blood of Gods: Where did your interest in wine originate? Was there an aha moment, maybe a specific wine or a wine-related memory that served as your gateway into the world of vino? Or was it more of a gradual evolution for you?

Brian Slagel: I was involved in a project with a couple members of the band Loudness years ago. I went to dinner with them and their manager/ promoter. Both the drummer and manager were big red wine fans. They ordered a few bottles worth over $500 and asked if I wanted to try them. I have tasted some red wine before but was not really into it. Of course I wanted to try some expensive wine! They were French Bordeaux and I immediately fell in love with them. I started trying more of those a week later and was totally into it.

BoG: What would you say are the wines you most typically gravitate towards? Any fave producers?

BS: Haute-Brion is my all time fave, but most anything from Graves or Margaux I really like. Lynch-Bages and Tour Léognan are also faves.

BoG: While there are plenty of stereotypes on both sides, what argument would you make to encourage more metalheads to try getting into wine?

BS: Just try it! I know a lot of metalheads who are big wine drinkers. I think you have to remember that there are a ton of great wines out there that are not super expensive. I have found that out and sometimes love the $20 bottles more than the expensive ones. Also, try different regions as everyone's palates are different.

BoG: Last year Metal Blade unveiled its fortieth-anniversary collaborative beer (an IPA from Revision Brewing) that tied in with Decibel magazine's Metal and Beer Festival. Will there ever be a Metal Blade wine? If so, what kind would you want it to be?

Jodie Muir

BS: We did some wine way back in the early 2000s. I would love to do one again. It is a bit complicated to get it done properly, but any kind of European red blend would be great!

BoB: Heavy metal and wine each have their fair share of elitism and gatekeepers. How do you handle egoism or pretentiousness when you encounter it?

BS: Honestly, I try to stay away from this at all costs. If there are artists or potential business partners we find with any of that, I prefer not to work with them. Makes life much easier. Luckily, there is not as much of that in the metal world as you might think.

BoB: Trends and innovation always seem to be met with suspicion in both wine and metal, where their respective audiences generally accept the more time proven institutions and practices the most. However, can you mention any new developments in wine and in metal that get you excited and keep your curiosity engaged?

BS: Well, I always like to embrace new ways of getting music to people. So whatever that might be, we like to try our best to make it work as best we can. Whether it is social media or the way people consume music now, we try to do the best for us and the artists. As far as wine goes, I try to stay on top of what vintages and producers are doing good things.

BoB: Sometimes fans, whether of wine or metal, can experience burn out or fatigue (e.g., keeping up with all the new stuff being released, or dealing with scene politics/drama)—does this ever happen for you? Do you ever require a "palate cleanser" or some kind of respite to reignite the passion? If so, what do you do?

BS: As far as metal goes, I remain a big fan and I am super excited by so many new artists coming out. 200 Stab Wounds, Capra, Entheos, Ingested, Lorna Shore, Creeping Death, and Frozen Soul are just a few new bands that keep me excited. I have to admit I did get a bit burnt out on wine for awhile. I also had some issues that made it harder to drink. Lately, though, I have been drinking a lot more wine and it's all good now!

FIRST TIME JUMPING INTO THE Metal Blade POOL?

HERE ARE A FEW ALBUMS BRIAN SLAGEL HANDPICKED FROM HIS CATALOGUE TO GIVE THE UNINITIATED A GOOD IDEA OF WHAT METAL BLADE IS ALL ABOUT.

SLAYER, *HELL AWAITS*
A classic album by one of metal's true legends.

ARMORED SAINT, *SYMBOL OF SALVATION*
Classic metal album that is in many people's Hall of Fame.

KILLSWITCH ENGAGE, *ATONEMENT*
Another one of metal's biggest bands with their latest chart-topping album.

AMON AMARTH, *TWILIGHT OF THE THUNDER GOD*
On the heavier side, but Amon Amarth is becoming one of metal's biggest bands and this is a classic.

Sigurd Wongraven a.k.a. Satyr of SATYRICON

Blood of Gods: Where did your interest in wine originate? Was there ever a particular aha wine moment where a certain wine just jumped out at you or changed your perception of wine?

Sigurd Wongraven: No. I find it hard to believe people who've said that there was one specific moment. I do, however, think a lot of the time there will be a chain of experiences that will lead to those one or two moments. In my case, I went through a handful between 1997 and 2003, where I started to feel that this is something more. Wine is culture, history, nature, people, philosophy, and so on. Realizing the depth of the wine culture, and all its layers, takes many years and that's what it did for me too. So you could say that there were many wines that jumped out over several years.

BoG: With beer being the typical drink to go along with metal, what factors have kept the metal and wine scenes and crowds so separate, in your opinion?

SW: Maybe because we metal people are mostly mainstream without realizing it ourselves. Anything we don't understand or fear we will label as trendy, commercial, or mainstream. That is how we respond to the unknown. Just like the mainstream does. However, when it comes to alcohol, it is rather a question of the party itself being the drug, rather than beer specifically. In the metal scene, we don't have a particular affinity for any type of drink—we just embrace the party culture. I see that changing though and we've got the future ahead of us.

BoG: Trends and innovation always seem to be met with suspicion in both wine and metal, where their respective audiences generally accept the more time-proven institutions and practices the most. However, can you mention any new developments in wine and in metal that get you excited and keep your curiosity engaged?

SW: Not currently. I think the change to organic viticulture that has been ongoing in Europe in the last decade is obviously for the better, but it is not an innovation or trend. It is rather a slow return to the roots, and I hope more will follow all over the world. In metal I am not sure. Seems like musicians practice more, though, and that is great.

BoG: While there are plenty of stereotypes on both sides, what argument would you make to encourage more metalheads to try getting into wine?

SW: Wine is not just a drink. It's a lifestyle, just like metal. There is a big package that comes with it, and I know it would appeal to the type of metal fan that is constantly looking to learn and discover. There are many of those too.

BoG: You have your own wine brand (Wongraven)—what was the goal/intention with making this wine?

SW: To use my knowledge, skills, and capacity on a different subject. I knew the things I am good at would translate into something useful in wine production. I wanted to produce wines that speak of the place they come from, that are classic in style, and that show elegance and finesse rather than power. I started very small with some bottles of Langhe Rosso and Barolo about ten years ago. Today I sell more than a million liters of wine annually, yet my attitude has not changed one bit. It has been very interesting and great fun so far.

BoG: What are some of your favorite producers in the U.S. and internationally?

SW: In the U.S. I would say Chanin Wines, Hirsch, Anthill Farms, and Lingua Franca perhaps. Elsewhere there would be too many to mention, but I have a particular affinity for Piemonte, Burgundy, Champagne, and German Riesling.

PAUL GRIECO

This is a meditation on PUNK ROCK,

but it's also a reflection on what it means to love wine unabashedly, be moved by it, and turn that passion into something transcendent.

This is a conversation with a New York punk, not one of the ones you might know, but one you should. Friends and admirers are quick to point out that Paul Grieco and his wine bar, Terroir, changed the New York wine scene. And, though Paul is too modest to say it, it's true.

We sat down to discuss punk music, winemaking, and where the two meet. The conversation lasted for hours but is presented here stripped down, condensed, lightly arranged for clarity, and with a touch of self-mythologizing—as punk an interview write-up as there ever was. But, to quote Paul, "Hopefully, it'll make you feel something, goddamn it."

Will Farley: Let's just go for it right off the bat. Can wine be punk?

Paul Grieco: I mean, fuck, is wine punk? Wine has been with us every step of human existence. I view it as something very simple, as something primal. You take grapes and turn sugar plus yeast into alcohol plus CO2 Can it get any fucking simpler than that? Anyone could fucking do it, and I think that DIY attitude is part and parcel of punk.

WF: When I think about punk winemakers, I think of people like Taras Ochota (Ochota Barrels) and Abe Schoener (Scholium Project) who have done their own thing, exactly the way they want. Who's in your punk winemaker pantheon?

PG: I think it would be easy today to focus on the natural winemakers who are genuinely practicing a "less is more" approach, but, for me, it's folks from the '70s, '80s, and '90s that were pushing at the establishment to get their shit known when the world of wine was relatively small: Angelo Gaja, Piero Antinori, Anne-Claude Leflaive, or even Robert Mondavi.

Fucking talk about punk, look at what Piero did with Tignanello. Maybe it's in the Italian philosophical zeitgeist to give the government the finger, but he comes along and is making good wine that sells, but says fuck it, that's not true Chianti. Chianti had become a commodity, and the wine itself was no longer true, so he said, "I'm going to do only red grapes, you call it Vino da Tavola, and I don't give a shit." That is punk rock.

Angelo took this small appellation that no one gave a shit about and made it into something. The most famous story of the Gaja family is that he took one of their top vineyards and grafted Cabernet onto the Nebbiolo vines. His father said *darmagi*, or "what a pity" in the Piedmontese dialect, when he drove by the vineyard, which is what Angelo ended up calling the Cabernet.

"To me, punk rock is the freedom to create, freedom to be successful, freedom to not be successful, freedom to be who you are. It's freedom."

—Patti Smith

Anne-Claude Leflaive in Burgundy with biodynamic farming took a grand, important estate and turned it on its proverbial ass. People thought she was out of her goddamn gourd, but look at where we are today. She's a rock star.

Robert Mondavi got kicked out of the family business, started his own thing, knocked on every goddamn door, and created new avenues to put his wine in perspective with wines from the Old World; he had the DIY punk approach.

WF: You've talked about this before, that some of your favorite bands went from playing rock clubs to arenas. Where does the burden of influence fit into this punk narrative or mythology—especially for regions like Burgundy or Bordeaux that are often prohibitively expensive for many new wine-drinkers?

PG: I don't begrudge anyone's success. As much as bands like the Sex Pistols became cartoonish over time, when you look at the lyrics or see footage of the energy at their shows, you can see that they really had a reason for doing and saying the shit they did. It was punk. So, with wine, I have no issue with Ochota Barrels being recognized or with their wines climbing to $50, $60, $70 and being highly allocated and impossible to find. Does that make them any less punk?

Is part of punk a lack of success? Are the Ramones still one of the great punk acts because their first album took four decades to go gold? Everyone who bought that album formed a band. The Clash's *London Calling* was massive. Are they any less banner-bearers of the movement because that was one of the highest-selling punk albums? No. No, no, no, no.

Is Lalou Bize-Leroy, who grows Aligoté on one of the most expensive parcels of land on earth, punk for growing that grape? She's getting an extraordinary amount of money for that Aligoté, but is she still punk, or is she part of the establishment?

WF: I love the idea of Madame Bize-Leroy as a figurehead of punk winemaking.

PG: If you and I were to pick up a bottle of the 2015 Tignanello, would it have the same revolutionary zeal from when I first interacted with it? Maybe not, and that's okay, but something about that wine is transportational and takes you to another dimension. Food doesn't often do that for you, with all due respect to Proust.

WF: My madeleine moment is definitely with a wine. The first time I had Paolo Bea's Sagrantino was sublime. It tasted like an impenetrable monolith. I sat and stewed on it. It was like a ringing chord, just sludgy, heavy metal.

PG: Ha. You're drinking that Sagrantino, and you're slowly beginning to headbang. It's a massive, heavy Tony Iommi Sabbath riff like "War Pigs."

WF: I most often think about jazz when drinking wine, records like Miles Davis's *In a Silent Way*, but this was just so rock and roll and, as you've said, primal.

PG: If a wine comes across as dark and brooding and impenetrable on my palate, Bauhaus, it's fucking Bauhaus.

WF: That's what *Blood of Gods* is all about, the interplay between things we love.

PG: I've been engaging with wine in some way, shape, or form for roughly thirty-five years, and I've yet to get bored. I learned on a trip to Italy in the '80s that, with wine, I could still dabble in history, philosophy, religion, music, culture, and civilization. And it's what keeps me interested and motivated and still very much in love with wine this entire time.

WF: You opened Terroir in 2010, and I still hear friends talking about how you changed the way restaurants in New York (and beyond) think about wine. It's evolved into more a full-service spot than the original that Jon Bonné called "New York's ur-wine bar," and you its "punk sommelier in chief." Was there a punk ethos involved in opening Terroir?

PG: For me, the first punk rock wine bar was Bar Veloce on Second Avenue. I remember being a restaurant guy in the '90s, and that was the bar that showed the rest of us that we could do it. It didn't require a lot of money, you could go into a space that no restaurant would have gone into previously, and you could make a life of this without doing fine dining. So when Marco and I opened up Terroir in '08 in fifty square feet, there was no way you could have done a full-service restaurant.

WF: Not to mention 100 wines by the glass.

PG: We never thought we were being different for the sake of being different. When we put together our first list, we did what we felt we should do. Numbers of selection don't matter shit to me, but do I have 100 wines by the glass now? Yes. Did I intend to have 100 wines by the glass? 110% not. What is original about a wine program these days anyway? We're all doing the same shit.

We're honored that people choose to cross our threshold and submit themselves to what we do. But I also accept the responsibility that I have to pull you into our little cult. I've gotta make sure you're comfortable with that. I'm still in the hospitality business. I believe that the team that comes to work here buys into that.

"I learned on a trip to Italy in the '80s that, with wine, I could still dabble in history, philosophy, religion, music, culture, and civilization. And it's what keeps me interested and motivated and still very much in love with wine this entire time."

WF: I think there's a shared choreography of entertainment in restaurants and music venues.

PG: Like with music, there's a bond between the band and the audience. Especially punk shows where band members jump into the crowd. That interplay is pretty fucking cool. But ultimately, what we do here is not done with the consumer in mind. Did a lot of the old punk bands give a shit if anyone loved their music? They did it for themselves. What we do here, maybe arrogantly, is for me and for my team.

WF: And I think that's a punk attitude, but it resonates, clearly. We've talked a lot about the past—who are some of the punk up-and-comers?

PG: I think it would be easy today to focus on the natural winemakers who are truly practicing a "less is more" approach. I think it's people exploring new areas, where there is no history of winemaking, but I'd reserve the moniker for those making still wines with hybrid grapes in a place like, say, England, and I'd say the same thing for Quebec.

I'd say the same for regions where they've been making wine for a long time but got no respect. We can go to central Spain, which was once only a source of bulk wine but in appellations like Manchuela Bodegas Ponce is taking Bobal and making it important. That's punk. Is a punk rocker in Spain the sherry house who's now making unfortified white wines? I think so.

WF: Or the winemakers reclaiming Marsala.

PG: Exactly.

WF: You heard it here first: Marsala is punk. So we know that winemakers can be punk, but can wine itself be punk?

PG: Is what is in the bottle punk? I guess it's in the eye of the beholder.

WF: There's some freedom in that.

PG: The entire world of taste is subjective, so I have no qualms jumping into it and making statements that are subjective. That's the freedom of taste.

WF: Choosing a side and planting your flag. I think that's pretty fucking punk. Maybe it's time to go find a good Marsala.

Lord of Rotter Towers

An Interview with Dan Keeling of Noble Rot

Blood of Gods: *Noble Rot* is now over a decade old with your 31st edition marking this monumental milestone. Congratulations, and what is your favorite memory?

Dan Keeling: It was a chance to look back on the first 3,650 days of *Noble Rot* with a few special lists (everybody loves a list, don't they?) including our "Essential Wines of the Past Decade," "Most Influential Restaurants", and "What We've Learnt from Humanity from a Decade of *Noble Rot* Interviews" (featuring Brian Eno, Mike D, Keira Knightley, and Nigella Lawson, among many others). We've also renovated our beautiful third restaurant on Shepherd Market (Mayfair's old red-light district).

BoG: You guys obviously see the crossover between music and wine where craft, obsession, and rebellion are often commonplace in each. Can you expand on how one can help understand the other?

EK: There are many comparable themes in music and wine, from natural wine's "anyone can do it" DIY punk spirit to the nerdy side of record and wine collecting. In a more practical sense, the fifteen years I spent working as an A&R man for Parlophone/EMI and Island Records helped develop the tenacity needed to do something different in wine and food with my business partner Mark. We applied many similar methods—and many old contacts—to launch the magazine, presenting what we love about wine culture in a different way.

BoG: *Noble Rot* seems to help remind wine lovers that this libation should be fun and actually enjoyed, not just an elite or austere niche. Is this a conscious effort, or simply a side effect of exploring and sharing your love of wine?

DK: It's been said that a brand is the most valuable real estate in the world—a corner of someone's mind. And whether it's *Noble Rot* magazine articles or our restaurants' service, it's always been our number-one aim that when people think *Noble Rot* they think "fun."

BoG: What are some newer developments, trends, or directions you see happening in wine that you are excited about?

DK: I'm excited to be meeting more young vignerons taking over their family domaines that have uncompromising approaches to regenerative farming. Winemakers such as Charles Lachoux in Vosne-Romanée, or Edgar and Louise Coulon in Vrigny, Champagne, are working hard to improve winemaking in their respective regions.

BoG: How do you handle egoism or pretentiousness when you encounter it?

DK: Knowing what we don't want to be makes our jobs easier.

BoG: You helped discover Coldplay and Lilly Allen . . . but how punk/metal/hardcore do your musical tastes get?

DK: There's a Carpenters album I really like called . . . But seriously, Nirvana was my generation's punk, and the best gig I've ever seen in my life. They played the 1991 Reading Festival on the second stage at three in the afternoon. I was sixteen years old, and I went to see them with my pal and his twenty-one-year old metalhead brother. Kurt started by playing the riff from "School" (*Nevermind* wasn't released at this point) with a half-naked, facially tattooed "interpretive dancer" called Tony slam-dancing to his side. My head felt like it had filled with helium and the crowd went *berserk*. The next half an hour was a blur of visceral energy. At the end, Kurt ran from the edge of the stage and star-jumped onto the drum kit, breaking his arm. I saw them a couple of times after (later the same year at the Kilburn National Ballroom, which still holds the record as the most crowded gig I've been to) but nothing else has come close. I love everything from the Clash and Sex Pistols to Sonic Youth and Led Zeppelin.

BoG: Despite the wine world slowly opening up and being more inclusive, it can still be intimidating and rife with stigma. What would you say to encourage more metalheads to give wine a try?

DK: Do metalheads need hedonistic encouragement?! If so, they need look no further than Megadeth's Dave Mustaine for inspiration. "I think some bands think their audiences don't like wine because it's not metal, not this or that, but I think they're missing the point . . . it's about the experience. It can be your background music, or it can be your theme song," he told *Noble Rot* back in 2018. Amen to that.

MAYNARD JAMES KEENAN

The Man, The Myth, The Winemaker

MAYNARD JAMES KEENAN IS AN UNASSUMING RENAISSANCE MAN. Best known for his musical contributions, via his bands Tool, A Perfect Circle, and Puscifer, his passion for musical creativity is rivaled only by his passion for wine—whether it's winemaking, grape-growing, or exploring the intricacies of the craft. True to his multifaceted nature, Keenan generously shared his insights with us, discussing wine, the challenges of winemaking, and his candid thoughts on the wine industry.

"Wine can be snooty. So-called wine experts can be even worse. If you ever hear me waffling poetic about a fuckin' bouquet or pointing out the legs on a wine, please punch me right in my fucking neck meat," Keenan quips, wearing his disdain for the pretentious side of wine culture like a badge of honor. But he's not one to sit on the sidelines and criticize. Instead, he's actively creating solutions and crafting experiences that celebrate the unique character of the Verde Valley in Cottonwood, Arizona, through the diverse range of wines he produces. »»»

James Daly III

BLOOD OF GODS: How have your wine preferences changed over time?

Maynard James Keenan: Well, you know, American palate, so initially it was the bigger, jammier things in the mid-'90s. A lot of Australian Shiraz, Californian Cabs, and Syrahs. But then I quickly discovered things like Lacrima di Morro d'Alba; it's just like rose water and aromatics, and barely any structure on the palate, but just impressive with what's wafting out of the glass. So I've kind of settled into Barbarescos, Barolos, and then some more '70s and '80s versions of Tempranillos and Garnachas from Spain. Earlier, when you could afford it, early vintages of Bordeaux, because of the subtlety, because of the restraint. I will kind of go back in time with some of the wines that were introduced to me initially, then I kind of go back to those wines that were more restrained in alcohol and had more structure and elegance. And all of those things have their place, the big steak wine Malbec has its place, and I can appreciate it, but I just prefer and respond more to the Pink Floyd versions of wines rather than Metallica versions of wines.

"I just prefer and respond more to the Pink Floyd versions of wine rather than Metallica versions of wines."

BOG: Ever since the Covid pandemic, there's been a subtle sea change in how wine is perceived and appreciated. Have you also witnessed any changes during and since?

MJK: The bigger issue with us in 2020 was not a lot of rain and quite warm for the season. In general, we were down. We were down in production just slightly, maybe 20% down. And we cropped it back quite a bit because we weren't sure what was going to happen with the pandemic. Which was the wrong choice to make, because we sold a lot of wine through our wine club. Of course, on-premise locations were way down nationally, but bottle shops were blowing through the wine, and of course all our tasting rooms were opened in a very limited capacity, but we were [open], and we were busy. We had to be completely closed for six to eight weeks, which was not great. But the appreciation for the wine, I think, came as a collateral benefit. And people just grabbing wine in general, and grabbing *local* wine. And now people are [doing that] in our area. I think that's always the trick, right? You might be popular in New York, you might be popular in other places, but in your own hometown sometimes people don't quite get what's happening in their own backyard. And now we're finding that there's some traction with that, with people realizing that the Arizona product is actually on par with other things they're used to drinking.

BOG: My sense was that wine provided a pressure-release valve or respite from the tension and stress of life during Covid. It seems that people's appreciation for wine deepened during 2020.

MJK: I think something that people don't quite realize about farming is that even though there is a pandemic, if you expect there to be food or grapes ready for you one at a time, that work doesn't stop. We have to continue paying those bills and making that effort. We have greenhouses, we have gardens, we have orchards, so we were feeding our employees with what we were growing. We still have to make it and grow it, and tend to the work, but we had it. So I think once people walk in they realize that, "Oh, you guys aren't just 'farm-to-table,' you're, like, your farm to table . . ."

BOG: We spoke with James from Rune Wines who gave us some insight and interesting observations about the region, the climate, and conditions for winemaking and how there are some excellent parallels for metal: baking away at close to 5,000 feet, sun glaring down on the rocky terrain, lack of nutrients, very little water, the grapes are tied to a trellis ... it's pretty brutal! Do you see some parallels between the two sometimes?

MJK: For me I see more parallels in the process. Some of my favorite bands are combinations of individuals who are good players, but they're better listeners. So, for being accurate with expressing a time and a place, you have to be a really good listener and get out of the way and let that kind of happen. And then when you see an opportunity to add, rather than subtract or cloud it with your personality, be able to step in and enhance something. Be the squeeze of lemon, be the dash of salt—don't be the jalapeño pepper.

"Be the squeeze of lemon, be the dash of salt—don't be the jalapeño pepper."

Mother Nature will always have the final say, but I love how the process exists at the intersection between art—where you have the ability to show some creativity and personality—but there's also the science, where there are rules you have to play by. But there is that element of chaos, just like in music.

Especially if your metal borders on jazz, so you're having to react. But you have to be really good at your craft, you have to be in your element, and be able to react in a relevant way, in a way that is going to add. So, yeah, that chaos .... I have a lot of comedian friends and they are able to handle hecklers very well because they've done it for so long, they know the response, and they know how to defuse someone who's going to derail their shit. So I guess that's kind of, in a way, like when you have some weather coming through and that minor bout of weather is your "heckler," or a leaky keg is your "heckler," ya know?

BOG: How did you find where that balance was between pushing your wine through wholesale and selling direct to consumer?

MJK: Just for Arizona, in general, to be able to survive, there are several elements that are hurdles for me. There's a couple elements that are hurdles for people like Dos Cabezas, Callaghan, and Rune, those hurdles are that: you're in Arizona. First and foremost: that you're making wine in Arizona, and once you explain it to people, that it's absolutely possible—"Oh yeah!" You know, the "duh!" moment, right? But you're up against having to make that explanation a million times over. They don't get the connection that making Malbec in Argentina is at the same elevation, it's just south of the Equator. Same thing. Same kind of heat, same kind of limited precipitation. But the added element that I have is that I'm making wines more like Taras Ochota. I'm picking early, I'm cropping less, I've extended macerating so ours are lower-alcohol, pretty, elegant, age-able, high-acid wines, which is not for everybody. A lot of people like higher alcohol, more extraction, a little bit more oak; kind of bigger, beefier wines. I'm not making those wines, I'm making something that's more on par with what you used to drink back in 1970, before Parker and *Wine Spectator* got involved. So that's a hurdle because that's not the common market. And third is that "It's a dude in a metal band, is he really making the wine? Or does he just have some Oompa-Loompas, and he's just kind of talking the talk?" So those are three hurdles for me. So I had to go down the route of direct-to-consumer as much as possible.

Courtesy of Anthony Mueller

Anthony Mueller

"Anthony Mueller, did we just become best friends?"

"Yep!"

Okay, that exchange didn't happen—that's a riff from *Step Brothers*—but the following Q&A did happen, and it more or less confirms it and confirms that only a true renaissance man such as he can blast Cannibal Corpse followed by Sarah McLachlan, espouse the merits of sherry, reference Pantera's older-than-old hard rock/glam era, and dish some history on Cinsault. The wine writer, formerly covering Washington State and South Africa for Robert Parker's *Wine Advocate*, kindly gave us some of his thoughts and insights in early August of 2021. >>>

Blood of Gods: Barriers are coming down more and more, and a lot of that seems to be happening because there are trends in wine with younger people coming on in, there's also some gatekeeping that's been coming down, and there's been the Court of Master Sommeliers having their own controversies; everything is feeling like it's been kind of stirred up, and I think that's a good thing. What are some of the first things that come to mind when you think of the growing pains and change that's happening?

Anthony Mueller: With the CMS and the misconduct, it's not just limited to the CMS, it's not just secluded to the wine industry. I think it's systemic, I think it's a worldwide thing in every industry, because it is a mentality and a thought process which we sometimes allow or turn a blind eye to. And I think the voices who have the courage to stand up and make their voice be heard and say, "This is not right, I will not accept this"—I think it is absolutely healthy. And, yes, it can be scary, but I think it's time that we have the courage to stand up and say, "This is not right, and we're not going to accept it." I think as far as the wine community, as it grows globally, right now is a really, really interesting time to be alive and to be in the wine industry, because there's been so much growth and currently there are some challenges looking forward to the future.

"The scariest place to be in the universe is my iTunes library on shuffle."

BoG: Wine and music can sometimes feel exclusive, making it difficult for new or younger voices to break in. I understand that both realms hold deep significance for those who cherish them, and there's a desire to preserve what makes them special. As a result, new influences can be met with resistance—because change can be unsettling. However, whether it's wine or music, we have a responsibility to give back, to support and sustain the community. Welcoming fresh perspectives and new voices is essential because they are the ones who will carry the tradition forward. Without that openness, these scenes risk stagnation—and eventually, fading away.

AM: Everything will evolve over time, and maybe what you like . . . maybe it just doesn't become cool anymore. That doesn't mean that you like it any less, it just means less people are interested in it, and that's fine. Speaking about music specifically, I've seen numerous heavy metal shows and was in a few metal bands growing up in high school and college, and it's one of those things where, heavy metal isn't nearly as popular as it was through the '80s, and '90s, and then kind of hitting its heyday in the 2000s, and then from the mid-2000s on it just became less popular over time, and that's all right. It's just about being fine with that because if music didn't evolve, where would we be today? We'd still be listening to only Bach and Beethoven ...

BoG: Do you feel like there are any wines that mirror that same sort of precept, where it maybe had its popularity or its heyday and then has sort of waned?

AM: Yes, absolutely. So, I love sherry. Awesome stuff—I cannot get enough of it. It's one of those things where sherry, back more than 100 years ago, was hugely popular. It was very stable; it could take the journey of being put on a boat in a barrel and then sent around the world, or to a far-off country, and still be fine. Over time, sherry became less popular, and still, if you think about who the average drinker of sherry is, they're probably British and more mature—in their sixties, seventies, or eighties—and I would be right there with them hanging out. That sounds wonderful. I think, honestly, one of the coolest things I could possibly do would be hanging out with Betty White and drinking sherry. That sounds amazing to me—call me a weirdo, I think that sounds great. Sherry has clearly become less popular over time, so much so that there's kind of been this resurgence of sherry, trying to get people interested in it, and there's a lot of mixologists now trying to make sherry cocktails to try and get people interested in the style again. So, sherry for sure, for me, is that style of wine that was far more cool and popular back in the day, but now it's not as important, but it doesn't give me any less pleasure today when I drink it. Same as listening to old Metallica or Slayer or Pantera. Still love that music, but Slayer is kinda retired, Pantera is now disbanded because Vinnie and Dime are no longer with us, and Metallica is still around but they're doing their own thing now and producing less music. Those are classic metal groups who were icons of the genre and [circa] now they're not necessarily as important, and that's cool. If Slayer came through in concert, or Metallica, I'd absolutely go see them in concert.

BoG: So, the cornerstone of *Blood of Gods*: why metal and wine? You can draw some parallels, or point out why these two actually make sense together.

AM: That's a great question. I have a good somm buddy friend of mine, Chris Sawyer, and he used to pair wine with music, like full albums, and I used to pair wine with movies, cause I'm a movie buff. I was thinking: if wine and food are a pairing, well, why can't we pair wine with other things, abstract things? Like movies? Cool! So what about having a movie where it gets better and better over time? Well, that's kind of how a wine will open up over an hour, hour and a half—it will evolve in the glass or decanter, and as the movie gets better to its climax, we drink the wine to its climax, and they're kind of in sync. And then listening to music, it's one of those things where I believe that there is a style of music for every time and place and music will enhance the moment to make it better. And this can be seen in almost every aspect of life. Graduation: there is the "Pomp and Circumstance" march. When you're accepting an Olympic medal, they're playing the national anthem. There's always music involved in amazing things. When you get married, you know the song, the wedding jam [hums the melody to "Here Comes the Bride"]. There's music associated with great moments in life, why can't that go well with wine? If music can elevate a moment or situation, why can't wine? So, it's one of those things where I think they do go hand in hand. It doesn't necessarily have to be metal—I'm a huge fan of classical music and I think most metalheads do have an affinity for classical music, especially if you listen to speed riffs and solos—a lot of those have been played by almost every classical music maker, going back two hundred years!

"I believe that there is a style of music for every time and place—and music will enhance the moment to make it better. And this can be seen in almost every aspect of life."

BoG: Oh yeah. Wagner is often referenced as being as a major metal-riff inspiration.

AM: Exactly, yeah! Think about Metallica, who did the San Francisco Symphony Orchestra album. There are all these amazing laterals, and it doesn't necessarily have to be metal, it doesn't have to be classical, but if you enjoy music and wine and you're listening to your favorite song and you have your favorite wine, that's a pretty good day! Because now you're listening to good tunes, and you're drinking good juice, then life is good. It's awesome!

BoG: What are you currently enjoying as far as wines and currently enjoying for music?

AM: Currently, I've actually been on this *No More Tears* kick—just listened to the album. I have a huge appreciation for Ozzy [laughs], as difficult as he is to understand these days—you know, what an amazing life. The guy started from meager beginnings and just followed his path. He's always been tried and true, I'm actually wearing a Black Sabbath "The End—The Final Tour" shirt that was supposed to happen... which, I've been going to the "final tours" for fifteen years now? [laughs] And every time he says he's going to retire, I don't believe him. I think for newer music that may not be as well known, I'm really enjoying *Dance with the Dead*. It's '80s synth, with a bit of a metal, slightly thrash undertones. Every time I listen to their music, I feel like it's pulled directly out of an '80s horror film—where the girl is running through the woods and there's a psycho killer with a big machete trying to get her and she finds an old, abandoned house and she's trying to hide and then the murderer jumps through the window and then she's back running through the woods—it's super awesome. My taste in music is incredibly wide and at some point esoteric. I used to be a season-ticket holder to Phoenix Symphony Orchestra and Opera, when I moved to Detroit I was a season ticket holder for Detroit Symphony Orchestra, and I've had season tickets for the San Francisco Opera. The scariest place to be in the universe is my iTunes library on shuffle, because you're going to end up hitting Exodus, then Cannibal Corpse, then maybe Sarah McLachlan, and then maybe Detroit Symphony Orchestra, and then you might get a little Tupac, and then like old Pantera, like *Projects in the Jungle*.

BoG: What about wineries and wines, though? I can't let you off the hook—let's say limit it to U.S. producers to make it easier.

AM: Every time that I try wines from Walla Walla they continue to get better, and I continue to see new players enter into the game and make some really great wines, and Walla Walla shows so much promise. And yet, in Walla Walla, Cabernet Sauvignon is still king but the Syrah and Grenaches are just stupid good. As far as producers that I see making more of an impact, moving forward in Washington, I think of Cairdeas over in Lake Chelan. And Côte Bonneville in Yakima Valley is doing some really great things and producing some amazing Cabernets and is one of the few places on the planet which actually grows really high-quality Cabernet and really high-quality Riesling from the same vineyard, which is unheard of—almost hardly ever happens. There's a lot of cool stuff going on in Walla Walla, and across Washington in general.

Marquis Sauvage of BURN COTTAGE

When we first heard of Marquis Sauvage, owner of Burn Cottage Vineyard, we were intrigued. First of all, the reputation of the wines from Burn Cottage is extremely good, helping cement the status of Central Otago and New Zealand as a whole. But perhaps most interesting was hearing that he's a dyed-in-the-wool metalhead—not just a casual fan, the real-deal lifer. The man even looks like he belongs in Amon Amarth belting out Viking metal anthems. His pedigree and palate in both camps make him a truly unique figure and one of the most qualified voices to illustrate how heavy metal and wine belong together ››››.

Illustrations by Alex Murd

BLOOD OF GODS: What was your first aha wine moment when you realized that wine was something special for you?

MARQUIS SAUVAGE: I started drinking White Zinfandel in college 'cause I liked to party and I was getting tired of drinking beer and mixed alcohol. So this college, sort of crappy, dive bar that we went to happened to have White Zinfandel, and I started drinking that. That was in 1992, and from that point on I became obsessed. And then in Burgundy with my wife, in 1994, I remember having a Henri Jayer 1985 Cros Paratoo which absolutely blew my mind—and it was before they were a gazillion dollars a bottle. And that's what led to the Pinot Noir obsession and eventually to what is now Burn Cottage nowadays.

BoG: Similarly, what was your first music moment when you discovered a taste for underground/extreme music?

MS: In the early '80s, probably when I was in junior high school, and my dad bought a satellite dish because we were living in very rural Kansas and did not have cable TV, and I started watching MTV, and then specifically *Headbanger's Ball*, and I was a huge hair metal fan. Bands like Mötley Crüe, Ratt, Dokken, Hanoi Rocks, which I'm not ashamed to say I still love those bands to this day. And then when I was a senior in high school, or a junior, it was like 1985, I had an art teacher and she would let us bring music into class. And some kid, I think Tom Wilson was his name, brought Metallica *Master of Puppets* and I remember putting in that cassette, and side one, track one, is "Battery," and it was like, "Holy shit! What is this?!" And somehow Metallica had escaped me, so then I went back and started listening to *Kill 'Em All* and *Ride the Lightning*, and then I think *Garage Days Re-revisited* had just come out about the same time. So that's what started that path into the more underground music and it led me to thrash, which is still my favorite genre of heavy metal, and then into more hardcore bands like Suicidal Tendencies and things of that nature, and it got me into Motörhead and Metallica and it just spun from there . . .

BoG: What principles from underground music have helped you in the wine world?

MS: I'd say specifically passion, because everybody who's doing this sort of music has to have the passion for it first, and that's the first thing with wine. And then I think determination and resilience, 'cause you just never take no for an answer and you just keep plugging forward and doing what you do. Passion, determination, and drive would be the main things.

BoG: Metal concerts and winemaking each have an element of "controlled chaos." There's some etiquette and rules, but there's also that unpredictable component where mayhem could erupt at any moment. Same thing with recording music and making wine. Do you see similar parallels?

MS: Winemaking is all controlled chaos all of the time. I don't pretend to be a winemaker or understand it near like I should, and I've always marveled at Claire Mulholland, who's a rock star of a winemaker, who's our winemaker on the ground in New Zealand, and Ted Lemon when he's helped us out. The stress to me is just unbearable, but they're cool as cucumbers and know what they're doing. But each vintage is a different vintage, especially in a place with an unpredictable climate like Central Otago—you'll never know what you're gonna get, or what you're gonna see, so there always seems to be something that can come up that you weren't expecting and you have to know how to handle that, and fortunately our team does. In the vineyard is controlled chaos as well. Any given season can give you multitudes of problems. Like in Central Otago, for instance, we deal with that—we can get frost in harvest, which can be a nightmare and not the easiest thing to deal with, but again, Shane Livingstone, who's our vineyard manager, is a rock star—all of our team are rock stars in their own right—of knowing what to do and how to handle things. So yes, all controlled chaos, all the way around.

BoG: Biodynamic grape-growing already sounds pretty metal: following the lunar/celestial cycles, burying a cow's horn stuffed with manure, honoring nature's relationship with all living things. Terroir is metal, right?

MS: That's a great question. I think everything is metal (laughs). But I guess in our case terroir is metal because our soils are very glacial and schisty in nature, so it seems pretty metal. And if you're familiar with our label, everything we did and do is metal-inspired—our t-shirts are metal-inspired. And I think with biodynamics it doesn't get much more metal than that, as you alluded to, burying cow horns full of shit in the ground. Biodynamics always reminds me of the Danzig t-shirt from back in the day with the cow skull and the horn—I don't why, but that always reminds me of biodynamics—but, yeah, there is some pretty crazy stuff you do when you're biodynamic.

A few years ago at Riot Fest, I was with Rick Sales, who's the manager of Slayer, Gojira, Ghost, and Alien Weaponry, amongst others, and we were with Slayer, 'cause they were playing Riot Fest, so we were all sitting around outside Slayer's trailer, and I brought a bottle of Screaming Eagle and nobody had any wine glasses or anything so we drank Screaming Eagle out of red Solo cups. That's pretty metal.

BoG: For the wineheads reading this, what would you recommend as some go-to metal albums and why?

MS: First one would be *Kill 'Em All*—that's my favorite Metallica album just because it's so raw—even though Hatfield's voice has gotten much better over the years, every song on that album is killer to me. *Piece of Mind*, that's always an argument from Iron Maiden fans—which is everybody's favorite Maiden album—mine is *Piece of Mind* probably just cause I love "The Trooper" and I love "Die with Your Boots On." *Next is Lights, Camera, Revolution!* by Suicidal Tendencies. I love Suicidal in general—songs like "Can't Bring Me Down" and "Go'n Breakdown." I remember when I saw them in 1989 in Denver, Colorado, when I was in college at some sort of deserted ice rink of some sort, and it was crazy. A band I don't think gets their due: Life of Agony, *River Runs Red*. They are just awesome—Caputo can freaking sing. Venom *Welcome to Hell*—doesn't need an explanation, I don't think. This might be controversial to some people, but Mötley Crüe's *Shout at the Devil*. I think that is a brilliant album, it's one of the first albums that kind of started me on my metal journey and it's one of those albums where almost every song is good. Since I was more raised in the '80s, I get accused of being stuck in the '80s a little bit, but for newer bands I love the band Gojira. I think the album *Magma* from 2016 is great. One of the songs on there, "Stranded," is one of my favorite songs of all time. And they are just the nicest, greatest guys, and they are way into wine—I guess it's their French heritage. Next, Motörhead. Again, it can be arguable which is everyone's favorite album, but I love *Overkill*—it's probably my favorite—I love Motörhead in general, but the song "Damage Case" is my favorite Motörhead song. One more, going back to the thrash era—Anthrax, *Among the Living*. I love that album, and those guys are just so nice, such cool guys. I've gotten to know Charlie pretty well, and he's into wine and so is Scott.

BoG: Trends and innovation are often met with suspicion in wine and metal, where their respective audiences generally accept the more time-proven institutions/bands and practices the most. However, can you mention any new developments in wine and in metal that get you excited and keep your curiosity engaged?

MS: I'm guilty of being stuck in the '80s, like I said before—I graduated high school in 1986 so that is my big metal year, and I still kind of get stuck in those years. I try to do my best to get into new bands and learn about new bands and I described not too long ago—someone actually had asked me what's one of my new favorite bands—and I said Killswitch Engage, who I love, but they were like, "That's not a new band." And I'm thinking, "For me, that's a very new band." [Laughs] My daughter turned me on to a band, she's sixteen and she's into a band called Bad Omens, and I had never heard of them and then I started listening to them, and I'm actually going to see them in concert with her next month. Love them. What I try to do to keep up with new bands is listen to Sirius Radio *Liquid Metal*—they always seem to have the newer bands. As far as innovations in wine, winemaking, and vineyard management, we kind of buck the system there because we do it, I guess for lack of a better term, very old-school. Biodynamics is about as old-school as it can get. And then, in the winery, we are completely minimal intervention and don't manipulate stuff, or do any of these new tricks that are being done nowadays, which are very much controversial and looked at with skepticism with new trends that are happening in the winemaking industry right now.

KRISTIAN ESPEDAL

A/K/A GAAHL

ILLUSTRATIONS BY ALEX MURD

KRISTIAN ESPEDAL, OTHERWISE KNOWN AS GAAHL,

is easily one of the most well-known figures in black metal, but his appreciation of craft transcends those boundaries. From his work in fine art and operating the gallery Galleri Fjalar in Bergen, Norway, to his collaborations with Viking folk group Wardruna and wine producer Anthony Tortul, he is truly a renaissance man. He kindly shared his thoughts and experience with wine in a conversation with us towards the end of 2021.

BLOOD OF GODS: **Hello! How are you?**

GAAHL: I'm good. I'm actually unwrapping a bundle of wines, so you're calling at the right time.

BOG: **Ahh, perfect. So, let's start at the beginning: where did your interest in wine originate? Was there a specific memory or moment, or was it more gradual over time?**

G: It was actually quite a moment, definitely. It was back in, let's see—I suddenly got a kind of reaction to alcohol where I couldn't stand the taste of alcohol, or my body just reacted against it. So I couldn't even drink things that had 2.6% alcohol—I still noticed the alcohol way too much. So I stopped drinking for a year at least, and then suddenly I met Pinot Noir [laughs], and then I started working outward from there, and this was back in '91 or '92. So that's basically how I started to develop the passion for wine. I was kind of more into the conventional [wine] universe for many, many years, and then—I think this was in 2004 or 2005—I came across a natural wine, from a Belgian producer, but producing wine from Mount Etna, from Cornelissen, and got really annoyed by how anyone could serve this terrible, terrible thing. But because I always have to see how the wine changes in this nerdy universe, and then I just fell in love with it. But it was wrong in the sense of how I knew wine. So since then I basically have to focus on natural wines, but it was very disturbing, and I fell in love with this disgusting bottle [laughs].

BOG: Do you ever go back to conventional wines anymore? Or have you written them off completely?

G: Well, of course, good conventional wines are usually very close to natural wines, anyway. But of course I drink with a very different focus now than what I did back in the day.

BOG: I'm glad you mention that, because our palates are changing. We as humans are changing, so our tastes in music and in wine are different now than they were fifteen or twenty years ago.

G: Yeah, and already I have many different kinds of focuses on regions and areas, and grapes, that constantly change. It's an endless universe, basically, but it's a pleasure, in a way.

BOG: You're so passionate about wine—have you ever thought about releasing your own wine or collaborating with a producer?

G: I did release two wines this year [2021]. It's a collaboration I did with Anthony Tortul, the wine house is La Sorga, from the Languedoc region. He's been listening to my music for years and years, and I've been drinking his wine, without us knowing about this shared passion. So I met him in Oslo when he was here for a couple of wine tastings, and we hit it off really well. And then Covid came, and of course it's a struggle for these wine producers because restaurants and everything are closing down and you're not able to sell in the market because no one was able to buy it. But we have a very different system here in Norway, and also in Sweden, so we actually sold more alcohol during the Covid period than prior. So we made two wines together, but it's only available in the Norwegian market, luckily, because otherwise it would be gone already.

BOG: What would you say to entice or encourage more metal fans to give wine a try?

G: Well, my experience is basically that wine is what artists are consuming the most. You have of course Sigurd [Satyricon], and Frost [Satyricon, 1349] is really into wine as well, but also different craft beers. So we always have good bottles. Same with Ted, Nocturno Culto [Darkthrone], we've also shared many, many bottles. So there's a huge passion for wine, at least within the Norwegian metal scene. It might be different for fans, but it might just have to do with accessibility. People go out to a pub and it's easier to, umm . . .

BOG: . . . just grab a beer!

G: Yeah, and there might be too many options with wine, and if you are unlucky with a bottle you kind of . . . it's just not the same. There are not that many differences in beer as there is in wine.

BOG: It seems like people have been talking about natural wines becoming more and more popular, but it's not really a trend, it's more of a return, a return to how wine used to be made before large-scale production . . . which I think is a great way to reframe looking at natural wine: as a time-honored tradition and practice that sort of got lost along the way but is slowly coming back.

G: We did start to pollute the wine with all of these chemicals, more of it recently. Of course, natural wines are natural wines. So it is definitely a return. But of course it's a new focus on it, but it is back to the old days. Of course it is a trend—it's the same with the "local food" and everything—"short travel"—it's the way nature itself is. So people are returning in a way, even though there's still a lot of transportation.

BOG: Before the pandemic you hosted a wine tasting in Hackney, in the U.K., is that right?

G: Yes, I had a couple of wine tastings in London, and also here in Norway. I often get these requests; if I'm traveling there I usually can do something, but I prefer to speak with the wines than speak about the wines [laughs].

BOG: Do you ever get to visit the United States or have any wines here in the U.S. you enjoy?

G: I do. Let's see—Scholium Project—it's in the Napa region. I don't remember the last name, but there's a character called Abe there who produces very decent wine. But in general I'm more of an Old World wine-drinker. But I think one of his wines that I really enjoy is called the Prince in His Caves—that's one of his wines. They are pretty decent wines. But I have a lot of focus on Eastern Europe, and also of course France, and especially Austria. Since 2014, Austria has really started to produce something very serious. But also Georgia and Hungary have quite a lot of interesting wines. They have a stupid rule that they are not allowed to sell wine that is unfiltered, so you kind of lose quite a lot of the best wines by just having this law. But I do know a few wine producers that kind of just produce some wine for themselves—they can of course have them outside of Hungary—but there is a lot of potential there. Romania—fantastic wines there. Slovenia, Czech Republic—a lot of interesting things, but these are more countries where you are almost kind of unaware of their wine industry, but they have certain ways of making wines that are probably older than the way we produce wine in the rest of Europe.

BOG: What are some of your current recommendations for wine and music?

G: Umm, let's see . . . we have an Austrian producer that I would like to mention, and that is Christian Tschida. He's a producer that, if you can get a hold of, I would definitely recommend. I think my favorite producer is Alice Bouvot for L'Octavin. She's from the Jura region, so close to the Swiss border, basically, in France. And of course I have to mention my friend Anthony Tortul for La Sorga. He has some really nice things from the previous vintage. There are so many . . .

BOG: Do you ever contemplate being a wine writer, doing reviews, anything else in the wine industry?

G: No. I was actually already asked this in the late '90s by one of Norway's most serious wine publications, to write about it. But, like I said, I like to talk with the wine, not about the wine [laughs]. It's something that I don't want to specialize in that field other than on a private basis. It's a passion that I want to stay on—I don't want it to turn into a profession.

BOG: You had your most recent release, *The Humming Mountain*, come out on Season of Mist towards the end of 2021. Do you take time to commemorate or mark the occasion with a special bottle to celebrate?

G: No, I'm actually celebrating all the time [laughs]. No, for me, the album was finished a long time ago. But I try to have some sort of celebration every day. We do things all the time, so there's always a good reason to open a bottle.

BOG: I just realized we never got to discuss any music recommendations . . .

G: I rarely listen to music. I don't spend a lot of time listening to music. It's become work, in a way. But, by all means, I really enjoy a lot of Bowie's music. If I've been listening to music during the production of *The Humming Mountain*, it's actually been quite a lot of Grace Jones. I like her—she never pushes things, she kind of keeps it on a mellow stage across this almost ska-like music. I find her energy very inspiring. Still, I don't spend a lot of time with music apart from creating it.

BOG: Are there any heavy metal albums you'd suggest to wine-industry folks as their first step?

G: There's quite a lot of wine producers who are metalheads as well, so I don't think they need any guidelines. I think people should dive into their own mistakes or happiness. But when it comes to wine, it's basically just: figure out which kind of grape you like and then follow that pattern. It's a very easy way to kind of get a certain form of understanding of both regions and differences. But find out why you like something instead of just hoping for a good bottle.

Not a Token but a Catalyst

Unyielding Feminine Power

Collin Estrada

Why Metal and Wine?

Lauren Buzzeo, Editor and Publisher, *Full Pour* magazine
Sarah E. Daniels, Wine Writer
Kristen Richard, Wine Writer

Crunchy and raw; layered and brooding; vibrant, textured and intoxicating. What two products of the human hand other than wine and music could be a possible fit for these and countless similar descriptors?

Both can be powered by or representative of a devotion, a pursuit of pleasure and/or an unbridled celebration of each artform unto itself. On the flipside, both also encapsulate a sense of chaos, albeit in different ways.

Metal excavates themes of discord typically shelved by "polite" society, charges them with high volume, and confronts them with imagination; wine is an artful translation of the organic chaos between vines, sun, soil, and altitude.

But the worlds of metal and wine have also both historically shared the same stereotypical audience: straight white males.

We are here to call bullshit on any remnants of that perception that may remain. For metal, for wine, for metal and wine.

There's room for everyone to enjoy metal and wine no matter who you are or how you arrive. We believe in the beauty of art and culture, and we believe in it being appreciated inclusively.

It makes no difference whether you prefer to take in some Mozart or Megadeth with your Merlot, read Plath or Palahniuk with a Pinot, watch Brando or Boseman with some Barolo. The intersectional possibilities of wine and art of all forms are endless and wonderful.

Though such pairings can seem worlds apart on paper, by applying different perspectives and understanding shared commonalities, we can achieve new, deeper insight and appreciation for both.

Think back on your first sip of good wine and how it made you realize you never knew wine could be this way. Similarly, maybe the first time you heard a killer album, like Truckfighters' *Gravity X*, you thought to yourself, "I never knew metal could be like this."

We've been fortunate to have those euphoric epiphany experiences many times over, both with beautiful wines from around the world but also with bands like Pantera, Sleep, Gojira, Weedeater, Electric Wizard, and more. As your palate and preferences continue to evolve over time, tasty experiences unfold around every corner, with endless paths of access into these ever-expanding worlds.

So why metal and wine? Well, really, why the fuck not?

BADASS WOMEN *In Wine*

BY EMILY WINES, M.S.

TWENTY-PLUS YEARS INTO MY CAREER, I CONTINUE TO BE SURROUNDED BY incredible female sommeliers, wine directors, winemakers, importers, and more. What kills me is that I am still being asked what it is like being a woman in the business and am put in roundup articles and panels to discuss being a woman in wine. How long does one have to do this in order to no longer be a novelty? Badass women have been in the biz since, I don't know, the Last Supper? It is time to pay some tribute to the real rebel girls and change-makers, as I am certainly riding their coattails. I also want to shout out to some of the new punk rock girls of wine that are paving the way for the future.

BARBE CLICQUOT PONSARDIN. This woman! Seriously, such a genius. At twenty-seven, after her husband died, she took over the bubbles biz. She was a pioneer in winemaking (she made that shit clear!), marketing (make my label the color of egg yolk so you can recognize it in a shop window from across the street, please), and sales. Following the French all the way to the Russian border in the Franco-Prussian War meant she not only got to sell her fizz to thirsty soldiers, she had product ready to sell to the Russians as well. Sure, the Agent Yellow jokes abound today, but you can't help but to admire someone so punk rock as Barbe.

MARTINE SAUNIER. Being in the right place at the right time ... it's everything. If Siouxsie Sioux hadn't been in London in the '70s, Joan Jett and Courtney Love might not be who they are today. Martine Saunier is one of the twentieth century's greatest tastemakers. Her curatorial prowess brought producers like Henri Jayer, Chateau Rayas, Domaine du Pegau, Emmanuel Rouget, and Meo-Camuzet to America. All proceeded to become some of the largest French blue-chip wines. In a male-dominated import world, this woman is so important that she can be referred to by her first name alone and everyone stops to listen to what she has to say.

NOT A NOVELTY

MADELINE TRIFFON. Picture it: Detroit in the mid-'80s. Is this where you'd expect a world-class female sommelier to thrive? Against all odds, in 1987 Madeline Triffon passed the master sommelier exam on her first attempt, *the day after passing the advanced exam.* That is metal as hell. She has continued to be the ferocious champion of the future generations of somms and an icon of the industry. Madeline eschews the "deification of the somm" and embraces the roll of a master sommelier as that of a master servant. A somm superstar with this much genuine humility is a rare thing indeed.

SHELLY LINDGREN. While it is a good idea to create wine lists that at least have some bottles with brand or varietal recognition, Shelly breaks all the rules. An advocate for Calabria and southern Italy as a whole, her Calabrian pizza joint, A16, is known for one of the most regionally specific wine lists outside of that region. It could quickly overwhelm even the most savvy wine drinker, but instead her well-trained staff and her personal delight in the region allow the guests to take a wild ride into a whole new level of wine appreciation.

JUNE RODIL. For all those who yawn at the old white-guy sommelier stereotype, June Rodil drops in like a Melissa auf der Maur bass riff. Deep in good-old-boy Houston, this fierce Filipina master sommelier brings a refreshing take on wine with a dollop of feminism and social justice. June was instrumental in forming the Court of Master Sommeliers' Diversity Committee with the goal of making the organization less old-white-guy.

SHAKERA JONES. Like a blast of A/C on a muggy summer night, Shakera is a refreshing, game-changing face in the world of wine right now. As her Insta handle @blackgirlsdinetoo says, there is too much assumption about what women of color, particularly black women, are likely to drink or where they are comfortable eating. Shakera's boundless enthusiasm for wine and food, which she addresses to the people instead of back at the wine industry, gives me life.

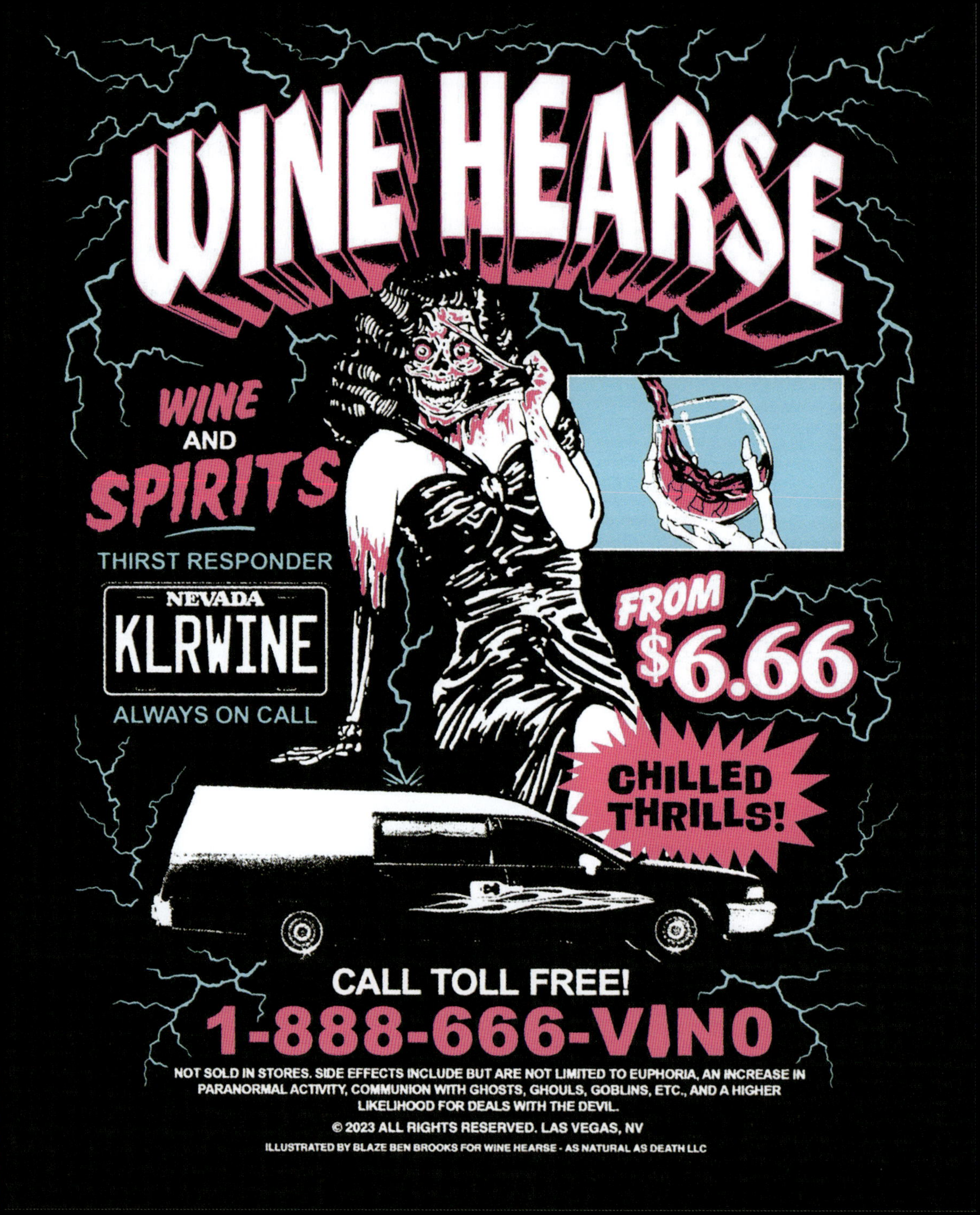

WINE HEARSE
WINE
AND
SPIRITS
THIRST RESPONDER
NEVADA
KLRWINE
ALWAYS ON CALL
FROM
$6.66
CHILLED THRILLS!
CALL TOLL FREE!
1-888-666-VINO
NOT SOLD IN STORES. SIDE EFFECTS INCLUDE BUT ARE NOT LIMITED TO EUPHORIA, AN INCREASE IN PARANORMAL ACTIVITY, COMMUNION WITH GHOSTS, GHOULS, GOBLINS, ETC., AND A HIGHER LIKELIHOOD FOR DEALS WITH THE DEVIL.
© 2023 ALL RIGHTS RESERVED. LAS VEGAS, NV
ILLUSTRATED BY BLAZE BEN BROOKS FOR WINE HEARSE - AS NATURAL AS DEATH LLC

Blaze Ben Brooks

Born from a lifelong love of the macabre, a flair for the dramatic, and a devotion to natural wine, **WINE HEARSE** is Lauren Tuvell's deliciously offbeat altar to all things dark and fermented. A Las Vegas native and certified sommelier, Lauren also moonlights as a female Elvis impersonator—because of course she does.

BLOOD OF GODS: What got you first interested in wine? Was there an aha moment? Or was it more gradual over time?

LAUREN TUVELL (aka WINE HEARSE): I've been an avid wine drinker forever but really dug in during the pandemic. I'd been laid off from my creative producing job and met with a wealth of unexpected free time so started casually reading about wine and listening to a couple of nerdy wine podcasts (shoutout to Helen of *Helen's Wines* and her pod *Wine Face!*). There was more opportunity for drinking, too, of course, and I think I realized I wanted (or needed) to be doing that more consciously. When the world started to open back up again, friends with a natural wine bar in Brooklyn, where I was living at the time, needed somebody to pour on their patio. I picked up a shift a week and totally got the bug. Certifications and a handful of other behind-the-bar gigs followed. If anything, my aha moment was about how simultaneously chill and very serious wine could be—sort of fun *and* academic in equal measure, depending on your approach.

›››

BOG: What was the initial inspiration and push to bring Wine Hearse to life?

LT/WH: A lifelong love affair with the macabre and the once-in-a-lifetime opportunity to buy a hearse from a friend! I wish it was more romantic than that, but I'd really just been looking for a way to marry interests and work for myself. I knew I wanted to pour natural wine exclusively and had already come up with a name for my LLC, As Natural as Death. When a friend decided to sell her hearse—previously used in promotion for a book she'd published, and prior to that in service with a California funeral home for many years—it was the obvious move.

BOG: Why the decision to focus on Natural wine?

LT/WH: It's always been my preference—I'm a big champion for sustainability and conscious farming practice (plus the only harvest I ever worked I was put in charge of additions and it was kind of terrifying)—but meeting my partner, James, really sealed the deal. He's an incredible bartender, but when we started dating he sheepishly shared that he "couldn't drink wine." Through much trial and error, we discovered his gnarly reaction was a histamine sensitivity that most natural wines don't give him! I appreciate that additive-free wine is accessible to him and lots of other folks who've told me wine is usually a no-go for them; plus, it's delicious.

BOG: What is a typical Wine Hearse experience for first-timers just learning about you and your offerings?

LT/WH: I love to show up in unexpected spaces. I'm a one-woman operation and the hearse is pretty full-service for what I have to offer—a pop-up bar that pours natural wine and cool craft beers. Because my bar top stores in the back of the hearse with a fridge and canopy, I've got a pretty sweet mobile set-up. I'd liken it to a food truck, but of course I only serve booze. Everything comes out of the back of the hearse including a casket, which is only for display at the moment (but I've got big plans for her in the future).

BOG: Combining something more macabre with wine is like music to our ears. What are most folks' reactions when first discovering Wine Hearse?

LT/WH: People think it's rad! And I'm grateful. I get occasional looks and bizarre questions—especially at gas stations, for whatever reason—but most folks seem pretty into it. It's been an awesome way to meet like-minded weirdos, too. I've met a bunch of cool tattooers, circus performers, and recently did a wedding reception for members of a band from Austin called the Coffin Fits. Building a network of ghouls is a definite perk.

BOG: So what kind of bizarre questions have you gotten?

LT/WH: Best one yet was, "Is that . . . a limo?" And I couldn't help myself but to reply, "In a manner of speaking." This guy's eyes got *huge* and he started backing away before he said, "Wait . . . it's not one of those ... dead people cars, is it?" Lots of "Do you have somebody in there right now?", "Is it haunted?', and a personal recurring favorite, "Can I get in?"

BOG: What are some of the typical grim and gruesome bands that are classics/constants in your rotation?

LT/WH: Lots of Joy Division and the Cramps, always. Screamin" Jay Hawkins, Bobby "Boris" Pickett (not just at Halloween)—and I was just turned on to Twin Temple. I've always got Angelo Badalamenti on rotation too, and the music David Lynch has released through his music project is deliciously dark.

BOG: Do you incorporate music into the Wine Hearse experience? What kind of tunes?

LT/WH: Most definitely; I think it's invaluable to the atmosphere I'm aiming to create. I use a pretty wide variety of things—classics from the '30s and '40s, New Orleans jazz, sweeping instrumentals (think Bernard Herrmann's Hitchcock scores), and more contemporary grunge. Anything that's got some spooky soul on it is fair game.

BOG: You're also the Queen Herself, a female Elvis impersonator. Please elaborate (and titillate for those reading who might wanna get hitched at the *Blood of Gods* Annual Merrymaking this summer) . . .

LT/WH: I moonlight as a female Elvis impersonator at Sure Thing Chapel here on Fremont Street and it"s the most fun job I've ever had. I could never have guessed that moving home would mean finding the most Las Vegas job ever (can you think of anything more Vegas than a minister in drag as Elvis?) but my parents are delighted that my B.F.A. is finally relevant! And I never tire of swingin' them hips or curlin' that lip, bunny.

THE COUPLE THAT DRINKS TOGETHER...

COURTESY OF CARLA HARVEY

BY CARLA HARVEY

Carla Harvey of Lords of Acid (and former co-vocalist of Butcher Babies), recalls her journey to the glorious world of wine. She and her fiancé, Charlie Benante, drummer for thrash-metal legends Anthrax, put their senses to the test to see just how far their palates have come, "during the pandemic of endless wine-drinking." >>>

I USED TO BE A WHISKEY DRINKER...

whiskey neat, to be exact. Or, if available, with one of those fancy, giant ice cubes. It started with Jack Daniel's at the Rainbow Bar and Grill when I was a precocious twenty-one-year-old that had just moved to Hollywood to be a rock star. I always had an affinity for Crown Royal, and drinking Japanese whiskeys in Tokyo was a highlight of my drinking life. Wine, on the other hand, was of no use to me. I had been wine-drunk once at nineteen when I drank a couple of glasses of cheap red at a wedding, so it always reminded me of veterans'-hall nuptials and bad bridesmaid dresses. Times sure have changed . . . Now, I'm the girl sending my Pinot back when it tastes like the last swallow out of the bottle. Luckily, I have myself a willing wino partner: my fiancé Charlie Benante from Anthrax.

I've been trying to figure out exactly when Charlie and I decided that we were going to become wine snobs. I believe I was hanging with him on an Anthrax tour through Europe and he had stopped drinking beer, so we started sipping on Pinot Grigio together at cute little cafés in places like Nice, Eindhoven, Nantes, and Metz. We got really into reds in Australia, and our obsession went overboard tasting Chilean reds in South America. When we got home from our adventures, we realized that we were opting for wine with dinner way more often than our Moscow mules or whiskeys on the rocks. We also started noticing that we had more metal friends into great wine than we realized. Our friends Kim and Jeremy Wagner (Broken Hope) got us hooked on Flowers and Golden Eye and our friend Marquis Sauvage, owner of Burn Cottage Vineyard, helped to develop our palates one indulgent night at Maple and Ash.

Nicholas Hartman

To see just how far our palates have come during the pandemic of endless wine-drinking, we decided to have a tasting for two at home, wherein Charlie and I would taste four wines and pick each other's favorites in order. We'd remain poker-faced during the tasting and really make the other guess. We had a sweet selection of reds: DRNK Pinot Noir, Time & Direction 2018 Syrah, Viv 2018 Petit Verdot and a Viv 2018 Malbec. We kicked things off with the Pinot. We knew we'd love it, as it's from the Russian River Valley. We frequent a wine bar by our house for a Russian River Valley Pinot that we can't get enough of. This one was no different—pure heaven! We tasted strawberry, spices, root beer . . . earthy and perfection!

We had the Petit Verdot next. Petit Verdot is indigenous to the western part of the Bordeaux wine region of France. I know this because Charlie and I got very drunk on Petit Verdot one evening in France in this swanky hotel bar. The bar was full of musicians (we must have been playing Hellfest the day after or before), and at one point the new singer of a very famous nineties band came in and sat next to us and told us a wild story about his girlfriend getting kidnapped from her taxi to meet him there. His solution? Drink more! This Viv Petit Verdot had a gorgeous bottle and smelled and tasted overwhelmingly like flowers! What broad doesn't like flowers?

We had the Syrah next. I brought my A-game poker face to this one. I never really mention Syrah, but I love a good one! Charlie would have no idea! We finished our tasting with the Vive Malbec. My former bandmate Heidi Shepherd, a wine connoisseur in her own right, introduced me to Malbec. She is always spot-on with what kind of wine I'll love. This one exploded with flavor just like the Petit Verdot by the same winemaker we had. I tasted raisin, maybe fig . . . so thick and full!

So how did our choices tally up? Let me preface our final lineups by saying all the wines were stellar. In order from favorite to least, I thought Charlie's would be Pinot Noir, Syrah, Petit Verdot, Malbec. Charlie thought I would like: Pinot, Malbec, Petit Verdot, Syrah. I thought we knew each other's tastebuds well, but we were both wrong! Charlie's personal picks favorite to least favorite were the Pinot, Malbec, Syrah, and the Petit Verdot. My personal favorites were the Pinot, the Syrah, the Petit Verdot, and the Malbec! The biggest surprise for me was Time and Direction's Syrah. I really loved it! I guess we will have to do some studying and have a do-over! Bottoms up, my friends!

Why Wine & Metal?

By Adahlia Cole

Adahlia Cole's abbreviated bio reads, "Bay Area commercial and editorial photographer with a focus on food, wine, and hospitality." That might not seem particularly edgy or metal, but one look at her résumé more than earns her street cred and metal horns raised. From working at the legendary 924 Gilman Street punk club in Berkeley, her formative listening habits—citing Asunder and Sleep as touchstones—and her DIY spirit and mentality, she has seen first hand the obsession, rebellion, and craft displayed in wine and heavy metal. Nowadays, one is most likely to see her photography and articles in the *San Francisco Chronicle*, *Forbes*, *Sunset Magazine*, and the *Michelin Guide*, but that same nerdy excitement, whether it's discovering a new band or restaurant, is ever-present.

Why wine and metal? I don't feel overly qualified to discuss such things, as I recently sold off all my metal records that had been boxed up in my mom's garage collecting dust for the better part of the past decade, though I did give ye olde Sleep *Volume One* and Asunder *A Clarion Call* one last nostalgic listen before I said goodbye and sent them off to be pawned away on Discogs. However, I do think there are some parallels that can be drawn between the wine and metal communities—some good and some bad.

Both metal and wine have a history in, and draw imagery from, the sacred and the profane. Both can be polarizing, both inspire devotion and sometimes obsession from their respective cohorts and enthusiasts. Both exist on a spectrum from the more commercial and easily palatable to the more niche, acquired tastes. Maybe you start off with Metallica, Black Sabbath, Slayer, or Iron Maiden but over the years find yourself starting to specialize, to learn what you like, maybe going down a rabbit hole of things that get darker, sludgier, doomier—with increasingly incomprehensible band logos. And wine is the same way—you likely started out drinking things that are a little more easily palatable before refining your tastes and figuring out what you're truly into. If I choose to look past my Sutter Home white Zin shoplifting teenagedom, the first wines I ever actually connected with were a 2005 Hexamer Spätlese and a very tropical Asatsuyu Sauvignon Blanc. I really loved those wines, even though they aren't what I would gravitate to now. But that approachable Riesling and California S.B. introduction paved the way to deeper exploration: dipping a toe into reductive white Burgundy, finding a penchant for left-bank Bordeaux, figuring out that I fucking hate Syrah,

>>>>

Photos courtesy of Colin Peck

40

Josh George

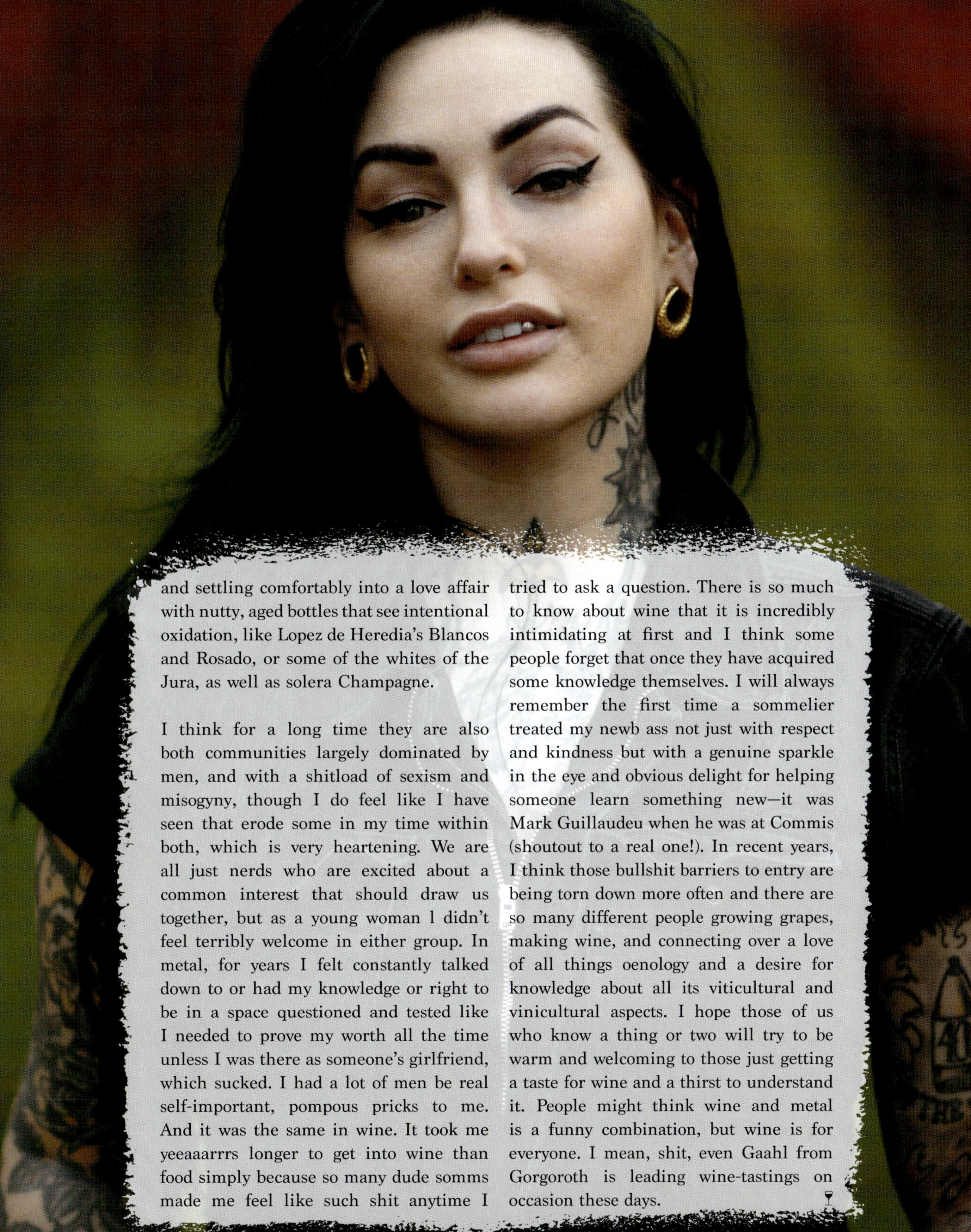

and settling comfortably into a love affair with nutty, aged bottles that see intentional oxidation, like Lopez de Heredia's Blancos and Rosado, or some of the whites of the Jura, as well as solera Champagne.

I think for a long time they are also both communities largely dominated by men, and with a shitload of sexism and misogyny, though I do feel like I have seen that erode some in my time within both, which is very heartening. We are all just nerds who are excited about a common interest that should draw us together, but as a young woman I didn't feel terribly welcome in either group. In metal, for years I felt constantly talked down to or had my knowledge or right to be in a space questioned and tested like I needed to prove my worth all the time unless I was there as someone's girlfriend, which sucked. I had a lot of men be real self-important, pompous pricks to me. And it was the same in wine. It took me yeeaaarrrs longer to get into wine than food simply because so many dude somms made me feel like such shit anytime I tried to ask a question. There is so much to know about wine that it is incredibly intimidating at first and I think some people forget that once they have acquired some knowledge themselves. I will always remember the first time a sommelier treated my newb ass not just with respect and kindness but with a genuine sparkle in the eye and obvious delight for helping someone learn something new—it was Mark Guillaudeu when he was at Commis (shoutout to a real one!). In recent years, I think those bullshit barriers to entry are being torn down more often and there are so many different people growing grapes, making wine, and connecting over a love of all things oenology and a desire for knowledge about all its viticultural and vinicultural aspects. I hope those of us who know a thing or two will try to be warm and welcoming to those just getting a taste for wine and a thirst to understand it. People might think wine and metal is a funny combination, but wine is for everyone. I mean, shit, even Gaahl from Gorgoroth is leading wine-tastings on occasion these days.

Anna Sweet

IN PURSUIT
of Vine Ripe Fruit

By Bree Stock MW, Winemaker of Limited Addition

Bree Stock's résumé checks just about every box of the wine industry. The Master of Wine, born and raised in Australia, has spanned the globe between consulting and education to writing and winemaking. That's like a skilled guitarist who also gives lessons, produces albums, and releases their recorded output on their own label. Oh, and bonus points: she's also really cool. She found time during harvest to pair six of our fave albums with some primo wine.

Drug Church, *Hygiene*

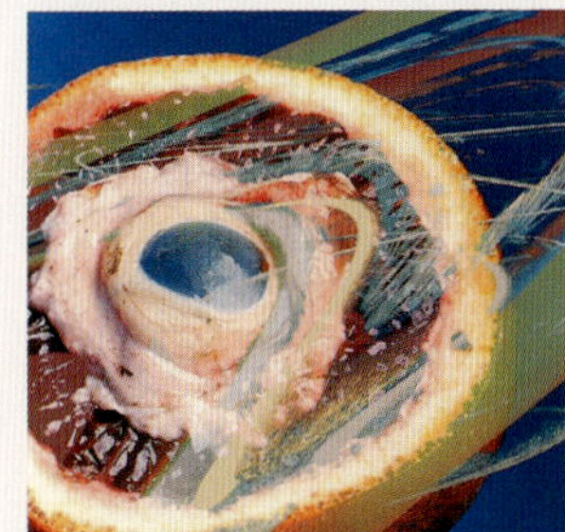

We swear this album didn't make the list solely because the first words sung are "In pursuit of vine ripe fruit." Drug Church went from a band whose name we'd simply heard of over the last decade or so to one of our most listened-to bands in 2022. Gloriously catchy, grungy punk (imagine a heavy, punk version of the Pixies, or maybe even the band Wavves) that has just a bit more dirt under its fingernails and gravel in singer Patrick Kindlon's voice to draw a through-line to their hardcore influences. The band somehow balances youthful energy with world-weariness and heartfelt sincerity with a feeling of wistfulness. It comes across as completely earnest and makes you a total believer and an instant fan. Last year it was Turnstile; for us, this year, it's Drug Church.

Notes: Youthful, Vibrant, Textured

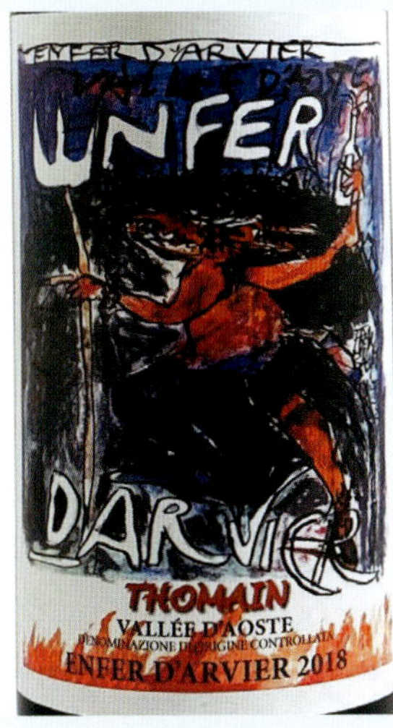

BREE: Wow! This album is so familiar it took me right back to my angsty high school and college days of the Pixies, Silverchair, and Nirvana with all the catchy grunge riffs—so enjoyable! However, the album has an old soul vibe and genuine sincerity. It reminds of the rustic and honest wines made by Danilo Thomain and his Enfer d'Arvier made from the alpine variety Petit Rouge high in the Valle d'Aosta. I love their wild alpine berry fruits and earnest rusticity. This is a wine that feels like it has existed for an eternity. There's no flash, it's not trying to impress anyone, which is exactly why it makes such a strong impression in the increasingly made-up world of wine. A wine for the ages.

>>>

Imperial Triumphant, *Spirit of Ecstasy*

They just keep getting better. The angular and experimental trio from New York have returned with easily their best album yet. It's wonderfully experimental, blending noir jazz freak-outs with blackened riffs that swirl and morph like Alice in Wonderland's disorienting fever dream as she falls deeper and deeper through the rabbit hole. But, rather than a fairy tale, Imperial Triumphant delivers their art deco motif more aligned to the futuristic, urban dystopia of the 1927 film *Metropolis*. *Spirit of Ecstasy* is more cinematic than anything the band has done before, blending strings and samples that really up the drama quotient.
Notes: Stately, Urbane, Refined

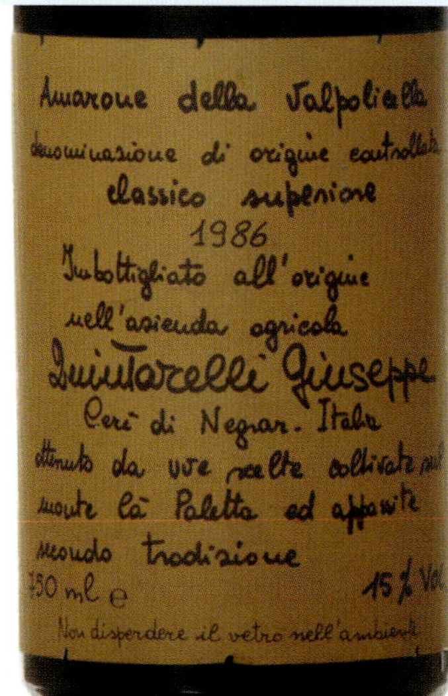

BREE: This album is a masterpiece; its deep, laminated, with multiple charred base layers supporting angular, energetic riffs are hypnotic and, like a good wine, continue to reveal more and draw you deeper with every listen. Imperial Triumphant brought to mind one of Italy's greatest wines and greatest wine minds, Giuseppe Quintarelli. Many of the greatest wines in the world cannot be compared to others in their region; they are more a product of the integrity of the person behind the wine than the regional benchmark. The Quintarelli wines never disappoint and are always an exercise in going deeper into the glass and craft of a master artisan and a lesson in patience. The eleven-hectare parcel nestled into the hills north of Verona, in the Valpolicella region of Italy, produces nearly a dozen wines from selective multiple harvests throughout the vineyard. The grapes are often made using the appassimento technique where a portion of the grapes are left to dry on mats in the barn before being pressed and fermented. This concentrating technique results in deeply flavored wines that have the most intense layers of fruit, herbs, spices, and fruitcake. Put on some headphones and grab a bottle of Quintarelli's Amarone della Valpolicella and sit in its generosity of spirit and allow it to share its secrets with you—you won't be disappointed.

Crown Magnetar, *Alone in Death*

This is deathcore—full stop. It's beefy and it's burly—there is absolutely no fat on this thing; it's all muscle. They're either tenderizing your solar plexus with blast beats or loosening your bowels with gargantuan breakdowns—that's it, those are their two modes. Is it original? Hell, no. But the band operates on such an unrelenting and destructive level it comes off as total panache. It certainly helps ensure the theme of brutality with vocalist Dan Tucker's performance, sounding like a rabid grizzly on uppers.
Notes: Meaty, Big, Punchy

BREE: Oof, this is chunky and dense and all I want is a Syrah or Grenache that's as meaty and gritty as this album. I'm immediately reaching for a northern Rhône Valley Cornas from one of the most understated producers that completely over delivers in the glass, Vincent Paris. The Granite 60, named for the soil and degree of the slope in this part of the vineyard, is everything you expect a wind-stricken, sun-drenched vineyard slope to deliver—there's power and energy in all the right ways. The fruit in this wine is excessively savory and sanguine, like eating salt licorice and biting the inside of your lip, releasing just a hint of irony blood onto the palate with the texture of this wine like biting into grilled bear meat, a dense kidney-textured mouthful. Rock this pairing while cooking outdoors over a sturdy flame.

Black Magnet, *Body Prophecy*

You know that lazy album review style where the writer says something along the lines of, "It's like *this band* partying with *that band* in *this other band's* backyard"? Well (deep breath), our apologies: Black Magnet sounds like classic-era Skinny Puppy partying with '90s-era Nine Inch Nails in Godflesh's backyard. Now, of course nothing is ever going to sound that good—us mortals wouldn't be able to handle it—but it's damn close. The three-piece's industrial crunch-n-thump runs parallel to overdriven cyber-goth electronics. With the album's crisp and modern production, the whole thing comes across like someone threw David Fincher's gritty filmography into a monochrome blender—flashy, alluring, startling, and thrilling in equal measure.
Notes: Crisp, Modern, Electrifying

BREE: This album has so much energy and crystalline layers and hypnotic grooves it takes me back to the mid-'90s in an instant. I can't help but think about the Grüner Veltliners and Rieslings of Austria's Wachau valley, specifically those with such clarity and energy like the fifth-generation estate F. X. Pichler. Their Steinertal Loibner Grüner Veltliner comes from one of the coolest parts of the Loibner vineyards buttressed by forest and the cool nocturnal breezes that emerge from them to cool the vineyard and keep the acidity high and the characteristic Grüner white-pepper spice ever present. The vibrant and crunchy tropical lychee and white-nectarine fruit will keep you bouncing along with the gritty-crunchy electronica riffs in this post-modern offering.

Sunrise Patriot Motion, *Black Bellflower Stream*

Featuring members of New York's Yellow Eyes, Sunrise Patriot Motion steeps post-punk and gothic rock in black metal just long enough to give the feeling of desperation, some teeth, and ire. There are moments that bring to mind Burzum, the minimalist lo-fi keyboards of "Warp of the Window," the vocals are reminiscent of Hateful Abandon with their intoned shout-sing delivery, but the absolute highlight is "My Father's Christian Humidor." The song comes across like the Church trying their hand at death rock—catchy and driving, but with just a dark touch of grit and gloom.
Notes: Achromatic, Hazy, Dense

BREE: This album reminds me of hot summer days in Australia's southern wine valleys and the hazy light that settles in the late afternoons. On a recent trip back just prior to the pandemic lockdown, I fell in love with a small producer in the Adelaide Hills Basket Range region called Gentle Folk. They make a delightfully smashable hazy red from a medley of varieties—mainly Gamay with some Pinot Noir, Sangiovese, Syrah, Merlot, Grenache and Mataro. The wine is all juicy red and black fruits laced with Christmas herbs and spices and a touch of grit, delightfully minimalist in its approach and dangerously quaffable with just a hint of a chill.

CHRISTOPHER HERNDON

SURFING THE CHAMPAGNE (SOCIALISM) SUPERNOVA: IN THE NEO-FEUDALIST WORLD WE FIND OURSELVES IN

BY SHAMIM DE BRÚN

AS OSCAR WILDE ONCE SAID, "PLEASURE WITHOUT CHAMPAGNE IS PURELY ARTIFICIAL."

Champagne, the OG sparkler once relegated to the realms of elitist circles and opulent graduations, has undergone a Kafkaesque metamorphosis, becoming the drink of choice for a new generation which is reshaping the landscape of luxury consumption and redefining what it means to indulge in the finer things.

At the heart of this cultural shift lies the concept of "little treat culture," a movement that champions the idea of celebrating life's small pleasures. Millennials and Zoomers alike have found themselves locked out of the traditional trappings of adulthood. Few can afford the white-picket-fenced-off house, car, and 2.5 kids of the generations before them. This, however, has left them in a strange limbo where they have more disposable income than their forebears. No matter how hard they save they will likely never have basic securities so instead they are imbibing in this kind of luxuries. They're consuming more caviar than ever. They book restaurants months in advance. They are highly engaged with experience-driven wine and culinary culture. They don't just want to drink it, they want to know about it.

With its effervescent bubbles and timeless elegance, the allure of Champagne is perfectly pitched for this. We live in an era where security and "the big joys" are not guaranteed, so indulging in these little treats is like a poor man's hedonism. Think, "Let them eat cake," but it's, "Let them drink Champagne."

As society teeters on the knife's edge of late-stage capitalism veering towards neo-feudalism, why not give everyone Champagne? Why not spend it while you got it, because it will only be worth less

>>>

next year. Who needs stability and security when you can have a delicious Blanc de Blanc to distract you from the impending doom of global warming and political unrest? Besides, it's not like a bottle of Bolly will solve all the world's problems, but it is a dependable win. If you want Champagne these days you can get it. So there's this guarantee that at least something will satiate you, while you deal with the cruel realities of rent and inflation.

Treats aren't exactly a groundbreaking idea; they hit their peak in 2011 when *Parks and Recreation* made "Treat Yo' Self" a thing and etched it into our collective consciousness. Fast forward many years later, and TikTok gave that moment a second wind. But the concept of small indulgences has been around long before the internet. This sort of little luxury can trace its roots back to the lipstick index. This theory suggests that, during tough economic times, sales of affordable luxuries, like lipstick, tend to rise. Despite tightening budgets, people still allow themselves these little pleasures as a coping mechanism. This theory held true during the Great Depression, the dot-com bubble burst of the '90s, and the 2008 financial meltdown. And now, with inflation having hit a forty-year high last year, we're undoubtedly witnessing it once more in the guise of the cheeky glass of Champagne.

"GONE ARE THE DAYS OF RIGID ETIQUETTE AND PRETENTIOUS SNOBBERY; INSTEAD, CHAMPAGNE IS EMBRACED FOR ITS ABILITY TO BRING PEOPLE TOGETHER AND SPARK MOMENTS OF JOY AND CONNECTION."

Champagne itself has also undergone a shift at the same time. Enthusiasts have been keeping tabs on it for decades, and the current level of interest is off the charts. Sure, the house Champagnes of yore still dominate the pop-cultural psyche, but the juice is no longer confined to stuffy boardrooms and exclusive soirées. Champagne has found its way into underground clubs, music festivals, and gatherings where the spirit of defiance reigns supreme. In this new era of Champagne consumption, the old rules no longer apply. Gone are the days of rigid etiquette and pretentious snobbery; instead, Champagne is embraced for its ability to bring people together and spark moments of joy and connection. Nothing on the deity-of-your-choice's green Earth brings people together like the popping of a cork.

Champagne's popularity is definitely in part because of pop culture. Its broader appeal can be traced back to its hip-hop links. Popping bottles of Champagne is so ingrained in rap culture that it feels compulsory. East Coast Emcees began referencing Champagne brands in their lyrics as early as 1985. Grandmaster Melle Mel's "King of the Streets" was the first to do so. This brought Champagne to a group that would have been locked out of the society that it was created for. Jay-Z catapulted Cristal into fame with his first mention in his debut album *Reasonable Doubt* in 1996.

References to Cristal surged in the genre, from twenty-one in the previous decade to 264 between 1996 and 2006, according to Tahir Hemphill's "Champagne Always Stains My Silk" hip-hop word-count project. As with all things celebrity, there was a trickle-down effect. A more ethnically diverse crowd began to see Champagne as something that they should, could, and would try. And once anyone tries a good Champagne they often become evangelists for it, spreading the bubbly word of Dionysus far and wide.

Of course, social media is a great place to share the good word of Champagne. As with all experience, Instagram became the place to see and be seen drinking Champagne. It became a self-sustaining ecosystem of wine experience and showed many people by modern word of mouth where to get your little fizzy treat.

To keep up with this diversifying demand, the Champagne scene has been bubbling over with new releases. According to Émilien Boutillat, Piper-Heidsieck's cellarmaster, the Champagne selection nowadays is broader than ever. Alongside the classics, there's a surge in premium non-vintage blends, extra-brut options, single grape varieties, and wines showcasing distinct terroirs. 2023, in particular, was a champ year for new Champagne offerings. Some houses are adapting to climate shifts or embracing sustainable practices. Others are riding the wave of Champagne's evolving reputation as a wine rather than just a posh staple. And some are simply giving their lineup a facelift to ride the wave of Champagne's growing popularity. Label design has never been more important.

Champagne has been embraced with the same fervor as Beaujolais, Burgundy, and Jura by the natty contingent—despite its house structure. Grower Champagne is leading the charge. More and more small-scale producers, known as *récoltants-manipulants,* are crafting their own "grower Champagne." While making wine from your own grapes is common elsewhere, it's relatively rare in Champagne, where most of the bubbly comes from big houses sourcing grapes from various vineyards. *Récoltants-manipulants,* however, grow and farm their own grapes, resulting in wines that showcase individuality rather than uniformity.

Take Champagne Egly-Ouriet, a family-run estate spanning nine hectares, mostly Grand Cru vineyards in Ambonnay, Bouzy, and Verzenay. Francis Egly, the fourth-generation owner, believes in working with nature rather than against it. His vineyards, mainly facing south or southeast, yield ripe grapes thanks to their sunny exposure and chalky subsoil, imparting a distinctive mineral character. Egly shuns insecticides and sticks to traditional methods like plowing, keeping the winemaking process as natural as possible. This family vineyard has devoted followers in the same way Gravner does. This is the bubbly that impresses at cork-dork gatherings. This is the Champagne-drinker's Champagne.

"REFERENCES TO CRISTAL SURGED IN THE GENRE [HIP-HOP], FROM TWENTY-ONE IN THE PREVIOUS DECADE TO 264 BETWEEN 1996 AND 2006."

It also happens to be mostly *brut nature. Brut nature* Champagnes and other low-sugar bubblies are growing in popularity at what could be considered an astounding rate. While food seems to be trending towards deeper and richer flavors, wine, particularly Champagne, is trending towards the opposite. The lightest, freshest, most delicate is what everyone wants.

Brut nature isn't a new concept either. In 1874, Madame Pommery unveiled Pommery Nature, following in the footsteps of Perrier-Jouët. This Champagne, like its counterpart, made a splash in London, capturing the tastebuds of high society and establishing brut Champagnes as the new pinnacle of sophistication. Before long, Laurent-Perrier introduced Grand Vin sans Sucre, the world's first dosage-free Champagne—*brut nature.* Both Pommery Nature and Grand Vin sans Sucre were ahead of their time, boasting a daring edge that still resonates today.

For much of the twentieth century, *brut nature* Champagne had a niche following. Unlike other Champagne designations, *brut nature* is where the climate, winery philosophies, and the personal touch of winemakers converge. These wines lay it all bare—there's no hiding behind dosage here. In fact, *brut nature* forces winemakers to confront any flaws in their craft head-on, as dosage can sometimes be used to cover up imperfections. *Brut nature* and other low-dosage options can challenge preconceptions about Champagne in exciting ways.

The wine industry in general was democratized by the internet. Where once you had to do expensive courses or have enough money to learn from drinking, when the internet got going, anyone could look up the story of a wine. More and more wine content appeared in increasingly accessible and approachable formats. WineTok is a testament to how far we have come from the gatekeeping of the "good old days."

Connoisseurship became somewhat par for the course. Shifting attitudes meant it was cool to know where the juice in your glass came from, who made it, and how they did so. Champagne has always told a good story. In fact, the region is so storied it has World War II legends and every wave of feminism entangled in it. It reaches as far back as the tsars and is the sponsor of every major celebrity event today.

There is a political and philosophical stance that we shouldn't numb the pain caused by late-stage capitalism with the same commodities that fuel this capitalism. Capitalist notions of self-care, like indulging in avocado toast, can distract from addressing structural issues. However, little luxuries aren't just about consumerism—they offer a moment of relief in a stressful world. Nothing feels like more of a "Fuck you!" to the crushing weight of responsibility as raising a glass of Champagne on a casual Friday night. Raising a glass of bubbly with your avocado toast is an act of defiance of the oppressive society that keeps you locked out of home ownership. Champagne, in other words, tastes like civil disobedience.

In a world that often feels divided and uncertain, Champagne serves as a reminder that even the most exclusive pleasures can now be shared by more people than ever. So here's to Champagne—the drink of renegades and revolutionaries everywhere. May its bubbles continue to break down barriers and pave the way for a more inclusive and egalitarian society. Cheers to the power of bubbles.

Terrestrial Ritual and Magick

Co-creation with Nature: Triumphant Decay

Jacob Belway

TRIUMPHANT DECAY

by Garett Long

WHEN WE LOOK OUT ACROSS A PICTURESQUE VINEYARD, we cannot see the land as it existed for an eternity prior to this moment. A keen observer might recognize a certain trellising or pruning approach, or approximate the age of the vines, but 99.999% of the history of this landscape is frankly unknowable by the human eyes that rest upon it adoringly.

The people who planted it may have died, or sold the vineyard and moved to Austin. Maybe their relatives lie buried beneath a majestic oak tree somewhere on the property. The rivers that seasonally overtopped their banks were likely redirected or dammed. In the United States, almost certainly all signs of the indigenous people who stewarded that land for tens of thousands of years before the arrival of European settlers were destroyed.

This Instagrammable sunset in wine country may have once been an old-growth forest or productive grassland—burned, grazed, flooded, trampled by migrating bison, and birthright to countless clutches of owlets. The cataclysmic effects of the asteroid impact that wiped out the dinosaurs 65 million years ago are most definitely no longer visible to our modern eye, wine glass in hand.

But if you look closely enough and engage all of your senses, the history of everything is detectable just below the soil surface . . . have a sip!

Lowly insects and microorganisms constantly eat and poop, releasing acids and digestive enzymes as biochemical warfare upon their microscopic world, nuking everything. Without microbes and their universal thirst for feeding on deceased comrades, all of the dead bodies and fallen trees would pile up endlessly, undecomposed. Instead, these unseen, often thankless microscopic organisms happily chew through rotting flesh, fallen leaves, and insect frass, converting all of it back into the basic building blocks of matter—amino acids, sugars, fats, minerals.

American astronomer Carl Sagan poetically wrote, "We are all star-stuff," a profound reflection on our place in the cosmos and the cosmic origins of life on Earth. Indeed, we are all one. The centipede, slime mold, and shark—living, dead, or in various states of decomposition—are made of the same atoms that were forged in the cores of ancient stars billions of years ago.

Oregon State University professor James Cassidy cheekily said, "We are all temporarily 'not soil.'" The bottom of the ocean, through tectonic shifts and millions of years, becomes the freshly hardened slopes of a nascent volcano, which weathers into the sand, silt, and clay we call soil.

Plants and their sugary root excretions, animals and their manures, compost and fertilizers applied by farmers—everything alchemizes belowground into the tiniest building blocks of life. Slaves and slaver are one. The blood of indigenous and colonizers are indistinguishable. The deceased Master of Wine and the lover of boxed white Zinfandel taste about the same

Morgan Robles

to the multitudes of microbes. Centipede, slime mold, shark . . .

So, if everything is made of the same fundamental ingredients, i.e. elements, what are the factors making wines from Burgundy so different from the Finger Lakes of upstate New York or Marlborough, New Zealand?

Terroir—a French term generally meaning "sense of place"—refers to the environmental factors, such as soil, microbiome, climate, and geography, that all contribute to the unique characteristics of a particular crop, especially wine. Scientific literature suggests strong evidence that soil factors such as temperature and the availability of nitrogen and water distinctly impact terroir. Other recent studies suggest that the soil microbiome, or the diversity and composition of microbial populations, indirectly influences vine growth and fruit composition and can directly contribute to distinctive aroma profiles in wines.

"Oregon State University professor James Cassidy cheekily said, 'We are all temporarily 'not soil.'"

While terroir traditionally focuses on natural elements, humans play a multifaceted and outsized role in shaping vineyard terroir, from site selection and cultivation practices to winemaking techniques. Humans can have both positive and negative impacts on the environment within and surrounding vineyards, which in turn affect terroir. For example, pollution, deforestation, and erosion can degrade terroir, while regenerative farming practices and habitat restoration can enhance it.

Cultural traditions and innovations in winemaking also shape terroir. Different winemaking regions have evolved unique traditions and practices over centuries, influencing the character and style of wines produced there. While the evolution of a new wine region or AVA is generally perceived as positive progress, it's conceivable that human actions, including acts of violence like slavery or genocide, could indirectly influence terroir through their impacts on the land and cultural practices.

For example, historical instances of slavery may have affected the development of certain agricultural regions, shaping cultivation practices, land-use patterns, and even the composition of soils over time. Genocide of the indigenous Americans similarly disrupted ecosystems and agricultural traditions, altering the relationship between humans and the land.

Furthermore, the cultural memory and social dynamics resulting from such events can also influence agricultural practices, including how crops are tended, harvested, and processed, which can, in turn, affect the expression of terroir in the final glass of wine.

While these connections may not be direct or immediately apparent, they do underscore the complex interplay between human history, culture, and the natural environment in shaping terroir. Profound human suffering associated with acts of violence and their lasting impacts on both individuals and communities have undoubtedly shaped our agricultural landscapes and traditions.

The next time you gaze upon the breathtaking beauty of a hillside vineyard, ablaze with purple, orange, and red wildflowers, be humble. Have gratitude for the vigneron that skillfully tended the vines and artfully created a sippable expression of this unique landscape—absolutely. As well, have reverence for the mighty rivers no longer flowing here. Recognize those who were murdered for the right to "own" these productive soils and prized vistas. Revere the legion of microbes, piles of bones, and fallen forests they converted into the stardust that became soil that is your rosé with subtle notes of strawberry and fresh spring flowers.

TERROIR IS SO METAL

The act of soil creation is one of constant destruction. Material melted in Earth's mantle erupts through holes, fissures and formations in a slipping and sliding surface, cools, and is broken down into ever finer soil, which contains the nutrients a plant, such as a grapevine, needs to survive. It's almost as if Bacchus himself coordinated this dance, directing geysers of molten lava to form hills, valleys, bowls, benches.

And eventually, sometimes, they become vineyards.

>>>

Illustrations by Jorge Corona

"Every act of creation begins with an act of destruction."

—Pablo Picasso

Surely, when Picasso said those words, he was not thinking of the eons of cataclysmic upheaval that formed the Earth billions of years ago. However, his sentiment still rings true: the old must be transformed (or destroyed) to create something new.

Our planet is a master of said transformation. It continually recycles, reshapes, and reforms itself, often violently so, like a pyroclastic Slurpee machine, churning the geologic goodies to the benefit of our vineyards. Perhaps the most commonly conjured example is the Earth's earliest formative origins, that is: a once destructive hellscape filled with massive volcanic eruptions, spewing lava and scalding ash raining down. "Think: the fires of Mount Doom," says Jackson Rohrbaugh, M.S., referring to the volcano of Mordor raining cinders and "rivers of fire" in *The Lord of the Rings* when describing the molten setting.

Not an *LOTR* fan? Then maybe think Disney's 1940 animated classic *Fantasia*, which provided a mind's-eye view of those tumultuous origins, set to Igor Stravinsky's *Rite of Spring*, which also conveys themes of renewal and rebirth, wherein the Earth's primitive roiling surface bears little resemblance to the planet as we currently know it.

And this was not just in many places, but *everywhere*. Earthquakes, volcanoes, and a general baseline of apocalyptic chaos was the order of the day . . . er, millennium. The calamitous, lava-ridden environment that led to many of the relatively calm vineyard vistas of today may seem incongruous, but they are essentially cut from the same cloth.

"It's hard not to think about the lava flows that were covering something like 63,000 square miles of the Pacific Northwest millions of years ago," says Todd Alexander, winemaker of Force Majeure. "It paints a harsh picture of the landscape, pretty stark." Based in the Walla Walla Valley, and sourcing fruit from nearby AVAs in eastern Washington, such as Red Mountain and the Rocks District, the name Force Majeure is itself a reference to the unrelenting power and transformative nature of the Earth that created the terroir where their vineyards grow.

Soil that is derived from basaltic volcanism, which is the dark, heavy end of the volcanic-rock spectrum, originates from partial melting of the Earth's mantle, and typically contains more minerals such as iron, magnesium, and titanium, along with other heavy metal oxides, more than your typical crustal rock. "Volcanic rocks are sort of the primitive starting point for pretty much all the rocks that we have on the surface of the Earth," says Dr. Kevin Pogue, professor of geology at Whitman College. "So granite and rocks like that are blobs of molten rock that cooled underneath the ground. All the typical rocks, even the calcium in limestone, ultimately was derived from minerals from the interior of the Earth."

These prehistoric fiery purges dredged molten rocks from deep within the planet—like when you need to shake up a fruit juice or hot sauce to bring the rich ingredients that have settled up to the surface. "The sandstones, limestones, the minerals and the elements that are in those, got to the surface originally during that time," says

Pogue, "and they've just been recycled a jillion times and spread all over. But they got out of the interior of the Earth through volcanic eruptions." Mother Nature, truly the ultimate mixologist.

Alexander's other wine label, Holocene, which sources grapes from acclaimed vineyards in the Willamette Valley, is a reference to Earth's current geologic epoch, the last 10,000 years or so, where the volcanism is the most recent. "In most cases, that's basalt, cinders, and ash," says Pogue. "That's really unique soil. It's not very weathered and it's very granular and it's well-draining, and it tends to be black, which absorbs and radiates heat to the grapevine. And so, in those cases, that's a very distinctive soil environment for grapes."

Volcanic terroir is just one example of the inexorable change the Earth routinely undergoes. What's old is new again, and what's new is older than dirt. But most geologists or winemakers will point out that volcanic soil only sets the stage. "Within the overall class of volcanic soils, you have lots of soil subsets and resulting nuance," says Alexander. "Combined with climate, cultivar, and winemaking, you can then have a wide array of wines that can still have a common thread between them." Pogue echoes the sentiment, noting that, whether a soil is volcanic in origin or not, climate and other factors are also important. "A soil derived from granite bedrock is massively dependent upon the climate that it's in because the granite can be deeply weathered and the minerals be breaking down into clays," he says. "Or it could be a super dry climate where the granite is just breaking down into grains of granite. And these are completely different soils—both derived from granite, but completely different in terms of cation exchange capacity, which refers to how easy it is for the roots to get at the nutritive elements they want."

The Earth's ever-unfolding fractal of becoming is most brutal and awe-inspiring when one considers that it never stops, it's relentless. Or, as the naturalist and environmental philosopher John Muir said, "Nature is ever at work building and pulling down, creating and destroying, keeping everything whirling and flowing, allowing no rest but in rhythmical motion, chasing everything in endless song out of one beautiful form into another." 🍷

Rodrigo Frêdes

WATAIN

WATAIN HAVE PROVEN THEMSELVES to be a black-metal institution over their two-decade-plus existence. With the core trio being the stable nucleus of the band that entire time, it's clear their creative vision is strengthened from a consistent like-mindedness and craft. Frontman Erik Danielsson, the lead visionary of the group, doesn't leave wine off his list of creative alchemy to praise. >>>

Blood of Gods: Where did your interest in wine originate?

Erik Danielsson: I've always had a thing for strong experiences originating from passionate and meticulous craftsmanship, be it with music, literature, art, philosophy, or what have you. Good wines take time to make, they can't be hastened together. The process itself has been refined and under creative progress for hundreds of years, which, to me at least, adds greatly to the whole experience. I've also always had an obsession with medieval monasteries and monk-hood, where wine had a special and interesting role somewhere between diabolical and divine.

BoG: Was there ever an aha moment where a particular wine jumped out at you or changed your perception of wine?

ED: The aha moments have been many, but, more importantly so, they have been quite diverse in nature. While it's often been about a fine-tuned array of tastes alone, many of my truly memorable wine experiences have been more about the circumstances. It is my firm belief that an exclusive bottle of the finest red might still not beat a cold jug of watery table wine if it's served at the right moment and in the right company.

BoG: With beer being the typical drink to go along with metal, why or what factors have kept the wine and metal scenes and audiences so separate, in your opinion?

ED: I think wine demands a bit more focus, maybe. Metalheads, myself included, often prefer to be fully immersed in the music and perhaps there is less room for savoring the intricate tastes of a glass of good wine while taking part in a loud and wild music experience. But I don't know—I've brought wine bottles to festivals and parties for as long as I can remember. Perhaps not because of enjoying the particular flavor but rather to have something sturdier and more severe than just beer.

BoG: What metal albums would you recommend to those in the wine world to help open up their eyes to the craft of extreme music they might appreciate?

ED: Hard to say since, just like wine recommendations, it comes down to personal taste, but generally speaking I'd say that if you give *Storm of the Light's Bane* by Dissection and *Sad Wings of Destiny* by Judas Priest a listen and still don't feel you get it, metal is probably not for you.

"...if you give* Storm of the Light's Bane *by* Dissection *and* Sad Wings of Destiny *by* Judas *Priest a listen and still don't feel you get it, metal is probably not for you."

BoG: Trends and innovation always seem to be met with suspicion in both wine and metal, where their respective audiences generally accept the more time-proven institutions and practices the most. However, can you mention any new developments in wine and in metal that get you excited and keep your curiosity engaged?

ED: I am a big fan of natural wines and really enjoy the DIY attitude that many of those new producers have. There's a lot in that scene that reminds me of what I like about the metal underground—challenging the established authorities and being driven by passion rather than monetary gain, ultimately with something quite unique as the outcome. Not that I consider myself an expert on the subject, but I see it as a welcome and interesting evolution. When it comes to metal, though, I belong to the ones who think everything was better before. It's quite simple really—just compare the front covers of *Kerrang* magazine 1983 and 2020. I like my metal old, raw, evil, and mean, something reserved for rebellious spirits who do not fear to live outside the boundaries of society. These days it's something else entirely, for the most part at least. With Watain we do our best to preserve and maintain the old feeling of danger and disaster, keeping things wild, challenging and unpredictable. It is certainly not about staying in or trying to resurrect the past, which many young bands seem very keen on doing, but about acknowledging it and letting it be one of the things that drive you forward into the great unknown.

BoG: While there are plenty of stereotypes on both sides, what argument would you make to encourage more metalheads to try getting into wine?

ED: For me it's quite simple—metal is music for people who want the most out of their musical experience. It's a genre that, unlike so many other music styles, is filled with true passion, variety, thoughtfulness, and raw power that reaches into the darkest crevices of your mind and takes you to places you didn't even know existed. When it comes to drinking, I'd say wine is the equivalent.

BoG: Current recommendations for wine? For music?

ED: Right now it's summer in Sweden and, while I'm usually a fan of stuff like heavy Italian reds that will crush your skull after two glasses, right now we're enjoying some great lighter but by no means sissy-tasting rosé called Pink Is Not Red from La Cave Apicole, which is a small natural winemaker in France. I'm also really looking forward to trying some natural wines from Japan's Fujimaru Winery that I just ordered. When it comes to music, the last album that blew me away was probably Concrete Winds' debut album *Primitive Force* from 2019.

Eric Sahlsten

Rakija

by Bill Gould

Illustration by Collin Estrada

IT WAS BUDAPEST, 1992. MY BAND, Faith No More, was on a massive tour with Guns n' Roses and Soundgarden. We had just released an album called *Angel Dust*. At the peak of our touring powers, we found ourselves in Hungary, a country in full transition after the fall of communism. The atmosphere was wild: neglected infrastructure, economic instability, and visibly nervous police trying to manage the massive crowds. The stadium was surrounded by what looked like a battalion of water cannons.

This wasn't just a big deal for Hungary; it was the most exciting music event stretching from Bratislava to Sofia, Skopje to Podgarica. Kids came on trains from Macedonia and buses from Serbia and Bulgaria, all pumped full of adrenaline—and their excitement was infectious. This show is where my fascination with the region began, and where a kid first handed me something in a plastic Pepsi bottle called *rakija*.

Rakija is a spirit distilled from fruit, more or less unknown in North America unless you belong to a Balkan immigrant community. It's also one of the world's most ancient spirits. Distillation, in fact, began in Mesopotamia, and its first contact with Europe came as it made its way from Turkey through Bulgaria as early as the eleventh century CE. The name *rakija* is believed to originate from the Arabic word *raq*, meaning "to sweat."

This process was a godsend for rural communities, allowing them to utilize every ounce of the fall harvest. Whatever fruit couldn't be immediately consumed could be preserved and put to use—as a cleaning solution, social lubricant, currency, or home remedy. Rakija is as versatile as duct tape. It's often labeled as a brandy, but this isn't entirely accurate. Brandy itself originated in France in 1313, at least three centuries after rakija. In terms of taste and character, it stands apart. To this day, rakija remains a staple for some 60 million people. Someone getting married? Break out the rakija. Someone passed away? Rakija. Breakfast before work? Rakija. And so on.

It turns out that when you work with the same climate, land, and fruit for several generations, you can get pretty good at it. Despite its humble rural origins, there are masters of the craft whose talents have evolved through generations of tradition and process. The results can be truly world-class.

I remember the "aha moment" that hooked me. I was in Belgrade, sampling a barrel-aged plum rakija (sljivovica) from a friend's grandfather's stash. It was

dark gold, having spent time in a barrel. It was clearly made by someone who knew what they were doing. Rustic but not "firewater" hooch—it was something penetrating, rich, and connected. I looked around at the room, the people, the smiles, and I felt a deep sense of place. A voice inside said, "You are in Serbia."

Others have described this experience as a connection to time and place. This wasn't just a drink; it was something deeper. Needless to say, from that moment on, I was hooked.

But I don't live in Serbia, so what could I do? I did what many immigrants had done for years: brought back as many bottles as my suitcase could handle. At the time, you couldn't just buy rakija in a store, even in Serbia. Most of the commercial stuff wasn't the same. You had to get it from a family who made it for themselves.

Not many people in California—or the U.S. in general—knew what this was. Each bottle I brought back had to last until my next trip to Europe, which wasn't often. I maintained this balance of travel and "smuggling" for about two decades. Then, in 2019, I realized that the only way I could regularly get my hands on real sljivovica was either to move to Serbia or import a proper one myself.

I had enough immigrant friends here in the same situation to convince me this could be a cool idea. So, with zero background in spirits or importing, I said, "Fuck it." I teamed up with a Serbian family producing impeccable sljivovica and created a label of handmade rakija that could proudly represent the category.

Rakija, in its premium form, is still a product of the land and culture. It is a living story—a real story—but it's not a "marketing" story. It's a bridge to a place we don't hear about often. And when we do, it's often very general, political, or negative. As I discovered in Budapest, rakija is something intensely personal. It has been a companion throughout countless harvests, generations of birth and death, tragic wars, and bleak economic uncertainty. I swear I can feel some of this when I experience it. There's a lot to rakija—and a lot to be learned through it.

Unplug your computer. Go outside. Get yourself some quality cold cuts. Some cheese. Have friends over. Fire up a grill. Crack open some rakija. (It doesn't have to be mine—just make sure it's a decent one.) Or take it to expert mode: travel to the region, make friends, eat homemade meals, and share something special. It's a real groove with gravitas and a doorway to a rich world. See for yourself.

CHRIS FIGENSHAU

FIRE IN THE MOUNTAINS WAS ORIGINALLY CREATED TO HIGHLIGHT the symbiotic relationship between heavy music and mountain landscapes. It was a way to bring people together to experience something extraordinary: the primal power of heavy music combined with the majesty and wildness of the Rocky Mountain Range. What has transpired is a truly unique and inspiring musical experience for the audience and bands alike. The yearly event is tied together through a deliberate curation of music and art that exemplifies the awe-inspiring beauty of one of the last intact temperate ecosystems that still exists. Festival mastermind Jeremy Walker needs no convincing that terroir, and nature in general, is metal. His background in wine and hospitality informs a curated, celebratory approach, elevating one of North America's most breathtaking outdoor festivals.

But Fire in the Mountains is becoming more than just a concert in the mountains. It deliberately blends music, art, education, food, and adventure to foster rewilding—reconnecting with nature to strengthen our ancestral roots. Culture, community, and tribalism evolved around fires, with food, drink, storytelling, revelry, and music. Tribal societies fostered deep social connections rooted in place, cultivating respect for the land—something often missing in modern life. Through music, art, adventure, local and foragable food options, and a social setting conducive to intellectual ferment, Fire in the Mountains offers a way to reconnect with nature's raw power—an experience increasingly rare in today's distracted world. Fire in the Mountains is not attempting to reinvent the wheel, but rather, to quote Einar Selvik, the intention is about "sowing new seeds while strengthening old roots."

BLOOD OF GODS: Please give a little background about how you got into wine and your experience with it.

JEREMY WALKER: I've been working in the restaurant industry my entire working life. I started in the FOH [front of house] and then moved to BOH [back of house] to learn about the cooking process, ingredients, flavor combinations, and, of course, hard work. Eventually, the process of learning culinary ingredients and flavor combinations stoked my curiosity in learning about liquid ingredients and flavor combinations. This curiosity led me to bartending and mixology, which, by the means of natural progression, ignited my passion for wine. I've been managing wine programs for restaurants and wine shops, as well as working the floors of restaurants as a sommelier, for the last ten years. My wife and I also started an experiential wine travel company called Taste of Place Travel. My greatest passions in life are metal, wine, travel, and skiing. Wine was the last of those four passions that I became interested in. The first three were a large part of my upbringing, with wine later resonating through my roles in the restaurant industry. Also, wine, culture, and travel go hand in hand together. Not only is visiting wine-producing regions a way to travel with a purpose, but every time I open a bottle of wine I'm transported to the place that wine was produced. I can be in my tiny cabin in the mountains of Wyoming, but when I open a bottle of Valpolicella, I'm immediately transported to that little area in northern Italy because I've visited there and experienced the wine culture there. I know the people there, I know the history, the topography, the climate, the food, etc. I can taste all this within the bottle of wine. Focusing my thoughts and senses on that, I can travel to any wine-growing region I want to at any point, simply by opening a bottle of wine. That experience makes wine incredibly special to me.

> "I CAN BE IN MY TINY CABIN IN THE MOUNTAINS OF WYOMING, BUT WHEN I OPEN A BOTTLE OF VALPOLICELLA, I'M IMMEDIATELY TRANSPORTED TO THAT LITTLE AREA IN NORTHERN ITALY ..."

BOG: There's the alchemy, ritual, ancient practices, and more in wine that seem right up metalheads' purview—what case would you make to encourage more heavy metal fans to take an interest in wine?

JW: Metalheads are deep people and old souls. Metalheads dig deep into the music world to find the music filtering through all the genres, sub-genres, and sub-sub-genres of metal to find the bands that speak to them. Metalheads tend to read the lyrics of the bands they love, they know all about the bands and their history, and travel to go see them. This experience and approach to music is exactly the same experience and approach a lover of wine has towards wine. We dig through all the crap and genres of wine to find the wine that speaks to us. We learn deeply about the wines we love and experience them the same way a metalhead experiences music. Plus, it's a great way to learn about

CHRIS FIGENSHAU

JAY NEL-MCINTOSH

culture, history, the earth, etc. while getting loose. I'm not sure you need much more of a reason to take an interest in wine than that.

BOG: Fire in the Mountains' "Communion with nature and the mountains that we call home" quote sounds like something you'd hear from a winemaker or grapegrower/vineyard manager. Terroir is metal, right?

JW: Damn right it is. That's literally the entire inspiration of Fire in the Mountains. It's a way to pair music with landscape—much like pairing wine and food together. The success of Fire in the Mountains goes much deeper than the bands that play, it is the experience of hearing it in such a raw and beautiful place. Metal pairs perfectly with the epic and dramatic landscapes of the Rocky Mountains. Fire in the Mountains started as a little party in the woods with an incredible Teton view behind a makeshift stage we built. When Wayfarer played on that stage for the first time, with the sun setting behind the Tetons as they played their American-Western-influenced form of black metal, everyone in attendance felt that pairing. It's similar to pairing sauternes and fois gras, sancerre and goat cheese, or Chianti and a ragu-style pasta. I would say, however, there are many forms of music that have specific terroir. For example, I don't love reggae music, but the few times I've been on a Caribbean island, reggae sounds particularly great in that terroir. Then again, so would some Norwegian bands like Emperor or Arcturus—that's probably unique to me and not felt amongst the local population of the Caribbean, though.

"MANY OF THE MODERN BLACK METAL AND NORDIC FOLK BANDS SING ABOUT THEIR CONNECTION TO THE NATURAL WORLD AND ITS SPIRITS. I HOPE THIS CONNECTION RUBS OFF ON THE GENERAL PUBLIC WHO LISTEN TO THE MUSIC SO SOME REAL CHANGE CAN HAPPEN IN THIS WORLD."

BOG: Trends and innovation always seem to be met with suspicion in both wine and metal, where their respective audiences generally accept the more time-proven institutions and practices the most. However, can you mention any new developments in wine and in metal that get you excited and keep your curiosity engaged?

JW: I love the way you tie metal and wine together with these questions. I treasure nature and am very concerned about the destruction humans cause to environmental systems, which is why Fire in the Mountains aims to be an environmental organization in addition to a music festival. Given my passion for environmentalism, I'm happy to see the path many domestic wineries are taking to focus on organic/biodynamic agriculture and the utilization of renewable energies. It's great to see the consumer demand for wines that focus on this (I do not love the term "natural wine," though). Similar to the wine industry, there is also renewed focus and demand for metal that is nature-based. This is obvious through the lyrical content of many modern black metal bands and the huge growth in popularity of Nordic folk music, like Wardruna and Heilung as the current leaders. Many of the modern black metal and Nordic folk bands sing about their connection to the natural world and its spirits. I hope this connection rubs off on the general public who listen to the music so some real change can happen in this world. Everyone knows that metal tends to be anti-religious, but spirituality in metal is a totally different thing, and very in line with not only the ethics but the deep feelings of connection expressed in the music. A part of Fire in the Mountains is to bring spirituality into the experiences people have with metal. 🍷

THE GRITTY, COMIC-BOOK-STYLED LABELS OF RUNE WINES IS WHAT INITIALLY DREW US INTO THEIR WORLD. HOWEVER, UPON TALKING WITH OWNER/WINEMAKER JAMES CALLAHAN, IT ALSO BECAME CLEAR THAT, LIKE HEAVY METAL, MAKING WINE IN THE UNRELENTING CONDITIONS OF ARIZONA CAN BE BRUTAL. BLISTERING HEAT, TORTURED GRAPES, DESOLATE ENVIRONMENT . . . TURNS OUT GRAPE GROWING AND WINEMAKING CAN BE AS EXTREME AS METAL. JAMES TOLD US A BIT MORE OVER THE PHONE DURING A HOT SUMMER DAY.

PILLSBURY MOUVERDE

WINES

BLOOD OF GODS: The imagery of Rune is strong and has a burly, Nordic influence of Vikings . . . What's the backstory with the branding and what you're trying to communicate with it?

JAMES CALLAHAN: I purchase grapes, as most wineries do, sourcing them from other vineyards. However, many wineries rarely credit these vineyards, leaving people unaware of their true origin. So it's important for me to showcase the terroir, especially in a new region like Arizona where no one is quite "there" yet—there's no concept of terroir here, so it's important to catalog that. So how do you weave all these different vineyard sites that you might get a ton or two from—because they're all small, there's nothing big here—how do you weave them all into a brand? You have these grapes coming in from all over the state in this really new region, and how do you take all those little vineyards and create a cohesive message? And the way I thought I could do that was by making a story. Because we make single varietal wines, each varietal from each vineyard is a different character [in the story]. And whenever I buy that fruit, because I might not get it every year, but whenever I buy that fruit, I can continue that section of the story. So I have an artist that I've been working with for seven years now, who helps me draft new labels each year. So, depending what I'm making, or what grapes I have, I just continue the story or make new characters into the story. It's like a science-fiction story based on how wine grapes came to be on this planet, but also it has some elements of human interaction and human history, but also it's based on this science-fiction world where there's this alien race that goes around to planets which have the ability to grow grapes, and they spread grapes to them. It's all about the way humans and nature discover these plants basically, and what they've done, that's really the core of it.

BOG: I feel like you could almost make a compendium of these stories and art and turn them into a graphic novel.

JC: Yea, it's basically a graphic novel that's on bottles. And it goes really slow, because one year is one picture, and one little blurb, right? But eventually, probably when we hit 100 or something, we'll figure something out to release. Right now people come tasting and they just see the bottles that we're selling and they don't really understand that there are vintages that have come before which are part of the storyline. So I want to

have all the bottles on display in the tasting room so people can finally see what's going on. Eventually probably publish a book, or make a book or compendium like you were talking about.

BOG: I feel like the first thing that comes to mind when people think of wine from Arizona is Tool vocalist Maynard James Keenan's winery Caduceus Cellars. I'm sure it casts a long shadow of influence, so I wanted to hear your thoughts and experience related to that.

JC: He's a celebrity and he's a good guy and he wants to make good wine, and I think he probably has a lot of financial assets to bring light to the state and what we're doing here. But beyond that, he has more of an influence among people because he's a celebrity, and I think he uses that to bring influence here from elsewhere. On that end, that can only go so far—people like him for his music, and the wine kind of comes second, and I think he wants people to know him for his wine . . .

BOG: He wants to invert that precept.

JC: Yeah, and it's hard to do that because he's spent his whole life doing music and that's what his fans are fans of. They're fans of music, not for wine. They like his wine obviously, but the idea of "there's no such thing as bad publicity"—we'll take anything we can get in Arizona! [laughs]

BOG: Yeah, and "When the tide comes in, it raises all of the boats" is what it sounds like to me. And for every wine-drinker they've gotta start somewhere. If it's a sweet Riesling or a celebrity's wine, whatever it is, everyone's got a day one. We've all gotta start somewhere.

JC: Yeah, I think people appreciate what he's doing in general. Despite whatever influence he has, and the people that kind of focus on him, especially people that are interested in his music, if it brings them to Arizona—it's great! They would never come here otherwise, so, it can't hurt anything [laughs].

BOG: What's something you would say to folks who are into metal, like we mentioned Tool fans earlier, to further encourage them to get into wine?

JC: I feel that people get tied up with their persona of who they are, and they automatically block out things. Like, "I'm a metalhead, I shouldn't like wine!" or "I'm a jock!" or "I'm a guy, I just drink beer!" I see it in my tasting room all the time. It's just a character trait of people where they just kind of feel comfortable with what they're doing. I think it's good for people to move outside of their box and challenge their comfort zone. Like you're saying, wine's pretty fucking metal. We're out here, in the middle of nowhere, we're baking away at 5,000 feet [elevation], with the sun glaring down on us, burning our skin, and the grapes are just out there. You wouldn't want to be out there in the sun all day—but the grapes are just out there, hanging on this twisted vine, as it's tied to this trellis, like some corpse to a cross . . .

BOG: . . . that we sacrifice!

JC: Exactly! That we give water to here and there, just to barely keep it alive, so you can get the best quality and most concentrated fruit. Then you plant it in the soil that's the rockiest and the poorest—you don't plant it where it can have all the nutrients it wants. You torture the shit out of it and then it gives you the best wine. That's basically how you make the best wine right there! [laughs]

BOG: We already know that wine and metal go together because there's a lot of brutality that goes on in each—especially when talking about terroir—just like you mentioned . . .

JC: Syrah in particular tends to showcase terroir more than any other grape, I think. You can grow it in France or Walla Walla or Arizona or Australia and it's all going to be different. In other grapes you can't necessarily get that type of expression from, that's why winemakers like Syrah I think [laughs]. It has so much character.

HUNTERS OF THE SKY

By Stacy Buchanan, *Blood of Gods* publisher

Illustration by Christopher Alliston

WHETHER YOU'RE ENJOYING A PATIO-POUNDER ROSÉ or savoring a complex red, one aspect of the vine-to-glass journey many grapes make that most don't consider, or are aware of, is the role birds of prey can play. That's right: deadly talons, dive bombing at 100-plus miles per hour, seek-and-destroy-mode falcons have been assisting winemakers and vineyard managers, mostly unnoticed, in a natural process called bird abatement.

As grapes grow on the vine and their consistency and sweetness develop, numerous birds are instinctually paying attention. Starlings, finches, jays, sparrows, and more snatch whole berries or peck at the seeds and pulp by the hundreds or even thousands. Beyond thinning grape yields, those pecked grapes can make great homes for fungus and bacteria and other pests, which can further damage grape crops.

"Harnessing the power of instinct, in both wild birds and raptors, falconry is the most effective method of bird abatement," notes freelance writer Denice Rackley, who specializes in agriculture, conservation, and science. "Birds are natural prey of hawks and falcons; the mere sight, sound, or shadow of raptors triggers the small birds to leave the area or fly to thick cover and hide."

"The amount of work, skill, and knowledge that goes into falconry is absolutely mind-blowing," says Sadie Drury, vineyard manager at North Slope Management. "While falcons flying over the vineyard to scare away pest birds seems simple, it's done with great precision and detail on behalf of the handlers. I will never cease to be impressed by the falconers themselves, who spend six to eight weeks on our site and work sun-up to sundown every single day during that period."

"As a kid I was obsessed with birds, so as soon as we planted Taggart Vineyard, my first question to Sadie was: 'How do we get some owls up here and can you call the falcon lady?'" says Doug Frost, M.S., M.W., of Echolands Winery. "The owl box got moved a while later and, though it had been empty for a couple of years in another vineyard, as soon as Sadie planted it in Taggart, little vole and gopher bones started showing up, scattered on the ground around the box. And every time the falcon lady comes by, if I'm around, I stop to take pictures."

No one is quite sure where or when the art of falconry first began. Long before the invention of bullets and guns, falcons were flown to catch prey too agile for mere humans to secure. Called the "sport of kings," falconry was the prerogative of royalty, but the tradition is much older, traced through writings, drawings, and artifacts to 2000 BC.

Artist and falconer Christopher J. Alliston adds, "After the Norman Conquest in 1066, new raptor species were introduced in England. The Normans restricted falconry to the upper classes, and peasants could be hanged for keeping hawks. Yeomen were allowed to use the short-winged hawks, like goshawks and sparrowhawks, to hunt for food, but only kings and nobility were allowed to have the more noble long-winged falcons, like gyrfalcon, peregrine, and merlins."

In most of the world, falconry has transitioned to a sport rather than a method of obtaining food. With the prominence of sustainable agriculture, another transition is on the rise: using falcons and hawks to reduce wild bird damage to crops. Falconry is seen by many as the most efficient and economical method of reducing the number of birds in orchards. However, the primal accord between our two species is an atavistic reward in its own right. Alliston continues, "It is rewarding—you always want the best for your bird, always. They are driven to hunt but not always capable of doing so at first. The gyr we fly came in quite horrible condition. Deck feathers we smashed up, never flown, never hunted. It took two seasons to get her to kill, and with the dedication and perseverance of my mentor, Geoff Kelly, she is now quite the duck hawk. It was like seeing a switch go off behind her eyes and her inner instinct to hunt, in life and death situations, turn on. It was completely awe inspiring and I will never forget seeing her come down with a stoop, hearing her cut through the air like a sharp blade through paper and catch her prey."

Chemical repellents, auditory repellents, balloons, kites, and netting are all used with some success, but each has its drawbacks. Birds became immune to loud air cannons and static scare tactics, soon realizing they don't pose a threat. Netting does work but is costly and labor-intensive and prevents air circulation needed for fruit health. Holding moisture close to the plants, netting promotes mildew and some birds still figure out how to get through the netting to the fruit.

"Falcons help the vineyards because we don't have to hang bird netting that prevents the pest birds from eating the grapes," notes Drury. "Not only does this mean we reduce labor, which is already scarce, but we also get to save on purchasing the bird netting itself, which is plastic-based and not great for the environment. Using falconry in the vineyard is very expensive, but in the end it's about a net even when all things are considered. Not only does this mean we get to produce a more sustainable bottle of wine, we also get to support people who are pursuing the passion of falconry for a living."

"I just can't imagine wanting to use rodenticide in Taggart," says Frost. "But having some raptors to keep the numbers under control gives me the sense that our plants can be part of the system there, rather than some foreign intruder protected against reality by a chemical wall." 🍷

"We do not train hawks to do the things they do. They do them quite well without us. The falcon is no arrow aimed at quarry, no extension of our capability, and certainly no commodity of our making. She is a near-perfect being unto herself, entirely unto herself. We do not extract her from nature and make her what she is not. Instead, we persuade her with gentle skill that she may trust us and share her life with us. That is the best we can do. Falconry is entirely different from all other forms of hunting; it is the largely passive celebratory participation in a richly natural process. Let us take care that it shall always be so."

——Grainger Hunt, scientist emeritus at the Peregrine Fund.

SPECTRAL WOUND

hails from the active black-metal hotbed of Montreal, Quebec. While their scene is relatively new compared to the genre's pioneers, their commitment to stylistic orthodoxy—acidic riffs tempered with equal parts venom and valor, racing blast beats like an arrow through a forest into triumphant marches—is delivered with confidence and passion. This tried and true approach mirrors the key tenets of wine that inspires them to more deeply mine the realms of creative exploration, expression, and craft.

Photo: Ben Zodiazepin

Blood of Gods: Wine has played a keen influence in Spectral Wound—where did your interest in wine originate?

Spectral Wound: For a long time wine remained—as it is for many—an opaque and impenetrable cultural signifier, and one not altogether trustworthy. This was owing largely to encounters with insipid, industrially produced wine from which one could learn nothing and about which one could say nothing, only than that it tasted more or less bad or that it "tasted like wine." I was not satisfied with this, I felt that it could not be all pretense and obfuscation, for I have at base a curiosity about the pleasures and obsessions of others. Certainly, there was some truer merit, some deeper attraction? What was the twitch on the thread that brought drinkers from antiquity onward to not only rhapsodize drunkenly but to discern and pronounce, and erect such an intellectual architecture of appreciation? It was only later, in the encounter with what is now called "natural" wine, that the doors to genuine interest began to creak open.

"The winemaker is not the author of his work. In order to create anything of worth, it requires entering into a relationship of uncertainty with the material world, the unruly living world, at a scale both greater and microscopically smaller than the human, the world of vital matter."

BoG: Was there ever an aha moment where a particular wine jumped out at you or changed your perception of wine?

SW: Indeed, I had a decisive experience many years ago with a wine so unlike anything I had tasted before that it suggested a new terrain of experience and a new method of approach. It was a bottle of 2011 Dinavolino from Giulio Armani in Val Trebbia, a blend of Malvasia di Candia, Ortrugo, and a fistful of other grapes traditional to that part of Italy. It was the aromatic complexity of the nose and the textural complexity of the palate, these lush stone fruits yet without sweetness, young gripping tannins, and bright acidity that captured me. It smelled and tasted of the land in all its roughness and polyphony, vital and wild. This was the click of the latch. The door was not fully open, but it was no longer barred to me. It was the beginning of entry into a space of exploration that continues still, an engagement with taste as both pleasure and problem.

BoG: The alchemy and transformation associated with wine, including ritual, magic of nature, mythology, and history seem primed for metalheads to enjoy, yet there persist outdated stereotypes and stigmas. What argument would you make to encourage more metalheads to try getting into wine?

SW: Simply to avoid industrially produced wine and turn toward wines from small producers who work close to the land, whether that means those with deep ties to the traditions of the vine, or younger vintners who are trying to reforge those connections. I am quite aware that so-called "natural wine" has become rather vogue-ish and something of a trend, but I see this as no different from the commercialization of underground music. The machinery that surrounds it is noxious, but the product is real—provided you access the real and not the imitation. If you seek out winemakers producing on a small scale, with conviction and without chemical intervention, who are trying to communicate something with their wine rather than simply creating a product for the market, you will have a greater chance of a meaningful experience. The truth is in the glass, but the understanding comes from deeper engagement with the craft, its history, and its traditions. In other words, bring the same ethos to wine as you bring to music, the same rigor and dedication, and it will be more likely to repay.

BoG: What metal albums would you recommend to those in the wine world to help open up their eyes to the craft of extreme music they might appreciate?

SW: I don't think that metal needs proselytizers. There is no particular reason that wine appreciators should be more attuned to heed the call than anyone else.

BoG: Recording an album, or even an intense live performance, and making wine have been likened to each other, both having an element of "controlled chaos." There's some etiquette and rules, but there's also that unpredictable component where magic or mayhem could erupt at any moment. Do you see similar parallels in your experience?

SW: I think that there is a quality of the ineffable, even of the sublime, to both, and the sense that one may arrive at a result quite different than anticipated, but that can be said of all art. It is not unique to music, let alone metal. In fact, I think that there is a still more important difference in the case of wine: that you are not the creator. The winemaker is not the author of his work. In order to create anything of worth, it requires entering into a relationship of uncertainty with the material world, the unruly living world, at a scale both greater and microscopically smaller than the human, the world of vital matter. The winemaker sets into motion a process that he or she can guide but cannot and should not hope to control. There are parallels surely, but I think these pursuits are more different than they are similar. I would say, however, that an element of openness to the unknown, an avoidance or refusal of the perfectionist imperative, is an important quality of both the wine and the music that speaks to me.

BoG: Trends and innovation always seem to be met with suspicion in both wine and metal, where their respective audiences generally accept the more time-proven institutions and practices the most. However, can you mention any new developments in wine and in metal that get you excited and keep your curiosity engaged?

SW: It is not innovation that keeps my curiosity engaged in wine, but rather the exploration of its already extant vastness—obscure local traditions, grapes, and styles that have largely been overlooked by the modernization of the wine industry, well-trodden forms imbued with new energy. One may or may not consider this an "innovation," but it is a relatively recent development that I see great value in, this attempt seek out, recover, and preserve the rich diversity of wines and wine knowledge that predates or escaped the post–World War II industrialization of viticulture and viniculture. For instance, people call orange wine a "trend" because it was turned into one, aggressively and deliberately, by marketers, but it is also the recuperation of both a technique and an aesthetic frame of reference that have long histories in regions like Georgia and Emilia Romagna. As winemakers throughout the world have explored this technique they meet with greater or lesser success owing to the peculiarities of their circumstances—their grapes, their climates, their soil.

For instance Zibbibo grown on the searing soils of Pantelleria off the coast of Sicily tastes as if it was born only to be made in this style, Alsatian Gewürztraminer gains texture and structure from skin contact, saving it from dull, formless opulence. But Chardonnay from the Jura seems confused and muddled by the process and tends always in my opinion to turn out as something less true to itself, its best qualities obscured rather than coaxed into expression. So, is skin contact an innovation or an ill-conceived trend? Both and neither.

Ultimately, I distrust the notion of innovation: it is too often fetishized, fetishized just as much as "tradition." Metal I think is always in a state of slow flux, but the changes are glacial, tectonic, hardly linear. Innovation is a word for history and retrospection; when I hear it used for the present, I know I am being subjected to a sales pitch.

BoG: Current recommendations for wine? For music?

SW: I listen to relatively little new metal, but Hellripper and Hällas are two bands I have recently come to love. Our compatriots, Verglas, Departure Chandelier, and Conifère in Québec, and Nächtlich and Nocturnal Departure from elsewhere in Canada. And in the spirit of recommending new wine-producers along with new(er) records, Lolita Sene in the Southern Rhône has caught my attention, and Shun Minowa in Val Trebbia is making fascinating wines in the vein of Il Poggio, Denavolo and La Stoppa but with quite their own identity. Maison Maenad is to me the most exciting new producer in Jura, but her already minuscule production was dealt a terrible blow when she lost her entire vintage to hail this year, so those wines are now next to impossible to find. And—not a new producer but a new cuvée from an important domaine—the Dinavolo Rosso from Giulio Armani is fantastic, and expresses much of what I love about wine—energy, sympathy, confrontation, edification. It is far from perfect, but it boasts a harmony of derangements.

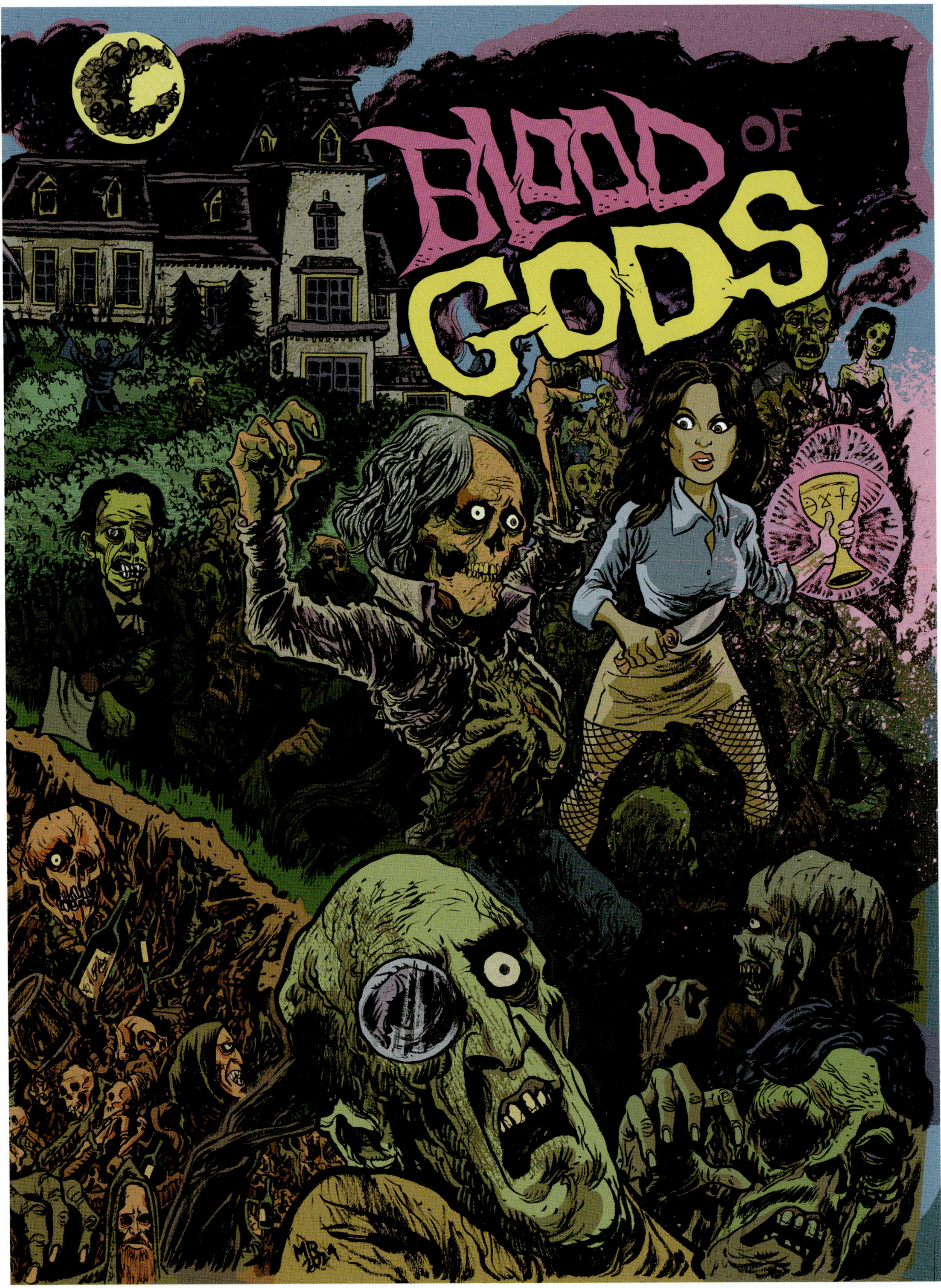
BLOOD OF
GODS

THERE ARE THE OLD WAYS--
TRIED AND TRUE METHODS THAT HAVE BEEN REFINED AND TESTED OVER GENERATIONS.
PROVEN WAYS.
AND THERE ARE THOSE THAT EMPLOY ARCANE RITUALS THAT CAN ACCELERATE GROWTH AND YIELDS.
PROPAGATION OF THE WICKED
PREMISE STACY BUCANAN
ART AND STORY: MARK RUDOLPH
THESE METHODS CARRY WITH THEM INHERENT RISKS. MANY OF WHICH DON'T REVEAL THEMSELVES...
...UNTIL IT IS TOO LATE!

THE CHAOS BREED TERRORIZE THE UNSUSPECTING PUBLIC.
LEAVING HAVOK IN THEIR WAKE.
RAISING THE DEAD TO PULL EVERYONE DOWN TO HELL.

BUT THE FOLLOWERS OF THE OLD WAYS HAVE TOOLS TO SEND THE UNDEAD BACK TO THE UNDERWORLD.
KEEPING THEM THERE IS ANOTHER STORY.
THE END

Bo Bradshaw

DEMYSTIFYING *the* ELEMENTS

By Justin Moore, Master Sommelier, wine consultant

THE MYTHICAL AND MISUNDERSTOOD element of sulfur (S) is one of the most controversial aspects associated with wine. This ancient and fundamental element was described as "brimstone" in the Old Testament. Other major religions played on this lack of understanding to gain power by striking fear into their gullible devotees. Dante Alighieri also used this imagery to depict Hell in the *Inferno* portion of *The Divine Comedy*.

Sulfur or Sulphur (both are correct) is one of the three principles of alchemy. Sulfur, mercury, and salt symbolize the spirit, soul, and body. Sulfur was first thought of as an element in 1777 and officially proved to be so in 1809. This pale-yellow brittle material just happens to be the tenth-most-abundant element in the universe. Our bodies use sulfur to build and fortify our DNA as well as to protect cells from cancer. True, it is used to make black gunpowder and sulfuric acid, but it is also used to preserve everything from fruit juice, pizza dough, and maple syrup to beer and, you guessed it, wine.

Due to its nefarious reputation, and the general lack of scientific knowledge in our day and age, sulfur often gets blamed for all sorts of consumption-related ailments, mostly hangovers. For those with real sensitivities (less than 1% of humans) it can cause redness and swelling, distress to respiratory and poor stomach function. My personal favorite side effect attributed to sulfur is a "sense of doom." In reality, far fewer people are negatively affected by both naturally occurring and added sulfites, and we are all far more exposed than we realize. In this country, up to 350 ppm may be added to wine which equates to 0.035% of the volume in the bottle. Organic wine is limited to 100 ppm or 0.01%. So the average human would need to consume enough wine to at least knock them out before suffering any major sulfur-related side effects, including the "sense of doom."

Why add sulfur to wine at all? It has functioned as a preservative to prevent spoiling and oxidation since Roman times. It has also been used to prevent bacteria contamination since the eighth century BCE. It's still commonly used for those same reasons today in wine and thousands of other food staples. Don't get me wrong, I'm not advocating for sulfur to be added to all wine all the time. Let's just try to diminish some of the hysteria and misconceptions when it comes to sulfur's relationship with my favorite dance-inducing beverage, wine.

>>>>>

In part, I'm writing this to better understand the subject because, honestly, I also know very little to nothing about sulfur. Digging in on the subject provided an opportunity to reconnect with one of the best winemakers in our science-deficient country. Ken Pahlow is the winemaker of Walter Scott Wines in the Willamette Valley of Oregon. I met Ken about ten years ago at a tasting and have been obsessed with his wines since the first sip. It turns out that good people make good wine and I can attest that Ken is guilty of both. His Pinot Noir, Gamay, and Aligote are all benchmarks of quality, but his Chardonnays are otherworldly and year after year get my vote for the best example this country has to offer. Not only do we pour them in all our restaurants, we drink them at home with cherished regularity. Here are some of the highlights and big takeaways from our conversation.

"I am not sure the general consumer knows any of the truths, because they have been beaten over the heads with so many misconceptions."

JUSTIN MOORE: How sick are you of hearing about sulfur?

KEN PAHLOW: The topic has slowed down quite a bit, but if it creates meaningful conversations then bring it on. I also think it has become similar to any other topic of discussion in wine. [e.g., ML [Malolactic Fermentation] or not, new barrels versus used, amphora versus any other fermentation vessel, etc.]

JM: What is a winemaker's relationship with sulfur really like?

KP: For most winemakers I know, SO^2 is a "tool" not really any different than a barrel, pump, destemmer, etc. Sulfur gets used at many different times during the winemaking process and for different reasons. Mostly during fermentation or pre-ferment, post-ML, and at bottling. We try to use it and think of it like how a chef would use salt, only more sparingly and when needed. The goal is to use this tool as minimally as possible, but it is also our best tool against oxidation and stopping wine from becoming vinegar, which is the most "natural" path for unfermented grape juice. As soon as we pick grapes, we are on a path.

JM: Do you think some grape varietals require sulfur, at least as part of their typicity?

KP: I don't really think of varietals here so much as "style" of wines. More "fragile" wines with higher pH, higher sugar, excess aldehydes (aroma of rotten or bruised apples which, for me, is a sign of lazy Chardonnay ferment). Wines being shipped internationally would likely show better when they land with a bit of an SO^2 dose. Wines that need less are typically low-pH wines (high acid), tannic wines, phenolic wines, fully dry wines without residual sugar, and wines that are well crafted. Basically, wines made with intention and care to detail. They do not make themselves! I am not talking "clean" or boring, but without dirty flaws that detract from the sense of place. Unfortunately, the wines that may benefit most from a small dose of SO^2 are those using more and more "natty" techniques like whole cluster, unfiltered, RS [Residual Sugar], etc. As a winemaker, if you think Brett [Brettanomyces], excessive VA [volatile acidity], etc. are a "purer expression of place," then you can skip the SO^2.

JM: What is your take on those culty, old-school, zero-sulfur producers?

KP: I don't drink a lot of those wines, but I imagine most of them have tidy-as-fuck cellars where they can ride the edge of making wine "naturally.' Most of the best wines in the world are made "naturally" (i.e., ambient yeasts etc). The best producers in the "natty" world are generally badass farmers too, and guess what their best tool for protection from mildew is? Sulfur!

JM: What are general truths and misconceptions the average consumer may believe?

KP: I am not sure the general consumer knows any of the truths, because they have been beaten over the heads with so many misconceptions.

[At this point Ken and I started to crunch some numbers. We agree that it would take at least 3-4 bottles of wine to be consumed by one person in a single drinking session to get anywhere near a negative side effect from sulfur. By the time you are on your fourth bottle, you can be certain that the alcohol will have more of an impact than a small dose of any naturally occurring element. We both agree: avoid overconsumption, RS [Residual Sugar] when possible, and don't drink shitty wines! Ken pointed out that histamines and tyramine, which are naturally occurring in wine, may cause more residual side effects (hangovers).]

JM: How much physical sulfur actually goes into a wine when you are talking 10 parts per million or 100 ppm? What does that translate to?

KP: In a 3,000-liter fermentation tank, I added a total of 63 grams of sulfur to protect the fermentation.

JM: 63 grams is 2.22 ounces, that's the size of a small plastic to-go ramekin for your takeout. How many bottles in a 3,000-liter tank?

KP: That's 333 cases of wine or about 4,000 bottles.

JM: What is something everyone could or should know more about on the subject?

KP: Sulfur sticks to things and there's always less in the finished product than you put in. If you are at 10 ppm in your tank prior to bottling, you probably lose 2-3 ppm in the bottling process alone. Sulfites occur naturally as part of the fermentation process as yeast gobble sugar—the main byproducts are sulfites, CO^2 and heat. Sulfur occurs everywhere in nature—soil, foods, plants, and water. Sulfur dioxide is gas produced when sulfur is burned and is bound to two molecules of oxygen. Sulfur dioxide is also preservative and it is everywhere ... check your OJ!

[Ken really brought it home with this next statement, and to me, it seems like a great place to wrap it up.]

KP: Like anything else, sulfur should be used only when absolutely needed and in balance with the wine—as it pertains to wine, wines made with care and detail, those that ride the edge but are stable due to clean cellar practices, not "clean" wine. We are a modern society and we have tools at our disposal that allow us to make life better. If sulfur allows me to better show off what my vineyards have to say, then why would I not use it? After a whole year of effort in the vineyard, why waste all that work because of shoddy cellar work? If we want the wines to taste delicious and not like vinegar, or some other bacterial spoilage, we need to embrace a small amount of SO2, period. Dance with the challenges.

I'VE LEARNED A LOT AND I HOPE YOU have too. The truth is, sulfur is a mysterious subject that the average consumer, sommelier, and even many winemakers don't know much about. People are afraid of what they don't understand, and sulfur is greatly misunderstood. It is a tool and, like a hammer or an ax or a paintbrush, some wield it with much greater artistry than others. Winemakers that care use sparingly little. Winemakers that don't care or don't know any better use it to cover mistakes or not at all out of misguided principle. And for the sake of a "natural" ideology, some will ruin their entire year's work in the vineyard, then tell you it's my least favorite wine word, terroir. Just like so many of the great pleasures in life, less is more.

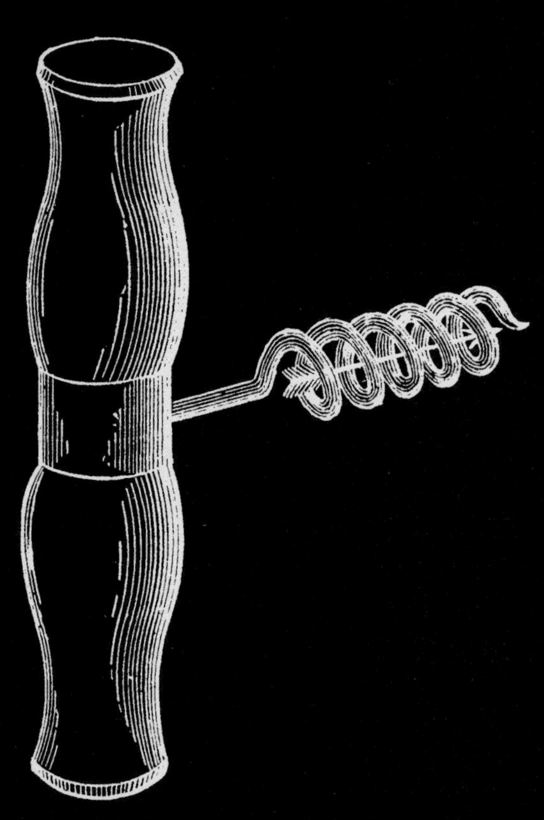

Brutality Is Law

Intense, Heavy, Extreme

This page and opposite: Matt Stikker

Death Metal Winery Name Generator

First letter of your first name		Last wine you drank		First letter of your last name	
a	Wretched	Barbera	Coffin	a	Canyon
b	Savage	Cab Franc	Battle	b	Sludge
c	Wolven	Cab Sauv	Abomination	c	Realm
d	Rabid	Carmenere	Lightning	d	Domain
e	Beastly	Chardonnay	Warrior	e	Power
f	Decomposed	Chenin Blanc	Sword	f	Ridge
g	Festering	Grenache	Funeral	g	Slime
h	Ruinous	GSM blend	Undead	h	Fields
i	Ominous	Malbec	Phantom	i	Reign
j	Spectral	Merlot	Scourge	j	Cellars
k	Skeletal	Mourvedre	Legion	k	Mountains
l	Iron	Petit Sirah	Armageddon	l	Creek
m	Rotten	Petit Verdot	Fire	m	Ooze
n	Desolate	Pinot Griogio	Void	n	Castle
o	Undead	Pinot Noir	Wraith	o	Hills
p	Thundering	Red Blend	Shadow	p	Wastelands
q	Razor	Riesling	Magic	q	Serum
r	Carnivorous	Rose	Dragon	r	Crypt
s	Deadly	Sangiovese	Shield	s	Blood
t	Grisly	Sauv Blanc	Chaos	t	Stream
u	Bludgeoning	Semillon	Barbarian	u	Valley
v	Maniacal	Syrah	Carnage	v	Road
w	Infernal	Tempranillo	Doom	w	Gates
x	Horrific	Viognier	Axe	x	Darkness
y	Brutal	White Blend	Wood	y	Horde
z	Cryptic	Zinfandel	Oblivion	z	Filth

Your death metal winery name is:

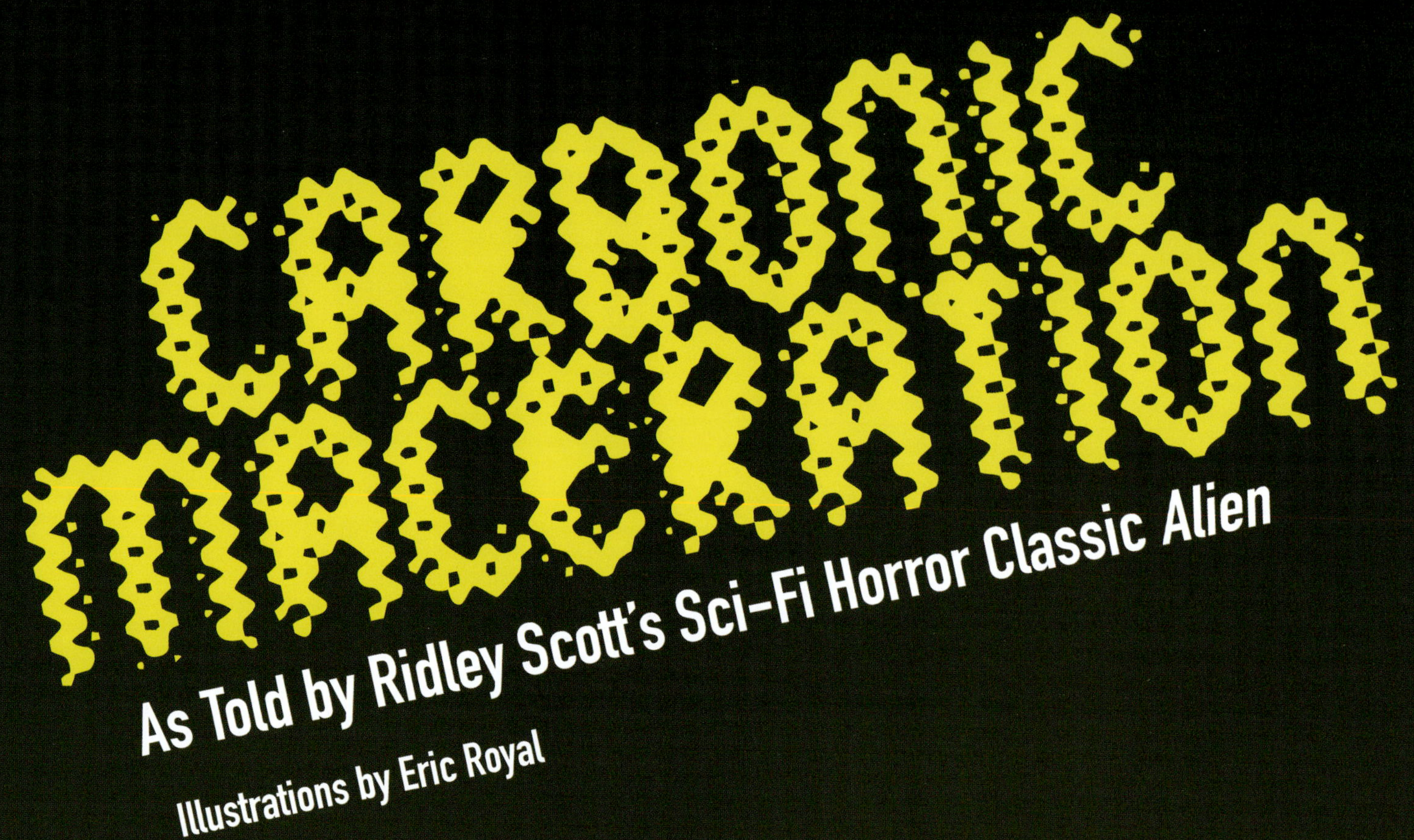

Carbonic Maceration

As Told by Ridley Scott's Sci-Fi Horror Classic Alien

Illustrations by Eric Royal

A HOST TO HARVEST

Unsuspecting grape clusters are targeted. Picked off by surprise attack, harvested at the perfect moment of ripeness, but not damaged, split, or crushed, for inside is the precious juice. In fact, the grape clusters are delicately handled but the Facehugger immobilizes/paralyzes the grape-cluster victim, removing oxygen and the ability to breathe, rendering the cluster incapacitated. The oxygen is replaced by carbon dioxide in the winemaking process, putting the grapes into a hibernative state of suspended animation in an anaerobic environment.

CLUSTERHUGGER

Cold, motionless, no respiration, dormant. Meanwhile, internally, something is changing and fermenting, a process within the debilitated grapes known as intracellular fermentation is happening. The victim is now host to this internal process that begins when the grapes start to release enzymes as a result of no oxygen. Since carbon dioxide is a byproduct of fermentation, the gas continues to build up while sugars and malic acid are broken down by the CO^2. As a result of this process, the grapes are becoming softer and infirm, meaning less tannin and less acid, i.e., more approachable when fermented.

GRAPEBURSTER

Once the alcohol reaches around 2% inside the intact berries, the internal fermentation has grown to its peak and the host's main body cavity bursts forth—typically the grape skins will split—and release their sanguine juice. The flesh of the grape cluster's individual berries has changed color and the delicious ichor gushes forth. The carbonic/anaerobic process promotes more candied and fresh-fruit flavors over the more complex flavors that come from aerobic fermentations.

VINOMORPH

Behold, the withered body, now a corpse, drained of its life-giving juice. Carbonic maceration extracts some color from the grapes but little tannin, generally creating red wines that are lighter in color due to the shorter period of skin contact, since the grapes remain intact during part of the fermentation. This, along with the lower levels of acidity and tannin, produces wines that are more aromatic and have a softer, lighter, more fruit-forward style, such as Beaujolais Nouveau, making an approachable wine that is often best when drunk fresh, young, and sometimes even lightly chilled.

Sindre Solem
of Obliteration and Nekromantheon

Courtesy of Sindre Solem

SINDRE SOLEM EXPERTLY PUSHES THE DIAL BETWEEN METAL AND WINE TO THE DEEP OPPOSITE ends of the spectrum. Hailing from Oslo, Norway, his extreme metal pedigree is balanced by his acumen for premium wines. On the metal side of things, he slings the guitar in murky death-metalists Obliteration and thrash speedfreaks Nekromantheon, both highly respected underground metal institutions. However, his skilled palate for tasty vino has seen him climb the ladder in Oslo's wine world, first starting at heavy metal bar Kniven before moving to Nektar and finally assuming position as wine director and restaurant manager of Arakataka. He graciously chatted with us about his experience in both metal and wine and the parallels of the two.

BLOOD OF GODS: Obviously at Kniven there was metal playing—what were some of the typical tunes patrons could expect to hear while enjoying some wine?

SINDRE SOLEM: Well, first off, Kniven was and still is a metal bar focusing on underground music and the less "hit-based" sides of metal but also hard rock and punk. It was supposed to be eclectic from day one, so you could hear everything from Mercyful Fate, Darkthrone, Swallowed from Finland, Cultes des Ghoules, and Deathhammer to Thin Lizzy, Slayer, Discharge, Rudimentary Peni, ZZ Top, Sleep, and Morbid Angel, with the occasional weird psych track etc. The focus was not really on wine either—more microbrew etc.—but we had a small, well-curated wine list that eventually people came for (wine interested people with little interest for metal, and metal people who cared about wine). It was small and eclectic but always included some great and extremely underpriced stuff, always some good Champagne, Burgundy, Piedmont, and Beaujolais etc. Thinking back on the insane producers we had at bargain prices still gives me the chills, but of course the times of getting cheap, great Burgundy are long gone.

BOG: Do you also get to play some metal at Nektar?

SS: Not really. We have some cool proto-metal, heavy rock, etc. on the lists, but there is so much more also. The focus there is not really the music, though, it's more the atmosphere and the food and wine. This fall I'm actually changing my workplace again, taking over as Wine Director (I hate that word—in Norwegian we say vinansvarlig, which just means "responsible for the wine") and restaurant manager at the classic Oslo restaurant Arakataka. Great New-Nordic food and a killer wine list!

BOG: Who is usually more surprised: wine industry folks who find out you're into extreme metal or metalheads that learn you've got a killer palate and work in the wine industry?

SS: Ha-ha, I can guarantee that *no one* in the wine industry is surprised that I'm into metal. With band shirts, long hair (until recently), leather jackets, etc., it's obvious that I'm a metalhead and in a band. It's by far more metal people who are surprised, and a lot of them don't get it. At all. It's considered snobbish and posh or whatever, but I don't care. A lifetime ago I got sick of the metal way of drinking warm beer, Jack 'n' Coke, and Jäger. Can't imagine anything worse, actually.

BOG: Metal concerts and winemaking each have an element of "controlled chaos." There's some etiquette and rules, but there's also that unpredictable component where mayhem could erupt at any moment. Do you see similar parallels?

SS: Sure, I get that. There are traditions, rules, and experience that lead things to be done a certain way, but elements of uncertainty can make it into something special, or completely destroy it. Would not drag this parallel too far, though—it can be more similar to recording an album, with limited time and budget, ha-ha.

BOG: Did you have a specific wine or a wine-related memory that served as your gateway into the world of wine?

SS: Hmmm . . . it was a gradual transition for my part. I remember enjoying well-crafted beers and wine much more than what the typical metal dudes drank, and I've been very lucky to be able to taste and drink some stellar "benchmark" wines. But I remember having a friend over after a concert I did in London, and I brought back a Nye timber, an extremely well-crafted British sparkling wine before it was possible to get it in Norway. We had that and a bottle of Araud Charmes Chambertin 2006 Grand Cru, and I remember waking up the next day thinking, "That is what I want to focus on and get deep into." Both wines were ethereal and so stunning at the time. I quit tobacco the next day also to get more cash for good bottles, ha-ha.

BOG: For the wineheads reading this, what would you recommend as some go-to metal albums and why?

SS: **1.** Black Sabbath, *Master of Reality*. Not a very original pick, but one of the most important records in metal. They took the heaviness to another level and brought doomy and slow elements into metal. It's like a Corneas that has gotten the correct cellar time and is peaking! A timeless classic.
2. Slayer, *Hell Awaits*. Another obvious pick, but this is for me one of the most important and perfect metal albums. It's fast, dark, slightly technical, and well executed, yet spontaneous, shabby, and raw. Perfect old-school production and a gloomy/evil atmosphere. An album I'd never get sick of. Like some crazy unicorn white Jura you'll only drink once, but be engraved in your memory forever.
3. Darkthrone, *A Blaze in the Northern Sky*. The epitome of black metal and Nordic extreme metal all in one. A cold, harsh, and difficult record to listen to, but this is the very essence of proper extreme metal and the benchmark all are striving after. The old, *old* world. Overjoy, Puffeney, Gravner, Coche-Dury, Rene Engl, and Accamaso all in one.
4. Repulsion, *Horrified*. The ultimate underground cult

DANIEL WARREN JOHNSON

classic and an early advocate of both punk and metal influences combined. Like a crazy co-ferment, on the natural, dirtier side. Partida Creus, Prieur Roch, and No Control for the ears.

BOG: For the metalheads, what wines would you recommend to give them some good places to start or expand their wine journey and why?

SS: This is mostly for expanding your journey into mystery (a Dream Death reference right there), as it's harder and harder for me to get excited on entry-level stuff, except Beaujolais ... Ulysse Collin,Les Roizes Blanc de Blancs Champagne. Oliver Collin makes extremely expressive and intense Champagnes from Citeaux du Petit Morin south in Champagne, and was mentored by Anselme Selosse. One of my favorite producers, Ulysse Collin's wines will challenge your senses and change the way you think about Champagne. Single-vineyard and single-grape-variety wines. Unfortunately, stupid expensive and hard to get your hands on, but you only live once. Extreme elegance à la Vemod, *Venter på Stormene* or Candlemass. Tissot, Patchwork Chardonnay (or any of his other Chardonnay cuveés, for that matter). A great entry into Jura and an elegant, yet expressive, Chardonnay. Smokey reductiveness and mature yet saline fruit—an absolute joy to drink that requires no knowledge or contemplation, just pure hedonistic bliss. Kinda like an Electric Wizard gig. Whitcraft Winery Santa Rita Hills Pinot Noir. Just an extremely well-made, juicy Pinot, with mesmerizing aromatics. Would pair well with Samhain's *November-Coming-Fire*. Rinaldi, Langhe Nebbiolo. Another perfect example of perfect, old-school winemaking. Rinaldi's wines will lure you into a dark place and rip you with perfect, tobacco-esque tannins. Another hard-to-get item, kinda like the yellow goat or Mayhem's *Deathcrush*, but it's well worth it . . .

COURTESY OF SINDRE SOLEM

BOG: Trends and innovation are often met with suspicion in wine and metal, where their respective audiences generally accept the more time-proven institutions/bands and practices the most. However, can you mention any new developments in wine and in metal that get you excited and keep your curiosity engaged?

SS: Well, not exactly new, but looking back to the way things were done in the past, going back to analog recordings, to have a raw punk-ish ethos, focusing on atmosphere instead of technicality, and taking the lyrics serious in ways that haven't been done before is all a new wave in metal where I feel at home, and this parallels the trends in wine I also really enjoy. Like looking back on old school winemaking, going organic/biodynamic, focus on local, ancient grape varieties, use of old casks and amphoras, stop using pesticides and fungicides, focusing on precise fruit qualities . . . Another trend in wine I'm excited about is the growing focus on co-fermenting red and white grapes, making juicy, fresh, yet complex wines that are highly drinkable. The Chardonnay and Gamay mix of Ganevat's Poulprix in 2019 vintage, or his girlfriend Maylis Bernard's Zeroine wines, are good examples here.

BOG: By the way, a friend from Relapse said, "I saw Obliteration on their last tour through Philly and Sindre was slugging a bottle of wine while onstage drinking right out of the bottle." Needless to say, we knew you were the real deal for wine and metal. By the way: you happen to remember what that wine was you were drinking?

SS: Haha! It was the second last show of the tour, and we were pretty beat and just had to soldier through—it had been a few rough weeks. My friends in Philly (Drew Elliot, who made the covers for Necrophagia and Blood Feast back in the day, and his wife) took me to a wine store, I bought one unidentified U.S. Pinot which I cannot recall and one Domaine de Lises Crozes-Hermitage, the domaine of Alain Graillot. Which I'm sure went down at the afterparty. Total class.

MICROBIAL MÊLÉE

OR: THE BATTLE IN THE BOTTLE

BY STACY BUCHANAN, *BLOOD OF GODS* PUBLISHER
ILLUSTRATIONS BY JAMES CALLAHAN

THERE IS A NO-HOLDS-BARRED throwdown in each glass of wine and the only law is brutality. Think we're kidding? Even in your most sophisticated and elegant wine, there first takes place an epic fracas on the microbial level that determines if your wine is going to be that stunner deserving of accolades and praise or a big uneven mess or worse: vinegar.

One such instance takes place in a crucial but seemingly quiet part of the winemaking process: aging. Sure, things seems calm, but under the microscope it can be anything but peaceful. While there are a number of factors, the key characters in this donnybrook are, first and foremost, the fruit, followed by oxygen, sulfur (SO^2, and VA (Volatile Acidity).

Master Sommelier Justin Moore breaks it down like this: "Oxygen is like the Undertaker, he has at one point or another chokeslammed all your favorite wines/wrestlers into a coffin. Meanwhile, Sulfur is André the Giant, completely misunderstood and underappreciated. Volatile Acidity brings intense zing, sometimes so much so, the only way to describe them is like a flying elbow drop from the top rope à la Macho Man Randy Savage. Fruit, the most important part of the whole brawl, is best represented as Hulk Hogan—pure personality where you always know what you're going to get."

As wine ages, it naturally evaporates because of the porous nature of barrels it is stored in. This can diminish the volume of the barrel anywhere from 1% to 10% over a year. The problem is that means higher levels of oxygen are introduced to the wine, which can negatively impact

the aging process, as well as create conditions for microbes to take root and damage the wine. Enter Sulfur: an antioxidant agent that, while also formed as a side effect during fermentation, is often added to protect against bacteria. This ties in with Volatile Acidity (the measure of a wine's gaseous acids) because the aforementioned oxidative process, as well as poor winery hygiene, can increase VA, which is known for aromas and flavors like vinegar and nail-polish remover.

"VA is the sneakiest," says Suzanne Harryman, former Assistant Winemaker at the Walls. "A hint of volatile acidity can appear to be on the side of the fruit helping elevate its character, while in reality it's waiting patiently for you to drop your guard so it can sneak in there and turn your wine to vinegar." Steve Wells, owner/winemaker of Time & Direction Wines, echoes the sentiment: "VA in small amounts can give a little bit of aromatic lift to the wine. It doesn't hurt anything and can be quite pleasant. However, when it's all hulked out, it's quite literally a monster, and it's now terrible and a huge rage-beast and something has to be done about it to get it under control."

They're all active characters with beneficial and detrimental attributes vying for the limelight, trying to elbow their way to center stage, while pounding each other into submission.

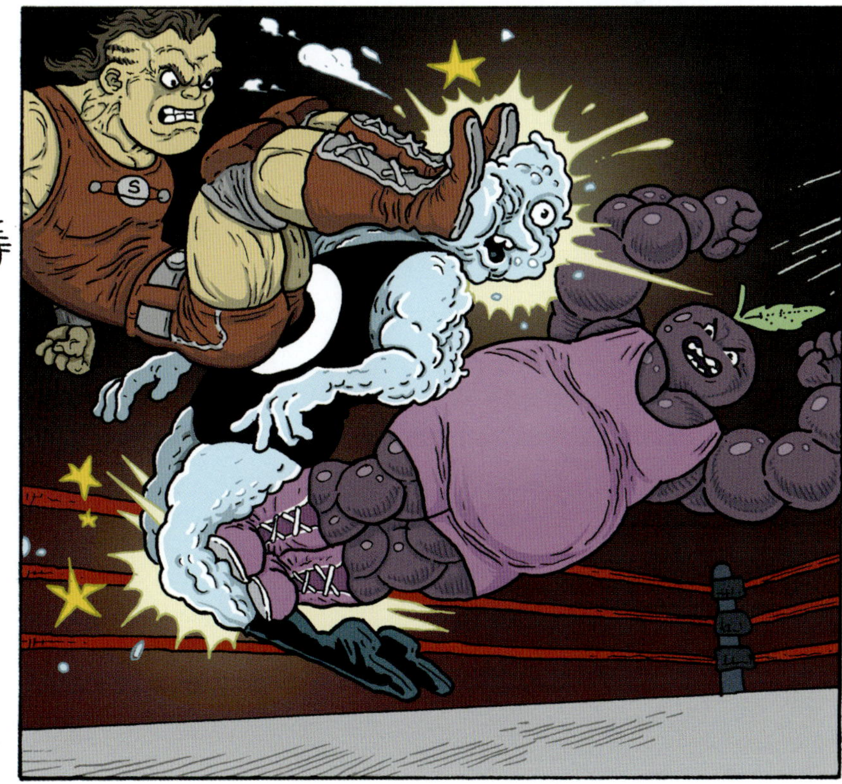

"Oxygen and Sulfites punching each other in the face, while VA is the asshole with the folding chair, sneaking up on Fruit, who has been watching from the corner," is how Doug Frost, M.S., M.W., sees the mêlée unfolding. "Then VA starts pounding Fruit over the head and Sulfites come to the rescue while Oxygen is still screaming in the middle of the ring about how 'I am the KING!' Then Fruit and Sulfites kneecap him."

No single personality in the fray is inherently bad. They're each keeping each other in check; no one character reigns supreme and steals the show, or least that's the goal. "Everything needs to be in balance," says Wells. "That's the most important part of the wine—everything needs to be in balance to make a really great wine."

(NOT) WORLDS APART

JOSEPH D. ROWLAND plays bass guitar in the Little Rock, Arkansas–based doom metal band **PALLBEARER**. However, he resides in Brooklyn, New York, and splits his time working in a fine wine (and other libations) shop, where his tasting chops have shown his palate is also skilled.

Ebru Yildiz

Having just completed a run of concerts in celebration of the band's debut album, *Sorrow and Extinction* (imagine Black Sabbath played at half speed with an extra does of heavy), he weighed in on his wine journey and some of the magic and mayhem it shares with metal.

BLOOD OF GODS: Where did your interest in wine originate? Maybe a specific wine or a wine-related memory that served as your gateway into the world of vino?

JDR: I was a fair-weather wine-drinker for a long time, usually spurred on by someone more enthusiastic about it than myself. After the height of the pandemic, and thus extended downtime musically, I ended up working part-time at a little boutique spirits shop in East Williamsburg. I knew a passable amount about whiskey and building cocktails but was sort of just thrust into the thick of it, particularly with wine; it seemed like it was going to be a hell of a learning curve. Even though I felt way out of my depth at first, I quickly realized that I had a fairly good palate and, perhaps even more to my advantage, a deep enthusiasm for exploration that mirrored my passion for music in a lot of ways. Since then, I've ended up doing it full-time when I'm not away with Pallbearer, and I'm still really enjoying the exploration.

Dave Kloc

BOG: While there are plenty of stereotypes on both sides, what argument would you make to encourage more metalheads to try getting into wine?

JDR: This may be kind of a pedestrian observation, but, considering the massive overlap that craft beer and metal seem to have developed in the past decade, wine could be an easy parallel. I believe the overarching macho mentality of metal's past seems to be fading, and with it the association of largely "cheap beer and booze" dominating. There are also many metal fans getting older, like myself, and appreciating more sophisticated things. There are so many good approachable wines in the world, and if you drink with the goal of finding things you enjoy, it offers a pretty endless pastime.

BOG: Who is usually more surprised: wine industry folks who find out you're in a heavy band or metalheads that learn you've got a killer palate and work in the wine industry?

JDR: It's probably not a massive surprise to people who encounter me at work; the little shop I work at has a small staff that includes multiple metal fans, and we're often playing heavy (or adjacent) music on the shop stereo and no one seems to bat an eye. I'm not the first touring musician in the heavy-music space to work at the shop either, so perhaps there's even a bit of a reputation around the store itself. Who knows? Thus far, most people in the metal scene I've talked to about wine seem to be nonplussed about it, but we've also only just started post-pandemic touring again less than a year ago. I'm sure my so-called elevated taste (read: snobbery) will crop up with more consistency as Pallbearer continues to regain some of our previous momentum.

BOG: Current recommendations for wine? For music?

JDR I tend to go nuts for virtually any Venn diagram of Gamay, Cinsault, or light fruity red blend that's produced with carbonic maceration. I love all the wines from the Les Vins Pirouttes portfolio, particularly Ultraviolet by David. Also Bloomer Creek Vineyards from the Finger Lakes in New York—their skin-contact Riesling from 2021 was a seismic shift for me in terms of a truly "creative" bottle. I still think about it frequently.

Music that's resonated with me lately . . . the Mournful Congregation catalog, Mindforce, *New Lords*; Chrome Ghost, *House of Falling Ash*; Badfinger, *Straight Up*; Bluetile Lounge, *Half Cut*.

BOG: Recording an album and making wine have been likened to each other, both having an element of "controlled chaos." There's some etiquette and rules, but there's also that unpredictable component where magic or mayhem could erupt at any moment. Do you see similar parallels in your experience?

JDR: I have been making music for a long time and I agree that there is a sort of intangible electricity that can manifest in writing and recording. In terms of controlled chaos, perhaps the touring element might reflect it in some aspects too. I've been on plenty of tours that were filled with euphoric highs and near-disastrous lows, but when everything is working and you just exist in the moment on stage it really does feel like magic sometimes.

WAR GRAPES

-An unimpeachable metal classic, injected with wine, frivolity, and nonsense-

Generals ______ (another word for drunk) in their masses
Just like ______ (fictional character) at ______ (color) masses
______ (adjective) minds that plot destruction
Sorcerers of ______ (another term for wine) construction

In the fields the bodies burning
As the ______ (another word for partying or drinking) machine keeps ______ (verb ending in -ing)
Death and ______ (least favorite wine varietal) to mankind
Poisoning their brainwashed minds,
Oh, ______ (person in the room's name) yeah!

______ (plural noun) hide themselves away
They only started the ______ (noun)
Why should they go out to fight?
They leave that role to the ______ (word that rhymes w/ last word of choice)

Time will tell them they are ______ (genre of music) minds
Making war just for fun
Treating people just like ______ (plural noun) in ______ (name of a game)
Wait 'til their ______ (wine descriptor) Day comes,
Yeah!

Now in ______ (favorite place to drink wine), world stops turning
Ashes where their bodies burning
No more war grapes have the power
______ (body part) of God has struck the hour

Day of Judgement, ______ (favorite singer/vocalist) is calling
On their knees the war grapes crawling
Begging mercy for their ______ (a type of party foul)
______ (favorite wine producer), laughing, spreads their wings
Oh, ______ (last person to text you) yeah!

"War Pigs" originally written by Black Sabbath (Tony Iommi, Ozzy Osbourne, Geezer Butler, Bill Ward)

THIS NEW NATURAL WINE PRODUCER HAS EVERYTHING...
COW HORNS STUFFED WITH MANURE
GANDALF IMPERSONATORS
VINE HEAVY PETTING
CELESTIAL WORSHIP ACCORDING TO THE ASTROLOGICAL CALENDAR...
DISGORGE PERFORMANCE
(THE BAND, NOT THE SPARKLING WINE PROCESS)
OH BABY!
ALEX MURD

Australia's death-metal titans **THY ART IS MURDER** pummel with aggressive heaviness. The drumming pounds like Thor's personal jackhammer, the riffs are lethal and enormous, and, despite their sonic barbarity, guitarist Andy Marsh and drummer Jesse Beahler also have strong palates for primo vino. When not tenderizing audiences' eardrums, the two members have also spent time in and around Sydney's wine and metal Mecca: Crowbar—rubbing elbows with owner Trad Nathan musically, professionally, and—more often than not—with some delicious fermented libations in hand.

[This interview was a rollicking chat between BoG, Jesse, and Andy. In some instances, they answer individually and in others, together. Joint answers are noted with Jesse and Andy's initials.]

Band photos by Thomas Savage

BLOOD OF GODS: Where did your interest in wine originate? Was there a specific wine or a wine-related memory that served as your gateway into the world of vino?

JESSE BEAHLER: Moving to Australia was the catalyst for me getting into drinking wine. I was a big craft beer drinker while living in the USA, but obviously beer culture is still in its growth phase down under. Our mutual friend Trad had started a music and wine business that was pairing bottles with vinyl records and our band did a collab release through it with a small winemaker called Konpira Maru, which really drove me to know more about wine.

ANDY MARSH: I got into wine relatively young through cooking my way through university, using it in the kitchen, and obviously drinking some along the way. Pairing food and wine is what I really love and was kinda of what gave me that aha moment, that the sum of the parts could be greater than either alone.

BOG: Who is usually more surprised: wine industry folks who find out you're in a heavy band? Or metalheads who learn you've got a killer palate and work in the wine/beer industry?

JB: Most people seem to be more surprised that I'm in a metal band, to be honest. A sizable percentage of the world consumes alcohol recreationally, whereas playing in a metal band is pretty niche. It's also pretty tough holding down a job or career path whilst keeping up a heavy touring schedule.

AM: For me it's a little bit the opposite, having come from the hospitality industry, where I spent a decade of my younger years, I now spend almost all my time working in the music business. There is some wine overlap amongst my peers but most metal bands on tour are drinking whiskey and beer. I did happen upon a bottle of Radikon before our last Italian show in Milan and Jesse and I drank that on stage. It's definitely more shocking when people know I keep a 200-bottle collection at home; on the flip side, I have plenty of metal head friends who still work hospitality.

BOG: Recording an album and making wine (or beer) have been likened to each other, both having an element of "controlled chaos." There's some rules and creative flair, but there's also that unpredictable component where magic or mayhem could erupt at any moment. Do you see similar parallels in your experience?

JB + AM: There are for sure some parallels, in terms of expression of ideas and the confluence of many working parts. What was the season like, how is the fruit, what process does the maker wish to deploy, etc. Sometimes you may walk into the studio with a distinct idea of what you want a song to sound like, but invariably twists and turns are encountered and you may end up somewhere totally foreign. Control and linearity can be found in refined bottles and songs, but sometimes there is unhinged, natural funk where you have allowed randomness to enter the equation. Sometimes the results come out amazing and other times you end up in a place you'd rather not be, so you start over and begin work on the next batch. Beer and wine do have some rules with respect to ingredients—music is a little less controlled by what you can use to make the sounds that form the songs—but ultimately we are in a death-metal band so there is some limitation to what we do.

BOG: While there are plenty of stereotypes on both sides, what argument would you make to encourage more metalheads to try getting into wine?

JB + AM: First off, it's fun and delicious! Metalheads pride themselves on being open-minded and there is a strong interest in diversity of culture and history. Wine and beer can be seen as a thread weaving through time, carrying culture (lol) and process through many civilizations around the world for thousands of years. It's a humbling feeling to drink the results of thousands of years of knowledge born out of pure chance, necessity, creativity, and conviviality, and feel your place in the wider world.

BOG: Current recommendations for wine? For music?

JB: I went to Nelson, New Zealand, recently and drank some Sauvignon Blanc that was a big passion-fruit bomb—it was my first time drinking at a vineyard and I had never experienced a wine so forward like that. I've been jamming a lot of Portrayal of Guilt this year, which is sort of this black-metal-meets-emo crossover band—I don't really know how to describe it as I don't listen to much music like it, but I dig it!

AM: This year I made a promise to myself to drink more German Riesling, Grüner and Chenin Blanc. I've been picking up a few bottles, but the only notable bottles I've drunk this year was a 2017 Nikolaihof Grüner which was ace and a 2016 Lavantureux Grand Cru that was hitting right—all the lemon brioche! Musicwise, not too much for me this year, the latest End record kicked my ass; otherwise I just get into the cycle of listening to the bands I'm working with.

BOG: Since you work with Trad at Crowbar, are there any funny anecdotes or gentle ribbing about him you care to share?

JB: Trad has really been the person who has introduced me to wine and guided me on my journey, so I love him for that. But there was this time when he forgot there was a water pan in the bottom of the smoker when we were barbecuing at Crowbar, and went to move it and spilled hot, fatty, grease-laden water all over his feet.

AM: Fifteen years ago I played in a band with Trad and at the time he lived in an apartment building located near a McDonald's that a fan worked at. He would get all the cheeseburger components from them and assemble what we called Trad Burgers in his kitchen, fill up a garbage bag with them, and bring them on tour. Trad Burgers kept us alive when the money was tight!

AN COLLAZO

SANDEEV REEHAL
SHINDY
DESIGN
MMXX

Wine Horror Name Generator

FIRST LETTER OF YOUR FIRST NAME		LAST WINE YOU DRANK		FIRST LETTER OF YOUR LAST NAME	
A	THE DEVIL'S	CAB FRANC	HARVEST	A	HORDES
B	GROTESQUE	SYRAH	VINEYARD	B	OF MADNESS
C	DARK	MALBEC	CHATEAU	C	FUNERAL
D	MIDNIGHT	MERLOT	GRAPE(S)	D	CRYPT
E	UNHALLOWED	CHARDONNAY	BUDBREAK	E	OF THE APOCALYPSE
F	UNDEAD	RIESLING	FERMENTATION	F	OF HELL
G	MACABRE	PINOT NOIR	WINE	G	OF THE DAMNED
H	EVIL	VOIGNIER	ROOTSTOCK	H	MASSACRE
I	TWILIGHT	SAUV BLANC	PRUNING	I	NIGHTMARE
J	TERRIFYING	ROSE	BEAUJOLAIS	J	CULT
K	CURSED	PETIT VERDOT	WILAMETTE VALLEY	K	INSANITY
L	HORIFFIC	TEMPERANILLO	BLENDING	L	WITCHCRAFT
M	INFERNAL	MARSANNE	VINTAGE	M	PHANTOMS
N	POSSESSED	SEMILLON	TERROIR	N	EXORCISM
O	BLACK	GRENACHE	RHONE	O	RITUAL
P	FRIGTFUL	CAB SAUV	SOMMELIER	P	SOULS
Q	HAUNTED	SANGIOVESE	VINE	Q	UNDERWORLD
R	UNEARTHLY	MOURVEDRE	WINEMAKLING	R	BLOODTHIRST
S	DIABOLICAL	CARMENERE	GRAND CRU	S	ZOMBIES
T	MYSTERIOUS	BARBERA	NAPA	T	CATACOMBS
U	HELLISH	ZINFANDEL	BORDEAUX	U	THIRST
V	WICKED	SPARKLING	BACCHUS	V	INCANTATION
W	CREEPING	PETIT SYRAH	CELLAR	W	CEMETERY
X	GHASTLY	ROUSANNE	BURGUNDY	X	SLAUGHTER
Y	FULL MOON	RED BLEND	VINIFICATION	Y	SPECTRE
Z	MALEVOLENT	WHITE BLEND	MACERATION	Z	SUMMONING

Your Wine Horror Name is

Bridging the Worlds of Metal and Wine

Fleshgod Apocalypse

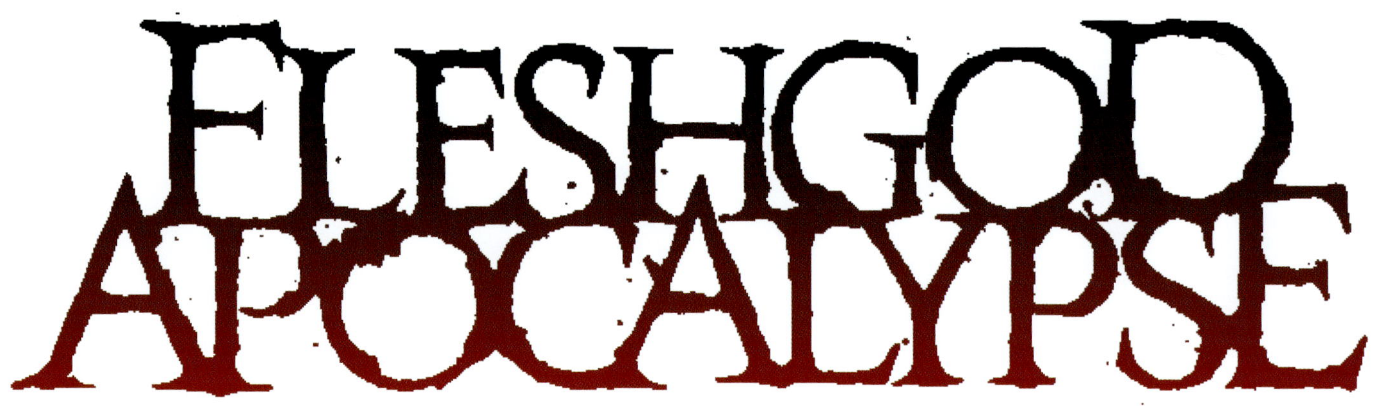

By Stacy Buchanan, *Blood of Gods* publisher

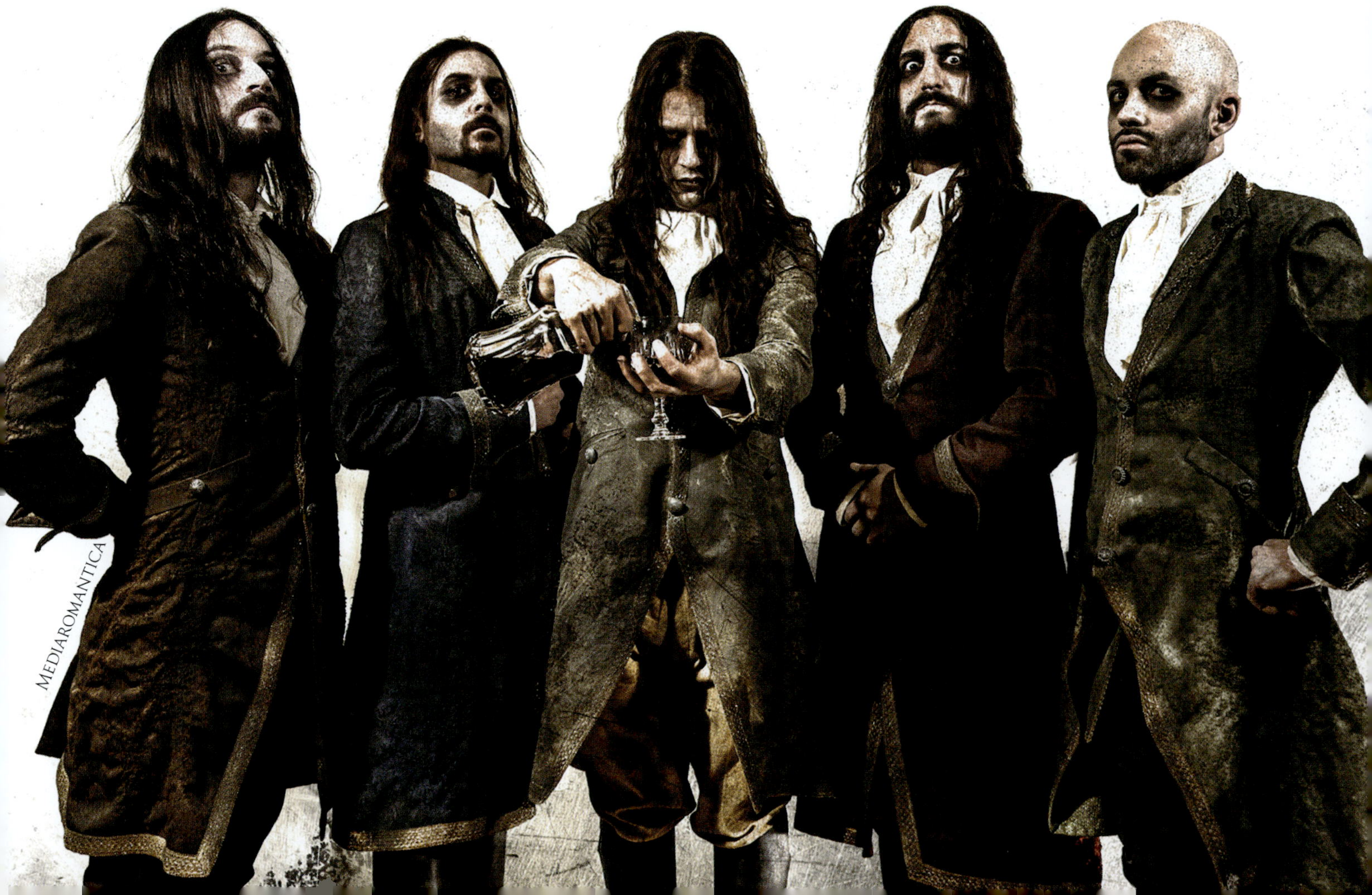

MEDIAROMANTICA

Few bands in the metal world can seamlessly blend the brutal ferocity of death metal with the grandeur of orchestral bombast quite like Fleshgod Apocalypse. The Italian five-piece has been making waves for years with their brand of high-intensity, symphonic metal. But, beyond their musical prowess, what also sets them apart is their appreciation for fine wine—a breath of fresh air in the metal world, where beer often reigns supreme. In fact, Fleshgod Apocalypse has gone a step further, offering their own red wine, the Fool, produced in Italy in limited quantities. This isn't just a novelty item with a slapped-on label—it's a reflection of their deep-rooted passion for wine culture.

ROBERT SAMMELIN

Francesco Paoli (vocals, guitars) shares his thoughts with us about wine's place in metal, the stereotypes surrounding both, and how their own wine project came to life. For him, wine appreciation is practically ingrained in his DNA. "As Italians, we are truly proud of our wines, especially those from our area," he explains. With Italy's vast winemaking tradition—one that extends across countless regions and varietals—wine holds a cultural significance that goes far beyond a simple beverage choice.

"Wine is in our genes, so to speak. There are so many great wineries in Italy, and our region, Umbria, is no exception. Wine represents the oldest and greatest tradition in our country, paired with a cuisine that is renowned worldwide. Each wine carries the history of its specific territory."

Despite metal's affinity for beer, Paoli believes wine has an untapped place in the scene. "Maybe beer is just more convenient at open-air festivals and packed venues. It's generally cheaper, refreshing, and easy to carry," he acknowledges. "I've seen people drinking wine at metal shows, but definitely not as many as beer-drinkers. Some might think wine is too 'sophisticated' for a metal concert—though jazz audiences probably think otherwise."

Geography also plays a role. "Beer is the leading drink in Northern Europe, where most of the biggest metal festivals take place, so that probably helps reinforce the association." That said, Paoli sees no reason why wine-lovers and metalheads should remain separate. "Good wine can be just as exciting, refreshing, and flavorful as a great beer—if not more so. Especially when paired with the right food."

Taking their passion a step further, Fleshgod Apocalypse launched their own red wine, the Fool. More than just a band-branded gimmick, this was a deliberate and deeply personal endeavor. "The winemaking tradition is deeply rooted in Italy, and we loved the idea of offering something unique for an extreme metal band," Paoli explains. "This wasn't about just selling wine—it was about giving our fans something truly meaningful to us as Italians. When you taste it, you're actually tasting our history and culture."

Currently sold out, the Fool was released in limited quantities, emphasizing quality over mass production. Much like their music, Fleshgod Apocalypse approaches wine with a sense of artistry and tradition. With their unorthodox pairing of metal and wine, the band is proving that tradition and intensity can coexist. Whether through crushing symphonies or a fine glass of Italian red, Fleshgod Apocalypse continues to push boundaries—one sip at a time.

CRADLE TO THE GRAVE
SURE, I LIKE MOTOR HEAD
COOL WHICH ALBUM DO YOU LIKE MOST?
THE ONE THAT HAS THEIR BEST SONG ON IT!
THE ACE OF SPADES!!
YOU DON'T KNOW MY MUSIC
APPEAR
DON'T LET THIS HAPPEN TO YOU— LISTEN TO MORE MOTORHEAD!

Josh Bayer

WICKED WINE TERM
OR
BRUTAL BAND NAME?

EXHILARATING, BRUTAL, UNPREDICTABLE, AND INTOXICATING. Now quick: are we talking *heavy metal* or *wine*? Therein lies the fun of the following word game ... of the words below, which are Wicked Wine Terms and which are Brutal Band Names? For each correctly picked Brutal Band Name you get +1 point, for each correctly picked Wicked Wine Term -1 point (no points for incorrect guesses). Make your picks, tally your score, and see where on the Vinohead-to-Metalhead spectrum you land.

WINE TERM / BAND NAME
(CIRCLE ONE)

1. (W -1 / B +1) Maceration
2. (W -1 / B +1) Acid Bath
3. (W -1 / B +1) Soilwork
4. (W -1 / B +1) Carbonized
5. (W -1 / B +1) Noble Rot
6. (W -1 / B +1) Batillus
7. (W -1 / B +1) Volatile Acidity
8. (W -1 / B +1) Burial Cane
9. (W -1 / B +1) Disgorge
10. (W -1 / B +1) Boytroitus
11. (W -1 / B +1) Fleshrot
12. (W -1 / B +1) Body Harvest
13. (W -1 / B +1) Crusher Destemmer
14. (W -1 / B +1) Oxidized
15. (W -1 / B +1) Umbra Vitae
16. (W -1 / B +1) Necrot
17. (W -1 / B +1) Phylloxera

Matt Kerley

(Vinohead) -9 -8 -7 -6 -5 -4 -3 -2 -1 0 +1 +2 +3 +4 +5 +6 +7 +8 +9 (Metalhead)

(Perfectly balanced and well cultured)

ANSWER SHEET:

1.W 2) B 3) B 4) B 5) W 6) B 7) W 8) W 9) B & W 10) W 11) B 12) B 13) W 14) W 15) B 16) B 17) W

We've all seen them at some point. Letters glimmering like retina-burning lasers, colors so gaudy they tempt one's gag reflex, and slogans so cheesy they force eyeballs to roll back in their sockets. That's right, we're talking about the bedazzled fashion ritual meets rhinestone spectacle of...
THE KITSCHY WINE SHIRT
But, one wonders: if pressed to choose (heaven forbid), which Kitschy Wine Shirt is the one for you...? Well ponder no longer because we've done the hard work and research to help YOU determine which tawdry, wine-themed t-shirt eyesore fits your bill. So, the first choice in determining which shirt to display your wine acumen to the public is to let 'em know your...
ATTITUDE or EXPERIENCE
MO WINE NO MO PROBLEMS
Do you own a wine themed shirt?
NO
YES =1
Dismember's Like An Ever-Flowing Stream =8
or
Dismember's Indecent & Obscene =9
Who listens to you best?
YOUR BESTIE =6
or
YOUR DOG/CAT =3
or
WINE =2=
WINE: (the cause, but mostly) THE SOLUTION TO ALL LIFE'S PROBLEMS
Black Sabbath's Master of Reality =5
or
Black Sabbath's Paranoid
Born before 1995?
YES =7
NO =4
Are you a Millennial?
YES
NO =4
VINYL =10
or
IPOD
or
SPOTIFY
1. WINE DIVA
2. WINES Constantly
3. WINE A Little... You'll Feel Better!
4. Makes Pour Decisions
5. It's Not Box Wine, It's Cardbordeaux
6. Love The Wine You're With
7. Sips About To Go Down
8. Rosé All Day
9. GIRLS GONE WINE
10. At My Age, I Need GLASSES!
Anelecia Hannah

Crossword of Madness
Across
1. Darkthrone drummer and all around loveable black metal icon.
7. European country with largest growing region.
8. Lost grape of Bordeaux
10. Sediment consisting of dead yeast cells.
13. Carcass, Napalm Death, Entombed and others made this label famous in the early 90s.
15. Wines grown organically & following a planting calendar.
16. Metal sub-genre Amon Amarth is known for.
17. "You've Got Another Thing Coming".
18. Motorhead frontman.
19. Principal grape grown in Australia.
Down
2. Dark Tranquility vocalist Mikael Stanne first sang in this other Swedish metal band.
3. Last step in sparkling wine production before final corking.
4. Part of the grape chiefly responsible for the color of a wine.
5. Major Red grape of Beaujolais.
6. "Run To The Hills".
7. Brazil's chief metal export.
9. "Iron Man".
11. Primary white grape in Champagne.
12. Main grape of Chianti.
14. Band that infected metal with industrial electronics, led by Uncle Al.
@austinwinsteadillustration
Austin Winstead

Solve et Coagula

Those Who Dissolve Barriers to Join the Disparate

FINAL GIRL

Heavy Metal and horror movies are like peanut butter and jelly. The crossover in fandom between the two is immense; in fact, when we learned of Final Girl Wines, who dovetail their love of horror movies and wine, it didn't seem like a no-brainer to include them in *Blood of Gods*, it seemed mandatory. The husband-and-wife-run winery makes fun, unpretentious wine and backs it up with serious horror movie chops and winemaking. Owner **PETER LANCUCKI** explained the craft that goes into each, and why.

BLOOD OF GODS: The first thing that came to mind when I saw your label for Final Girl was the movie *High Tension*. Are you familiar? Is that what you were going for, or something different altogether?

PETER LANCUCKI: I am familiar with the film but have not seen it as yet. I know about it, though, and missed it when it was doing the rounds at film festivals all those years back. My goodness, so young back then. *High Tension* was part of a wave of French films that were pretty violent, *Martyrs* and *Irreversible* perhaps being the most famous.

The trope of the gritty, dirty final girl is canon for horror, so the fact that you see it in the label means we are getting it across. We wanted it to be iconic, without it being referential to one specific movie. Our old housemate Kaley is an artist and comic illustrator, and she did a fantastic job on the silhouette and the imagery.

BOG: Metal and horror are two niches that rarely infiltrate the wine world—however, what similarities do you see between these realms?

PL: It's funny, we have been at winemaking for some time, Anna much longer than myself, but the label only started just last year on *Friday the 13th* in September (this will be relevant in a second). I thought this [concept] was clever because they are so unrelated, but, funnily enough, the more you look into it, the more you see people working in it. You have Pink, who is a neighbor making wines from the same area as us, Maynard James Keenan from Tool, Dave Mustaine from Megadeth, Les Claypool from Primus ... all making wines and actually getting their hands down and dirty in the process.

We also have found so many in the horror community who appreciate good wines and love the fact that they have a brand like ours they can be proud to share with others. There are other winemakers, too, holding the banner of horror, like Adrienne King of Cristal Lake Wine, who played Alice in the first *Friday the 13th* movie (this is the payoff from earlier).

To answer the question though: nerdism. I see it in horror, metal, and wine fans. Everyone knows their stuff in great detail. I sometimes think I'm the dumbest guy in the room in all three genres. Never do horror, wine, or metal trivia nights. It's a great way to find out how little you know compared to other fans out there. But I think a secondary element, which is more serious, is that all three have an appreciation of craft. They have an appreciation of hard work to get a small glimpse of a beautiful creation in their respective art, and there can be a lot of failures along the way. It's part of the process. There is also a pragmatic, practical characteristic to it all. Perhaps that's why you see crossovers.

BOG: Have you found it at all difficult for some folks to take the winery and your wines serious because of the branding or theme?

PL: I think there certainly are elements who would not take our wine seriously because of the imagery and the labels. But you have to be authentic to who you are and what you're trying to do with a wine label. We wanted to have quality wines that don't take themselves too seriously, that people in genre, particularly horror, would be proud to share with their friends and family. I think we've achieved that, and we have found that, even if at first some people dismiss it, once they taste the wines, they are impressed. We've even had some great reviews in the established wine review magazines here in the U.S. I think on our Instagram we highlight one reviewer who treated us as a joke label and then ended up saying that "These are ridiculously good wines." All we ask is for people to try them and make their minds up for themselves.

BOG: Fortunately, there are some legit niche wine producers, but there often also seems to be "merchandisers" that just slap a label on some cheap swill they know fans will buy, making it a tad daunting to stick your neck out there in terms of image and branding.

PL: There are some people who like to slap on a label and are more like marketers rather than winemakers. Don't get me wrong, you need both those elements for success, but wine is a competitive industry and, while gimmicks may work for a little while, they are soon called out if there isn't good winemaking behind it. There are some high-profile examples at the moment, but I would rather focus on good winemakers, including those famous for other reasons, who nonetheless get their hands down and dirty in the winemaking process and try to improve year on year. So in terms of sticking your neck out ... it's only a problem if it's not authentic to you. For us, our label describes us pretty well and it's reflected with the fantastic people who support us as wine bars, cellars, customers, and our all important wine-club members.

BOG: To the uninformed, what's the flagship wine you'd pour for someone from Final Girl and why?

PL: We are more likely to pour a wine that suits the palate of the person who is asking or for the occasion. We used to have ideas about the ones we make—which is the more popular, which goes with white on certain occasions—but largely we let our fans determine it. Funnily enough, we have fans within our wine club and community for different wines. For example, there's an even split between our Grenache-Syrah and Petit Verdot in the reds. Some really love our Rosé of Pinot Noir, because they love the acid and summer flavors. We have a Jurassic Park Chenin Blanc coming out soon, and I reckon that's gonna be a bit of a favorite.

But if I was to say a personal favorite of mine, it's probably the Petit Verdot. Our winemaker Anna (my wife) fell in love with this wine that is often referred to as a Bordeaux blender. But when it is by itself it stands out boldly. Fans of Cabernet Sauvignon and Cab Franc will appreciate this style. This is why we often refer to it as Barbara from *Night of the Living Dead*. It has so many characteristics of the iconic final girls in horror.

BOG: What's your favorite horror movie soundtrack?

PL: This question is unfair and borderlines on harassment—LOL. There are so many iconic greats. *Halloween*, *The Omen*, *The Crow*, *Psycho* . . . if I wanted to tip a hat to metal fans, I would highlight a movie where the music is an integral part of the actual story plot and characters themselves. It's a quirky, dark horror comedy that is so damn New Zealand: *Deathgasm*. Fans of horror or metal should definitely go see it. Fans of both . . . this is a legal requirement. Next choice would be *We Summon the Darkness*. That's a movie with metal and Satanic panic baked into the mix.

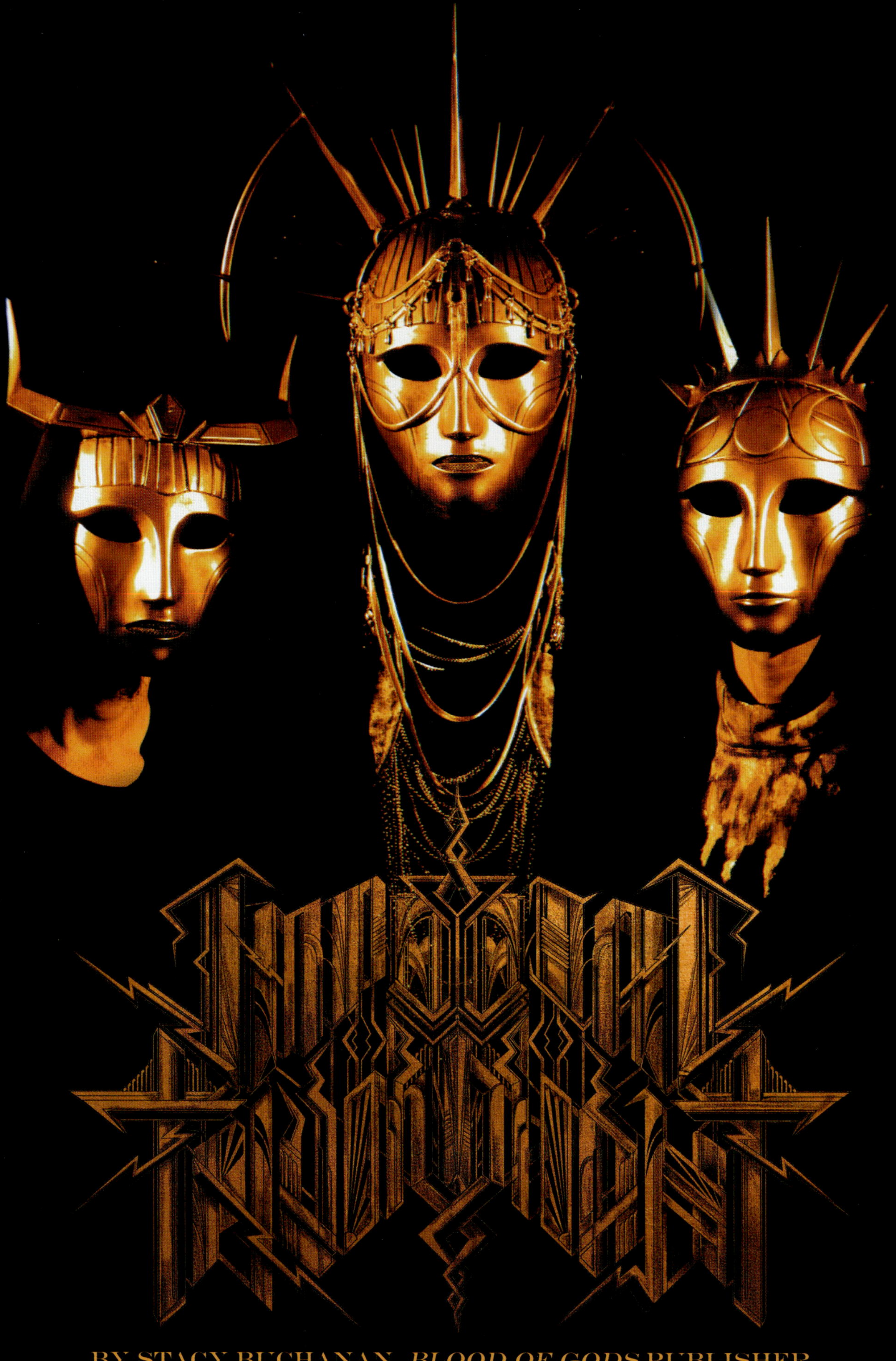

Courtesy of Imperial Triumphant

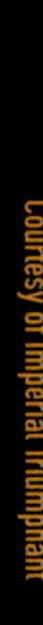

BY STACY BUCHANAN, *BLOOD OF GODS* PUBLISHER

The sonic black metal nucleus of power-trio **IMPERIAL TRIUMPHANT** is hanging on by a thread. That is to say, the New York band's ambitions and experimental drive are outpacing their stylistic origins. Black metal mostly serves as shading or a bit of semi-opaque overlay to the otherwise progressive and exploratory terrain they cover. Of course, one look at the band, and you know this is going to be a far cry from traditional or orthodox metal. There are free-jazz freakouts, avant-garde experiments (i.e. featuring Meshuggah's Thomas Haake playing Japanese Taiko drums), piano, saxophone, and more. It's a lot, and return listens yield exciting rewards via easter eggs and hidden layers. Oh yeah, and they like wine. We spoke with vocalist and guitarist Zachary Ezrin to dig deeper into the band's ever-evolving sound, aesthetic, and tastes.

BLOOD OF GODS: Let's start things off straight outta left field: after confirming this interview, I learned about your bassist's live solo with a bottle of wine while performing last year (before the Covid shutdown). After checking the video out online, we knew we had made the right choice to connect with you guys—how did this come about?

ZACHARY EZRIN: The live bass solo typically uses a slide, but over time our bassist, Steve Blanco, started using whatever local beer bottle was available at the club. Now we usually use Champagne or wine as the slide of choice. It makes for a most luxurious solo.

BOG: So now backing up to the beginning: where did your interest in wine originate? Was there a turning point or more of a gradual growing appreciation and interest over time?

ZE: Just as I'm getting older and cooking more, I'm starting to appreciate good wine pairings. In the last few years, I've been drinking way more wine. I wouldn't say I'm well versed in it, but I like what I like. Lately I've been checking out the organic wines, orange wines, and even enjoying some occasional Lambrusco.

"IF YOU APPRECIATE JOHN COLTRANE'S *ASCENSION*, YOU WILL LOVE PORTAL'S *ION*."

BOG: How do you go about discovering wines? Bottles shops, online, elsewhere . . . ?

ZE: Living in New York City is really great for wine-drinkers since a lot of European imports are first distributed into the city before they make it to the rest of the country. I mainly go to my local shops and see what's new.

BOG: I can see a lot of wine fans digging the free jazz, experimental flourishes, and other progressive tendencies laced throughout your music—are there any suggestions you'd offer for those just getting their feet wet with metal who might be drawn to those qualities?

ZE: Metal has a wide spectrum of offerings nowadays. There's a lot to explore and the adventurous listeners can enjoy metal just as they appreciate free jazz and other extreme sub-genres. If you appreciate John Coltrane's *Ascension*, you will love Portal's *Ion*.

BOG: While there are plenty of stereotypes on both sides, what argument would you make to encourage more metalheads to try getting into wine?

ZE: Honestly, I love beer as much as I love wine, but the best argument is you don't have to use the restroom every thirty minutes with wine.

BOG: Any current recommendations for wine? For music?

ZE: My go-to for an affordable good wine has become this Bourgogne Pinot Noir by Louis Latour. The extravagant Vile Luxury [2018 Imperial Triumphant album] bottle would be a Sassicaia Super Tuscan. For music, I'd say you can't go wrong with John Zorn Simulacrum's new album *Baphomet.*

BOG: It seems like the prohibitive conditions of Covid, which obviously have been a major bummer, have also put people in a position to experience and try things, like wine and music, in all new ways or with a new perspective and appreciation. Has this notion been true for you?

ZE: Not really. I've been exploring wines before Covid. I just drink at home now instead of at the bar. Balance is key to elevating a craft from being one-dimensional, be it wine or metal.

BOG: When it comes to Imperial Triumphant, your experimental influences always seem to be balanced, never so much that it's experimental for originality points or as a novelty, but always present to add uniqueness to your brand of extreme metal. Can you talk about the balance in your music? What helps keep things in service to the song and not tailspin out of control?

ZE: We're a trio and all three of us are the writers. There's power in that. The triangle. It allows for a healthy filtering process when we write. We all are pushing towards the greater good. Having all three of us as writers makes it so only the best of the best songs, riffs, and ideas stay alive. Balance is truly everything when it comes to songwriting, dynamics, lyrics and, "avant-garde moments."

METAL ICONS PAIRING

Lemmy
Motörhead

Few humans become legends yet remain as humbly consistent throughout life as Lemmy. When the Kilmister wasn't slugging four fingers of Tennessee's finest over ice with a splash of cola for color ("the Lemmy") in the Rainbow Room, he reached for the grape that put Australia on the international wine stage. Shiraz is strong, spicy, meaty and bold, with just enough ABV, likely over 15%, to kick you in the ass. Good luck finding the actual Motörhead brand though: its not in the States.

George "Corpsegrinder" Fisher
Cannibal Corpse

Only the finest will do for Corpsegrinder to soothe the growl box and thigh-thick neck after a brutal show. He keeps it trendy with orange wine from Slovenia and Italy, pinky held high. There they make white wines but treat them like reds by leaving skins in contact with juice, adding texture, complexity, and richness to this polarizing style. Many encourage further oxidation by not topping up wines as they age in large barrels or amphora. While not for everyone, they can be incredible with food.

By Justin Moore   Illustrations by Ryan Caskey

Ozzy Osbourne
Black Sabbath

Though you may find the Godfather's likeness on a bargain bottle of blended California wine, I doubt the Prince of Darkness pops that cork. When dealing with years of overindulgence, one finds that less is more and quality is preferred to quantity. The Sabbath himself deserves the best, so Grand Cru Red Burgundy it is! Pinot Noir originally comes from this small sixty-mile stretch called the Côte d'Or, or "golden slope." There are only thirty-two Grand Cru (best) vineyards producing only about 2% of the region's total output. You can find a solid bottle of Corton for about $100, but the best bottles go for over $10K. Go get some of the best.

Dani Filth
Cradle of Filth

When Dani Filth isn't composing concept albums or belting out a rock opera with his most impressive five-octave range, he is likely chugging Tanat. This grape is literally Total Fucking Darkness and produces the famous black wine of Madeiran, France, though it can be found in tiny amounts the world over. With a deeper-than-black, impenetrable, ink-like hue and a symphonic range of fruit paired with some of the most brutal tannins on the planet, Tanat is likely to make your eyes as vivid as the frontman of Filth.

WINES *For the* BEER GEEK

"GIVE YOURSELF THE OPPORTUNITY TO FIND SOMETHING YOU DON'T LIKE," says wine writer Anthony Mueller, "because within that context of expanding your mind, you're going to find something that you do like and that only increases your enjoyment of the world's beverages." In the same spirit of those words, we asked two Master Sommeliers, **Andy Myers** and **Doug Frost**, to select wines to serve as "gateway wines" to appeal to the more beer-savvy drinker. And we mean SAVVY with all caps—**Nick Nunns**, founder of Trev Brewing, along with his cohorts E.J. and Zach, weighed in on the picks. We also enlisted drummer extraordinaire and beer fanatic **Dave Witte** (Municipal Waste, Discordance Axis, Burnt by the Sun, Human Remains, and about a thousand other bands) to try the selected wines. Read on to see how and why the wines were selected by the Master Somms and the thoughts, quick takes, and anecdotes from our beer-loving compatriots.

Echolands 2020 Pet-Nat Sparkling Cabernet Franc

DOUG FROST

Echolands 2020 Pet-Nat Sparkling Cabernet Franc—as for the pét-nat, it is in fact more about the making of it (yeast and such) than it is about the origin material. But this is a very unusual wine in that it is made without any sulfites at all; in the parlance of the day, it is a natural wine. And pretty tasty (unlike some of them). So, I thought a beer expert might find it interesting.

DAVE WITTE

Dry, crisp. I'm a sucker for carbonation and dryness. Fruity but not overly sweet. Reminds me of Orval kinda in a weird way, which is one of my favorite beers. I had Dare Vegan Roasted Garlic Brie and Pepperjack Brie. The sweet and heat combo was nice. I listened to Cinderella Night Songs while drinking.

TREV BREWING

A nice gateway into the natural side of sparkling wines. Most pét-nats we've drunk taste a lot like Saison; as much as we love Saison we're thankful that isn't the case with this one. Green apple and shelled peanuts evolve into crisp cantaloupe. Super high carbonation that mellows nicely. If you're a fan of brett beers or Belgian Goldens like Duvel, this would be a good start.

Courtesy of Dave Witte

DAVE WITTE

Courtesy of Nick Nunns

NICK NUNNS

Barboursville, Vermentino

ANDY MYERS

Barboursville, Vermentino, Monticello, Virginia—you usually only find Vermentino in Italy, but my friend Luca Paschina makes this great example in Virginia. I sent this over for the beer fellas because this version has super tasty, leesy notes and great bitter fruits. It struck me as akin to delicious Pilsners (or beer-flavored beers in general). It's a really well-made wine, but it's also just crushable, so it had me hoping the beer crowd would find this sessionable but also get a bit geeky about the yeasty notes and the hints of winemaking on display.

DAVE WITTE

Soft and smooth. Pear again. Dry and fruity. Not much bitterness and it is also good with Dare Caprese Brie. I would drink this again. Made in Virginia, so I may actually visit where it's made. I listened to Daryl Hall's *Sacred Songs* while drinking. Pairs well with Frippertronics.

TREV BREWING

We went into this with pretty low expectations, as we've yet to have any stellar wines from Virginia, but this was a pleasant surprise. Tropical fruits, petrol, and dried stone fruit make this profile pretty similar to some New Zealand Sauvignon Blancs (and Nelson Sauvin hops). Pretty chewy, almost borderline claggy on the palate (think NEIPA in texture), but that mouthfeel and the acid of this make it a great wine to pair with food.

Sigalas Santorini Classic

DOUG FROST

As for why I chose these wines, it has much to do with intensity and personality—the Sigalas Santorini Classic is a Greek wine and is as mineral-rich as any wine you will ever find. That makes it a world away from beer, which is derived more from the action of the yeast, the character of the malt, and the environment in which the beer is aged. I thought that the contrast might be curiously compelling to beer experts.

DAVE WITTE

Light, tart, a little sweet—I feel like I taste pear, maybe? Mild acidic burn on the way down for me. I had it with Dare Vegan Cheese. The Gouda and Caprese Brie were very nice with it. I listened to Turnstile, *Glow On* while drinking.

TREV BREWING

This wine arrived a bit later than the others, so unfortunately we didn't have the opportunity to taste it together, and my notes aren't as detailed as I'd like. From what I recall, it was somewhat restrained in expression but shared similarities with some of the table Saisons we've enjoyed.

Failla, Bjornson Vineyard, Gamay, Eola-Amity Hills

ANDY MYERS

Failla, Bjornson Vineyard, Gamay, Eola-Amity Hills, Oregon—Gamay always makes me happy. It's not too heavy, not too light, has great acidity and delicious, tart red-berry flavors and usually carries a nice, rocky minerality. I was hoping beer drinkers would find this pleasant like those killer red-fruit-based sour beers. This version is a bit more robust than French versions, so you get a little extra boozy bang for your buck here as well. Ultimately, it's a super juicy, fun red from my buddy Ehren Jordan.

DAVE WITTE

I've always thought I enjoyed red wines more for some reason and it rings true here. Bear with me here on my notes. Kinda hot, dry, smooth. Dark cherry, rose petals. Drank it with seared Tempeh and sautéed cabbage, apples, and onions with a little barbecue/sriracha sauce. I think it paired well. It brought out the nuttiness, I think? I listened to the new and really great Iceburn, Asclepius. The wine and record together was really special.

TREV BREWING

Blindfolded we could have guessed this was a Pinot Noir from the Pacific Northwest. Dark fruit, black pepper, a light smokiness, and earthiness are on the trajectory to leathery without getting the whole way there. Definitely a little more on the rustic side, but the sweetness and acid are nicely balanced. Definitely one to try if you're into mixed fermentation sour beers, especially those aged on cherries.

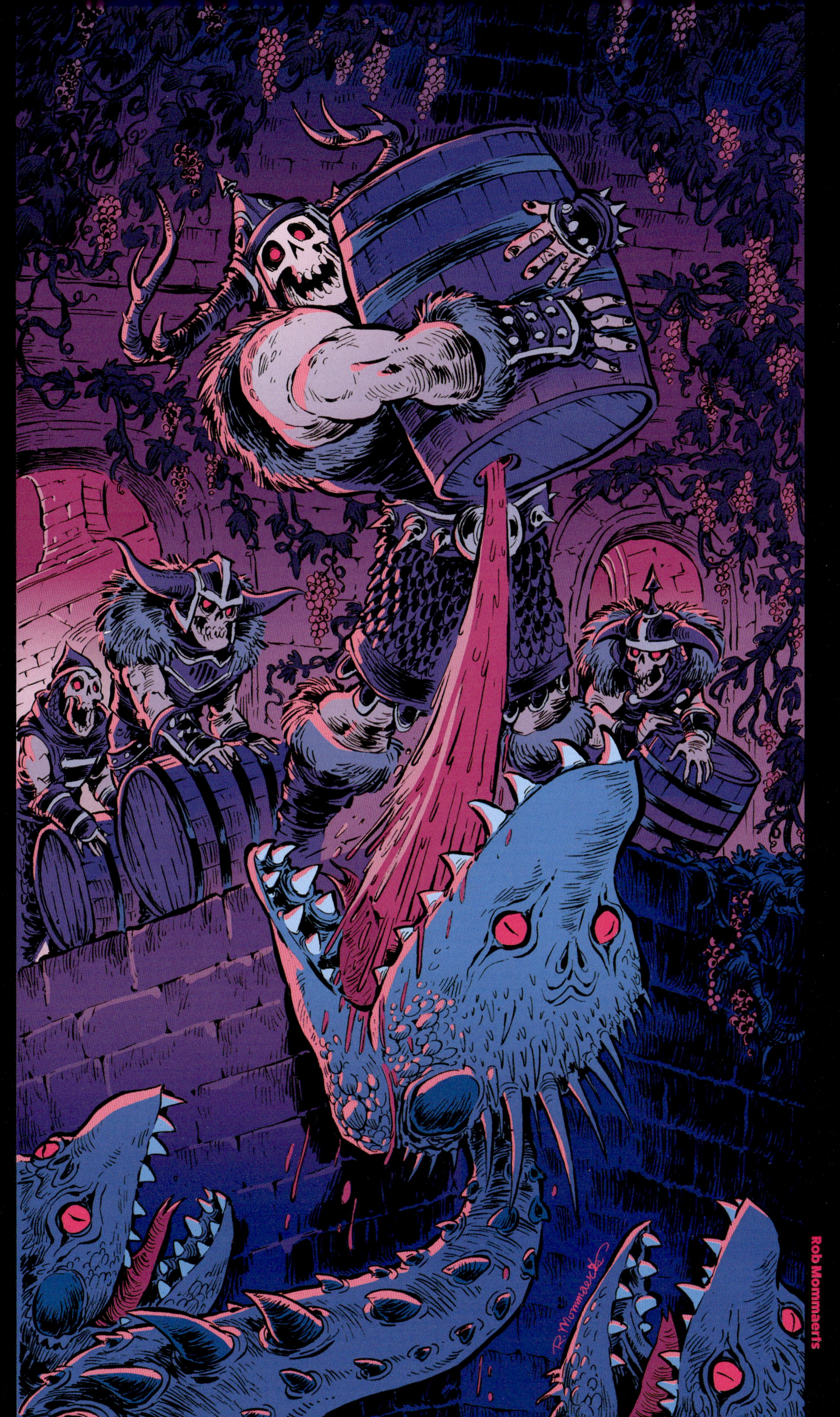

Rob Mommaerts

ALEXIS
MINCOLLA
OF
ILL
TEETH

CULTURE:
THE ARTS AND OTHER MANIFESTATIONS OF HUMAN INTELLECTUAL ACHIEVEMENT REGARDED COLLECTIVELY

When considering the above, the industrial metal band 3Teeth is very much a band that traipses in the past, present, and future manifestations of human achievement. Sometimes it's exhilarating. Sometimes it isn't pretty. But fret not: vocalist Lex Mincolla is your Sherpa on the mountain of art, alchemy, sonics, and creativity. Like the many others documented in these pages, he can see and appreciate the throughlines of craft, whether it's music, wine, food, or story. We sent him some wine, sent him some questions, and received some wonderful insight in return.

BLOOD OF GODS: Not long ago, it would seem much more taboo in the metal world to show an appreciation for other creative endeavors, such as wine, or even coffee, fashion, or cuisine. But in recent years it's starting to feel like walls are coming down and fans are seeing the same passion for craft channeled into other artistic outlets. Would you agree?

ALEXIS MINCOLLA: It may come as a surprise to some that fans of heavy metal can possess sophisticated tastes in other areas of life, highlighting the widespread misunderstanding of the metal genre. Personally, I believe that Bach and Mozart would have been avid metal enthusiasts if they were born under different circumstances. I even recall from Psychology Today where they presented actual research that heavy-metal listeners tend to exhibit more logical and complex thinking patterns compared to non-listeners and that metal music significantly enhances focus. Therefore, the revelation that the metal community harbors a richly artistic side is, to me, entirely expected. Is the metal world finally stepping out of its artistically refined "closet," shedding light on the depth and complexity that has always existed within its realm? Maybe . . . but either way I'm here for it. I think people should remember that humans are complex creatures and filled with nuance and just because some dude walks in with long hair and battle vest doesn't mean he's not a brilliant, inspired artist.

BOG: Jumping off from the previous question: seeing you front an industrial metal band, enjoying high-caliber wine, blowing up shit in the desert, and referencing astrology—sometimes all in the same day!—makes me feel hope for the future. You and 3Teeth seem to exist at a creative nexus of this cultural, cross-pollinating renaissance. Does it feel this way to you?

AM: The older I get the more I just find myself relentlessly drawn to being out in nature with good food, fine wine, great company, and the thrill of aiming a high-powered rifle at five pounds of binary explosives. I'm not sure if this is a nexus of cultural, cross-pollinating renaissance but

PHOTOS BY JIM LOUVAU

like to believe that Hunter S. Thompson would be proud.

BOG: Transformation, alchemy, and ritual—all important things in music and wine. Can you chat a bit about how these things play a role in creating art to you?

AM: Each album we've created emerges from a profound need to articulate and release something deeply personal, serving as a catalyst for my own healing process. To me, these albums are akin to diaries, meticulously chronicling my emotional and spiritual journey. They're not just collections of songs; they are alchemical processes through which raw, unfiltered emotions are transformed into musical expressions. This transformation mirrors the ancient practice of alchemy, where base materials were purportedly turned into noble metals, aiming not just at physical but also at spiritual purification and enlightenment.

The creation of each album, in this sense, is a ritualistic act. It's a deliberate, thoughtful process that involves delving into the depths of the self, confronting and embracing the shadows within, and then emerging with a piece of art that encapsulates those experiences. This ritual—much like those found in traditional alchemical practices—serves not only as a method for personal alchemy but also as a bridge connecting the artist to the listener. Through this connection, the healing and transformative power encoded within the music can extend beyond the creator, reaching others and potentially facilitating a similar process of transformation and enlightenment in them.

In essence, the act of producing an album is both a personal and universal ritual grounded in the principles of alchemy. It's an intimate process of converting personal trials and tribulations into something transcendent, which, once shared becomes a medium for collective healing and understanding.

BOG: There are a lot of hidden layers and nuances on the new album, a lot of "Easter egg" surprises in there. How do you know when what you've created is done? How do you know when is the best time to walk away and something you've created is finished? Is this ever difficult to definitively know for you?

AM: I personally feel a work of art is never finished, it's only abandoned when you feel it's strong enough to live on its own. This act of abandonment is not one of negligence but a profound acknowledgement of the work's readiness to engage, provoke, and exist beyond the confines of its creator's imagination. It's in this deliberate release that the artwork begins its true journey venturing into the open where its strength

"THE OLDER I GET THE MORE I JUST FIND MYSELF RELENTLESSLY DRAWN TO BEING OUT IN NATURE WITH GOOD FOOD, FINE WINE, GREAT COMPANY, AND THE THRILL OF AIMING A HIGH-POWERED RIFLE AT FIVE POUNDS OF BINARY EXPLOSIVES."

resilience, and ability to resonate or repel are put to the ultimate test. Therefore, the notion of finishing an art piece is a misnomer; it is, instead, a courageous act of letting go, allowing the piece to mature, influence, and weave itself into the fabric of cultural consciousness on its own terms.

BOG: Chaos versus order—whether in the studio creating music, creating wine in a cellar, performing music live, working with nature in the vineyard ... sometimes there's an unexplainable factor that guides the process. What's your experience been like with this duality?

AM: For me, the creative process is akin to navigating the delicate equilibrium between chaos and order. Venturing too far into the realm of chaos, one risks losing grasp on the project, letting it spiral into disarray. Conversely, exerting excessive control stifles creativity, choking the life out of the work and preventing the serendipitous occurrences of magickal mistakes. It's about mastering the art of balance, allowing just enough disorder to invite unexpected moments of brilliance, while maintaining sufficient oversight to steer the project towards its envisioned completion.

NONE SO VINO: MATT McGACHY OF CRYPTOPSY

WE'RE SUCH FANBOYS FOR CANADA'S CRYPTOPSY that we've just gotta get something out of the way right at the jump: the band's second studio album *None So Vile* is very likely, quite possibly, one of the greatest death-metal albums of all time. If you're new to death metal, this album checks all the boxes with aplomb. Singer Matt McGachy is a craft-beer expert who also hosts *Vox and Hops*, a podcast that features casual conversations with creative people involved in the metal scene as well as craft-beer artisans. We tasted some wines we thought would appeal to the beerheads and discussed the parallels of our love for brutal tunes and fermented beverages.

BLOOD OF GODS: We draw a lot of through-lines that connect wine and metal, and we'll tell you till we're blue the face why it makes sense. But because you're talking to the beerheads, what are those through-lines and connections that you usually talk about?

MATT McGACHY: I see it as a sense of community. There's nothing more encompassing or bringing people together more than a beer, or an alcohol in general. Same thing as a show. We roll up into a town, and it becomes, like, the event of the city, and there's a bunch of people here tonight. So, same thing with a beer. You get together with some friends, you sit down with a beer, all of a sudden the conversation goes in a different direction. Everyone starts loosening up a bit. Same thing at a show with metal, or even just listening to an album with a friend, it's the same sort of thing, it's like a conversation-starter, for either alcohol or metal. Bringing people together, a sense of community, a sense of kinship. "You like beer, I like beer. You like this band. I like this band." There's definitely those two things going on, for sure.

SUSAN MOSS

BOG: What do you think is cool about wine that you wish would be more prevalent in beer?

MM: I guess the little side of sophistication there. It'd be nice if there was a little bit more. And it's probably the way they package them too. I wish there was a bit more sophistication in craft beer. One other thing that I love about wine is the complexity of barrel-aging. That does come across in some beer styles but not as prevalent as it is in wine. I think it's because it's a gamble and it is more expensive for the breweries. Most breweries just want to do IPAs because they can get a product out on the market within three weeks. Wine is a more patient investment that people have to take chances with. I'd like to see more of that in the beer world.

BOG: Some of that packaging is similar to the natural-wine movement in the wine world. The natty-wine crowd is somewhat like the folks in the beer world who are into the sours and mixed-culture kind of beers.

MM: Yes—which is delicious by the way—they will get into that, totally. So I wish there was a bit more sophistication, but then I also don't, because I don't even like going into craft breweries that are too trendy, 'cause then I feel like I'm the outcast.

BOG: Like, "I'm not cool enough to be here."

MM: Elitism sucks. People will grow out of that, I hope, and then there will be a new generation of elitists [laughs]. I try to just relax and enjoy what I want to. People will always have a lot of options. My friends in Despised Icon, they run one of the best breweries in Quebec, Messorem Bracitorium—they've been open for five years. I went there for the first time expecting it to be a metal bar, and it's not, it's like super hipster trendy. They've leaned even more into it now—the beer is phenomenal, though, so I put up with it.

BOG: I think also with metal and with wine there's also a class thing, where beer feels more working-class, whereas wine can feel more snooty or snobby.

MM: That is true. It's also, you'll go to a bar and typically they'll only have, what, like a house white or house red. What is that? Who knows. So it's hard to get wine into everything everywhere, just like it's hard to get good craft beer because there's monopolies on distribution and who puts what where.

BOG: Metalheads are like collectors—they have this encyclopedic tendency where they want to know more, and who's in the thank-you credits, and what shirt was the guy wearing. It's the same thing with wine. They want to know all about tannins, they want to know about terroir, and they want to know where it comes from. And I love that wine is not just old, rich, white dudes with a monocle. And metal is not all denim, leather, bullet belts, and spikes. And I'm just trying to push the dial and normalize it a little bit. I think that's what you're doing, too. What's been your experience in general with finding commonalities or normalizing these niches?

MM: Well, I think craft beer is just so everywhere now. I feel like the bubble popped, and now it's trickling over into more normalcy. So I think that more often you go to the grocery store now, it's just full of decent craft beer—people are more aware that there's more to explore beer-wise than the standard Budweiser, Coors, Molson products. So it's interesting. It's an experience, right? You go up and you take a chance on the branding that you think is interesting. There are a lot of metal breweries which speak directly to metal heads, so they'll be more gravitating towards picking up that can versus another can. You can only hope that what's inside the can is decent.

SUSAN MOSS

BOG: You don't sound like you're wine-averse. You're like an equal-opportunity, open-minded imbiber . . .

MM: I like to drink, but I need to watch what I drink, because I don't want to feel like garbage the next day.

BOG: Absolutely. It's a quality thing. There's sugars and alcohol involved . . .

MM: I became vegan in 2017 and doing wine and cheese when you're vegan sucks a bit more. So we're doing them less. So I'm drinking a little bit less wine. When I do go to get wine, I'll go to the SAQ, which is our government-run liquor distributor up in Quebec, and I try to not buy shit, you know. I'm a beer expert, so if I walk into a beer store I know what will be the most recent, what is fresh, what is good. Wine, I'm still taking chances, you know. I ask for recommendations. So we're lucky that we have certain SAQs where the liquor store has a more specialized section with higher-quality wines. So I try to pick in there, but never too expensive, because who knows.

BOG: What about your bandmates? Are they like, "Oh, Matt's just a crazy guy. He's so into it!" Or are any of them also into beer?

MM: Oh no, they're all really into it, and they're very happy to not have to go and spend their money on beer. I didn't do it this tour, but what I'll do is I'll exchange beer for guest-list spots. I did that on our last tour, and the first day of the tour I walked onto the tour bus and I told the tour manager, "We don't need beer. No one's gonna need beer, trust me." And he didn't believe me. And then the first day I got over 100 beers. And then at the end of the tour when he was leaving he goes, "You know what? You told me that, and I didn't believe you, but I've never—and I've been touring for twenty years—and I've never seen anyone get as much free beer as you." The whole bus drank for free, and there were two vans that were following us, and I would make them little four-packs and send it off to them.

But I'm always very appreciative when people bring stuff out—it's a nice little comforting thing at the end of the night to sit down and crack a beer, not having to have spent my day hunting for beer—people are bringing me primo stuff that they love. There was a dude that came out in New Jersey last time with a full cooler of beer sharing with me, and then I was like, "Hey, well, I gotta get ready for the show . . ." and he just went home. He came to drink beer with me. He didn't give a fuck about the show [laughs].

JOE KEINBERGER

WHERE NEXT TO CON~~QUER~~ SUME?

Wine has been consumed, contemplated, loved, adored, and obsessed over by humans from every walk of life for thousands of years. Kings and queens drink wine in celebration and defeat the same as you and me. Thankfully for us, the quality and diversity of wine available today are at an all-time high.

Great as that is, it can be immensely frustrating when you can't read through the jargon on most labels from Spain, Germany, Italy, and France. These Old World wine-producing countries historically label by place of origin rather than by the grape in the bottle. That means it is up to you to remember that Chablis is Chardonnay, but so are Champagne, Puligny-Montrachet, and even Beaujolais Blanc. There are code words, but they are not in English and not everyone has the time to memorize the legal implication of terms like Joven, Trocken, Sforzato, and Sur Lie.

Most wines and regions from the New World (countries that were at some point colonized) have found a way to be less intimidating. They most often label wines by the grapes rather than where they come from. Knowing the bottle in your hand is full of Pinot Noir is important, but so is knowing the difference between Central Otago, Ahr, Walker Bay, Eola-Amity, and Gevrey-Chambertin.

"Heavy metal" was once an all encompassing term for people that liked things a little louder, a little angrier, and a little more in-your-face. It didn't matter if you were into Motörhead, Metallica, Morbid Angel, or Tool, you were part of the group. Headbangers associate with music more strongly than most groups, and those groups multiplied as more heavy music became available. First came thrash metal, death metal and the hair/glam thing in the '80s. Then there was industrial, prog, doom, and before we knew it we had Viking, folk, Kawaii, and every other subgenre of metal you could imagine. Metalheads are likely more familiar with these subgenres than they are with the major wine-producing regions of Europe. Likewise, wine geeks are probably more understanding of regional varietal requirements than with the many phases Opeth has gone through.

Let's try to make some sense of both by comparing the two and seeing how much metal and wine really have in common.

THRASH METAL = BURGUNDY

Thrash may be the first subgenre of metal and certainly deserves a top-notch region to match. The "Big Four" pioneered lightning-fast riffs with dueling guitars, dive-bomb solos, and anti-establishment lyrics. Burgundy produces Pinot Noir and Chardonnay of such high quality they are emulated the world over. The first single vineyard of outstanding quality in Burgundy was recognized in 630 CE, and entire countries have modeled their vineyard management systems and laws after the Burgundy standard. Both the music and the wines are as classic as they are inspirational.

Pairing Suggestion: Slayer, *Reign in Blood*
+ Domaine Berthaut, Fixin 1er Cru

PROG METAL = SPAIN AND PORTUGAL

The endless stream of concepts, creativity, and polyrhythms you get from bands like Meshuggah, Tool, and Intronaut parallel the vast diversity of the Iberian peninsula. Both countries are rich with quality-minded producers, expressive indigenous varietals, and unique styles to explore, not to mention the absurd quality-to-price ratio.

Pairing Suggestion: Meshuggah, *obZen*
+ Bodega La Senda, La Barbacana

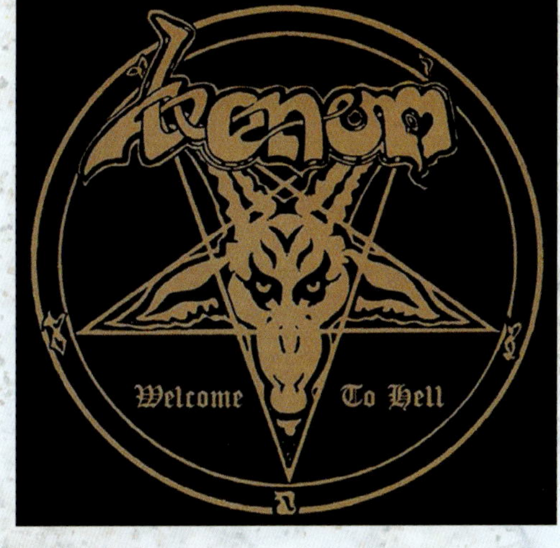

BLACK METAL = SORRY, IT'S TOO COLD TO MAKE WINE IN SCANDINAVIA

Pairing Suggestion: Venom, *Welcome to Hell*
+ Strongbow Cider

DEATH METAL = BORDEAUX

Death metal has spawned numerous genres on its own thanks to the legacies of bands like Cannibal Corpse, Death, and Deicide. These detuned, massive-sounding, throaty bands have more in common with Bordeaux than one might think. Similarly full-bodied and complex, Cabernet Sauvignon, Cabernet Franc, and Merlot have inspired winemakers the world over. All originally from Bordeaux, these grapes now produce some of the best wines in the world from Walla Walla, Washington, to Coonawarra, Australia.

Pairing Suggestion: Fulci, *Opening the Hell Gates*
+ Château Poujeaux, Moulis

HAIR/GLAM METAL = CHAMPAGNE

Pop-influenced (pun intended) Mötley Crüe, Poison, and G n' R are notorious party bands, and, when it comes to celebration, no wine is more synonymous than Champagne. Pro tip: look for "grower producer" Champagne and leave Agent Orange to the posers. Friends don't let friends drink Veuve.

Pairing Suggestion: Whitesnake, *Still of the Night*
+ Pierre Peters, Chetillions

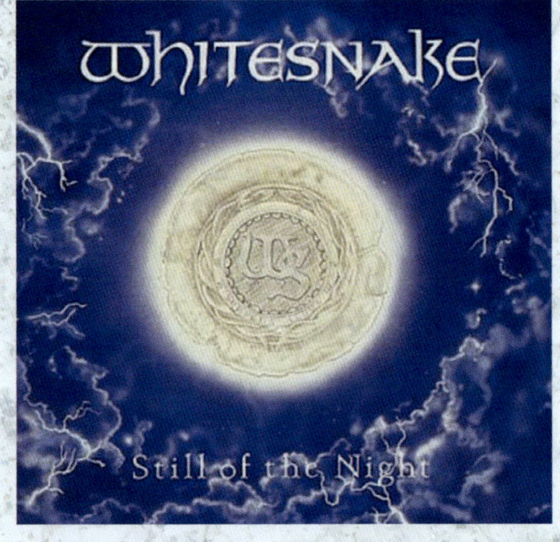

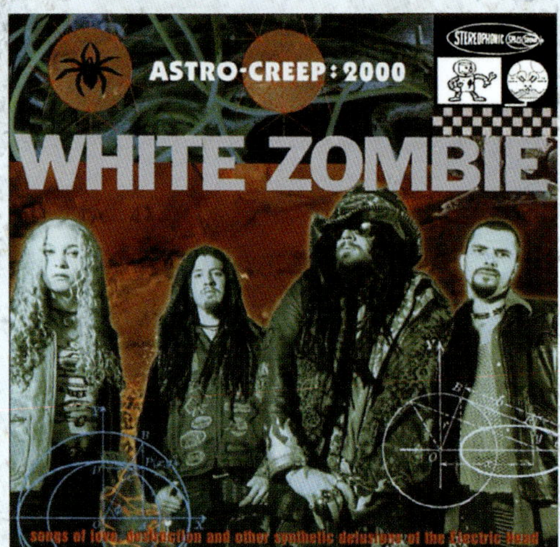

INDUSTRIAL METAL = GERMANY (DUH)

When I hear "industrial" I immediately think of NIN, Fear Factory, and, of course, Rammstein. The important thing to remember about German wine is that the Mosel and Rheingau make the best Riesling on the planet, and they are not all sweet. Look for "Trocken" if you want dry and "Kabinet" for the best expression of the grape. Save the sweet Riesling for spicy Thai food and keep an eye out for Spätburgunder, a.k.a. Pinot Noir.

Pairing Suggestion: White Zombie, *Astro-Creep:2000*
+ Egon Müller, anything

NU METAL = NATURAL WINE

Just like the music, you may find some expertly crafted guilty pleasures, but most are not for everyday consumption.

Pairing Suggestion: Sepultura, *Roots*
+ Pierre Cotton, Glou Glou VDF

DOOM METAL = ITALY

From the originators like Black Sabbath to goths like Type O Negative and stoners like Sleep, doom metal is about as diverse a genre as it gets. Comparatively, Italy has around 2,000 indigenous varietals, twenty fiercely independent regions, and over 400 legally defined wine styles. Nebbiolo from Piedmont and Sangiovese from Tuscany are excellent places to start exploring, but stay on the lookout for lesser-known varietals, including Sagrantino, Aglianico, Vespolina, Teroldego, Trebbiano, Verdicchio, Cortese, and Garganega. Don't be afraid to try something that is difficult to pronounce.

Pairing Suggestion: Monolord, *Vænir*
+ Tiberio, Trebbiano

COLLIN ESTRADA

Dedicated to my incredible wife, Heidi. Thank you for your love and support on this wild ride.

ACKNOWLEDGEMENTS:

Thank you to my two sons, River and Rune, and my parents, Jim and Sally. Thanks also to everyone who has subscribed, ordered merch, attended the *Blood of Gods* Merrymaking, or said a kind word. Special thanks to all of the artists, contributors, well-wishers, and benevolent forces who have guided me.

"My mind is open to new ideas. The divine mind is inexhaustible. The spirit is ever active in me. There is no weary or monotonous action in spirit. It is forever new and vibrant with ideas. I know that I am continuously receiving new impressions from life. New, better, and fuller ways of living. I let the newness, freshness, and originality of spirit permeate my entire consciousness."

—Ernest Holmes